MW01089959

DISCIPLINING WOMEN

DISCIPLINING WOMEN

Alpha Kappa Alpha, Black Counterpublics, and the Cultural Politics of Black Sororities

DEBORAH ELIZABETH WHALEY

Cover photo of Delta Chapter, Alpha Kappa Alpha, 1930, women in front of AKA house in Lawrence, Kansas (Dorothy Hodge Johnson Collection). Courtesy of the Spencer Research Library, Kansas Collection, University of Kansas.

Published by State University of New York Press, Albany

© 2010 State University of New York

All rights reserved

Printed in the United States of America

No part of this book may be used or reproduced in any manner whatsoever without written permission. No part of this book may be stored in a retrieval system or transmitted in any form or by any means including electronic, electrostatic, magnetic tape, mechanical, photocopying, recording, or otherwise without the prior permission in writing of the publisher.

For information, contact
State University of New York Press, Albany, NY
www.sunypress.edu

Production by Diane Ganeles
Marketing by Michael Campochiaro

Library of Congress Cataloging-in-Publication Data

Whaley, Deborah Elizabeth.
Disciplining women : Alpha Kappa Alpha, Black counterpublics, and the cultural politics of Black sororities / Deborah Elizabeth Whaley.
p. cm.
Includes bibliographical references and index.
ISBN 978-1-4384-3273-1 (hardcover : alk. paper)
ISBN 978-1-4384-3272-4 (pbk. : alk. paper)
1. Greek letter societies—United States. 2. African American Greek letter societies. 3. African American college students—Societies, etc. 4. Alpha Kappa Alpha Sorority. I. Title.
LJ31.W43 2010
369.082—dc22

2010004840

10 9 8 7 6 5 4 3 2 1

CONTENTS

List of Illustrations vii

Acknowledgments ix

Introduction 1

CHAPTER 1
Stomp the Yard, *School Daze*, and the Cultural Politics of Black Greek-Letter Organizations 13

CHAPTER 2
Alpha Kappa Alpha, Black Counterpublics, and the Ambiguity of Social Reform 29

CHAPTER 3
Stepping into the African Diaspora: Alpha Kappa Alpha and the Production of Sexuality and Femininity in Sorority Step Performance 59

CHAPTER 4
Disciplining Women, Respectable Pledges, and the Meaning of a Soror: Alpha Kappa Alpha and the Transformation of the Pledge Process 87

CHAPTER 5
Voices of Collectivity/Agents of Change: Alpha Kappa Alpha and the Future of Black Counterpublics 117

Conclusion: *Sorority Sisters* 143

Appendix: Alpha Kappa Alpha Fact Sheet 151

Notes 153

Glossary 177

Bibliography 181

Index 201

ILLUSTRATIONS

FIGURE 1
Delta Chapter, Alpha Kappa Alpha, The Jayhawker, 1921. p. 178. *Courtesy of the Spencer Research Library, Kansas Collection, University of Kansas.* 55

FIGURE 2
Delta Chapter, Alpha Kappa Alpha, 1930, women in front of AKA house in Lawrence, Kansas (Dorothy Hodge Johnson Collection). *Courtesy of the Spencer Research Library, Kansas Collection, University of Kansas.* 55

FIGURE 3
Alpha Kappa Alpha house, 1011 Indiana Street, Lawrence, Kansas, 1940. *Courtesy of the Spencer Research Library, Kansas Collection, University of Kansas.* 56

FIGURE 4
Delegates to Tri-annual YWCA Conference, including AKA members Dorothy Hodge Johnson and Maxine Jackson, who aided in the adoption of the YWCA to end its policy of racial segregation, 1946. *Courtesy of the Spencer Research Library, Kansas Collection, University of Kansas.* 56

FIGURE 5
AKA Rushees paying pledge fees, Kansas City, Kansas, 1955. *Courtesy of the Spencer Research Library, Kansas Collection, University of Kansas.* 57

FIGURE 6
AKA Delta Chapter, University of Kansas from The Jayhawker, 1959, p. 118. *Courtesy of the Spencer Research Library, Kansas Collection, University of Kansas.* 57

FIGURE 7
AKA Delta Chapter, University of Kansas from The Jayhawker, 1963, p. 166. *Courtesy of the Spencer Research Library, Kansas Collection, University of Kansas.* 58

ACKNOWLEDGMENTS

Alpha Kappa Alpha (AKA) sorority members offered me support, guidance, and interviews. Cheryl Washington, the former graduate advisor of the Zeta Psi AKA chapter, made it possible for me to sit in on AKA meetings and locate internal publications of the sorority through her contacts. AKA member Tajuana (TJ) Butler granted me an interview and encouraged me despite her busy schedule as she toured in 2000 for her book *Sorority Sisters*. Other AKA women helped me, and their voices were the heart of my project. Although most asked that I not name them in the book, they know who they are and how much I appreciate their help.

Many scholars, mentors, colleagues, and students supported this project and offered their scholarly advice. I appreciate their important work and time and their emotional support and for pressing me further along intellectually and creatively. My editor at State University of New York (SUNY) Press, Larin McLaughlin, believed in the merit of this project; her detailed attention to and suggestions for the manuscript, in addition to the comments of the press's anonymous readers, helped make this a better book. My thinking through of Black sorority activism and symbolic and ritualistic practices was shaped by the wisdom and feedback of two of my earliest academic mentors, Michael Cowan and Ann Lane, at the University of California, Santa Cruz. David Katzman and Maryemma Graham at the University of Kansas were persistent champions for this book project and provided advice during various stages of its advanced development in dissertation form; they have been consistent and positive guiding forces in my career. The Center for Cultural Studies (CCS) at the University of California, Santa Cruz, provided office space, resources, and a community of intellectuals with whom to engage while I began revising this study during my year (2003–2004) there as a Visiting Scholar. I thank Gregory S. Parks, Tamara Brown, Clarenda M. Phillips, and Craig Torbenson for providing the opportunity to publish in their collective and individual projects on Black Greek-letter organizations (BGLOs).

Portions of chapter 1 appeared in Brown et al., *African American Fraternities and Sororities: The Legacy and the Vision* (Lexington: University Press of Kentucky, 2005), and in Parks and Torbenson, *Brothers and Sisters: Diversity in College Fraternities and Sororities* (Madison, WI: Farleigh Dickenson University Press, 2009). I am especially grateful to Gregory Parks for his colleagueship, for our many discussions about BGLOs that helped sustain my momentum for this project, and for putting me in touch with a wonderful network of scholars working in the field. Parks continues to define, contribute to, and press the boundaries of BGLO studies.

I was lucky to complete the proposal for this manuscript while I was a faculty member at the University of Arizona in its Africana Studies Department, where I had intellectually engaging, caring, and collaborative colleagues. I extend heartfelt thanks to Geta LeSeur in Africana studies for her mentorship and to the members of my writing group—Beretta Smith-Shomade in media arts and Dana Mastro in communication studies—for their friendship, conceptual advice on this and many other research projects, and professional encouragement that nurtured me. My research assistant at the University of Arizona, Carmella Schaecher, was also of great assistance.

I have a strong institutional support base at the University of Iowa, which provided financial assistance for this project in the form of research funds. Thanks also to my colleagues, mentors, and friends at U of I who compose the American studies and African American studies units. In particular, I am appreciative of Horace Porter, who offered his help and advice and regularly sent me BGLO resources that came across his desk. Gyorgy Ferenc Toth, a doctoral candidate in the American Studies Department at the University of Iowa, aided in identifying sources on Alpha Kappa Alpha sorority's 2008 centennial celebration, which led to a new, exciting direction for the framing of the interviewee voices in chapter 5.

I am thankful to the editorial board of the journal *Contours*, including its editor Barry Gaspar in the History Department at Duke University, and two anonymous readers for their helpful review comments on an earlier portion of chapter 2, published there as "We Strive and We Do: The Counterpublic Sphere Work of Alpha Kappa Alpha Sorority," *Contours* 3:2 (Fall 2005). Hank Nuwer, an independent scholar, helped me tackle the legal, ethical, and writing issues that arose in my discussion about hazing and the pledge process. His encouraging, detailed, and thoughtful responses to e-mail queries in the late 1990s about hazing were invaluable. I was also fortunate to receive feedback on a condensed version of chapter 3 by a group of scholars that attended a talk I gave on sorority stepping at the 2000 American Studies Association meetings in Detroit, Michigan.

Several librarians and archivists at the University of Kansas Law School, the Kansas Collection on Black history at the University of Kansas, and Kent State University worked with me long distance. The University of Kansas Law School helped me obtain and research AKA hazing cases. Deborah Dandridge at the Kansas Collection aided me in identifying AKA members' personal papers and collections at the University of Kansas. Kent State University sent me copies of its college paper, the *Kent Stater*. Ivy Center in Chicago, Illinois, allowed me to read and photocopy its sororal magazine, *The Ivy Leaf*, in the winter of 1995.

I thank the San Jose State University chapter of Phi Beta Sigma fraternity and the Long Beach State chapter of Zeta Phi Beta sorority for allowing me to film their step practice sessions and step shows and for granting me interviews in the spring of 2000. On many occasions, Steven Millner at San Jose State University put me in contact with fraternity and sorority members for interviews and other resource information on stepping.

Finally, I am eternally indebted to my parents, Emma and George Whaley, and to my sisters, Lisa Whaley and Twilynn Whaley-Collins. I thank them for their love and support and for making my career in academia possible. I dedicate this book to them.

INTRODUCTION

Although I received yearly invitations, I never pledged a sorority when I was an undergraduate. I did my undergraduate work at the University of California, Santa Cruz (UCSC), a place known for making the linkages between being a public intellectual and community organizing. My chosen field of study, American studies, functioned as a site for the critical study of America and for debate among cultivated scholars who sought to intervene in the problems of public life. For many of us, our crusades for human rights and social justice were and still are personal. At the same time, UCSC was not Greek-fraternal friendly.[1] White sororities and fraternities represented the elite conformists, and despite other conservative factions within the university, most students opposed fraternal affiliations because they perceived them as the epitome of cultural and political conservatism. Black Greek-letter organizations (BGLOs), in contrast to White Greek-letter organizations, were involved in generating and organizing a great deal of activist work at UCSC. Their work was largely invisible to the larger campus because the majority of their activism was within the arena of Black civic engagement, otherwise known as the Black public sphere. Yet, as I would come to know through my research and ethnographic inquiry, BGLOs also encompass conservative and problematic aspects.

As the title of this book suggests, the work of this study is to consider the dual aspects of BGLO life and, in particular, the individual and group commitment to social and political engagement for women who are members of the first historically Black sorority, Alpha Kappa Alpha (AKA). To this end, the history of fraternals in general and the major nine BGLOs are resources for this book, but the main focus of this study is AKA, for several reasons worth mentioning. The first reason to focus on AKA concerns matter of access; information about this sorority was available to me because of the generosity of friends, family members, referrals, and colleagues who pledged AKA and granted me interviews and open inroads into this social and political subculture and movement among Black women. Second, AKA was established in 1908 and is the oldest Black Greek-letter sorority; it has thus contributed to the cultural work performed in the Black and wider public sphere from the first decade of the twentieth century to today. All Black sororities have cultural, social, and political elements, but AKA remains the most visible for its community efforts and for its cultural mistakes, with Delta Sigma Theta arguably running a near second in terms of these critical issues of visibility. In 1999, AKA faced public scorn and gained national attention, for example, after a local chapter of the sorority refused to let a brown-skinned teenager with African locks take part in its cotillion, unless she altered her hair grooming to what the chapter deemed a suitable style.[2] AKA is also the only Black sorority to have had alleged pledges die during a hazing ritual (to be discussed in chapter 4). AKA's cultural, social, and political elements are true to this book's title, then, insofar as their calculated cultivation of sorority life demonstrates their personal and group-directed discipline, which illuminates how culture collides with politics and Black public life in dubious ways.

My interest in writing about the history and culture of a Black sorority stems from my memories of the spring of 1989 when my sister pledged the AKA sorority.[3] During my first year of college, I witnessed my sister, then a senior in college, and her fellow pledges, wearing the same clothes and hairstyles and walking in unison during their pledge process. At that moment, I thought she was relinquishing her own self-identity, and I was ambivalent about what this meant. Later, I realized that she was in search of something very valuable: a sisterhood with a group of women from various classes, women with different personalities, ages, skin complexions, and ethnic pluralities who shared in common a gender identity and, predominantly, as opposed to exclusively, a racial identity.[4] Throughout this book, I refer to this work and element of Black sorority life as the making of and engagement with *cultural politics*, that is, the site where culture and politics meet in productive, although certainly at some junctures counterproductive, ways. More than the celebratory acts of individuals and collective groups, cultural politics entails realizing the cultural aspects of political mobilization, and the politics of maintaining cultural identity as a salient site to act from and cohere. That AKA sustains its organization through ethnic rites, collective mobilization, and local and global activism locates the sorority as having additional cultural elements that are not as prevalent in White sororities and fraternities. This is the lesson that observation of sorority cultural practices and politics—both personal and ethnographic—taught me.

Although I have a family lineage of sorority and fraternity members—indeed, most of my family's social activities were in relation to my father's fraternity, Kappa Alpha Psi—I never fully evaluated the political and cultural uses of such an organization until my sister pledged in 1989. After her induction into AKA, I began to see a fundamental change in her, and I acquired a window into the organization. I also began to understand the richness of culture, pride, and activism that Black sororities entail: I witnessed her achieving a sense of community with the rest of her sorority sisters as she actively served the Black community. My understanding of the Black Greek-letter organization extended beyond childhood memories of my father wearing the Kappa colors of crimson and cream to social functions and joining his fraternity members in Kappa sweetheart songs at yearly Greek conventions, picnics, and other social occasions. I had not known as a child that those social and cultural events were also fund-raisers for our community. I benefited from but did not initially see these events as a space for same-race interaction in a racially intolerant world, which had allowed everyday people to feel comfortable in their own skin and to perform cultural work within the Black community. Put another way, because of my young age, I was unable to articulate what meanings membership in such an organization entailed for its participants and the effect it had on the larger social structure. My understanding of Black Greek-letter organizations as an adult, though, metamorphosed into something more complex than fragmented childhood memories. I began to see the Black sorority as a way to reconceive the Greek-letter experience and rethink the social as political, and the political as a being dependent on cultural practices that, when fostered appropriately, can begin the work of social, cultural, and political transformation.

An interdisciplinary book-length study of Black Greek-letter sororities does not exist. This study thus extends BGLO scholarship. Much of the existing work on Greek-letter organizations is within the realm of social journalism or is by members of fraternities and sororities. Studies about Black fraternals include the engaging journalistic work by Otis Graham, a member of the Boulé, and Lawrence Ross, a member of Alpha Phi Alpha.[5] BGLO members and cultural critics Ricky Jones and Walter M. Kimbrough have written on the challenges of BGLO life with a focus on Black men; Jones writes on Black masculinity and hazing, and Kimbrough paces through the customs and relevance of BGLOs.[6] Other authors who are members of Black sororities have written strong sorority histories, the two most popular being historian Paula Giddings's book on Delta Sigma Theta (DST) and educator/activist Marjorie Parker's book on AKA.[7] Giddings and Parker were forerunners in Black sorority scholarship and were invaluable resources for this book. Giddings laid the conceptual foundation to understand the Black sorority as a social movement through her case study on DST, and Parker laid the foundation to make known the details of AKA history and political action in the twentieth century. As an interdisciplinary project, *Disciplining Women* departs from the aforementioned studies.

Giddings's book is a solid historical case study that asserts Black sorority politics as embodying the characteristics of a social movement, and Parker's book is a concrete review of the political participation of AKA. However, neither of these studies discusses cultural practices, colorism, hazing, and the performance of femininity for undergraduate and graduate members of the sorority nor entertains the effects of popular culture on how the larger society views BGLOs. *Disciplining Women* fills these intellectual gaps and includes an analysis of the contradictions present in Black sorority formation and identity. Although it is a case study on a particular sorority, *Disciplining Women* makes a comparative analysis to other White and ethnic women's organizations and Black benevolent and social organizations and uses multigenerational interviews with AKA members. In juxtaposing existing books on BGLOs, this study provides an analysis of film, popular literature, dance, and initiation rituals, and it employs participant observation, police reports, court records, legal documents, questionnaires, and a broad age and regional range of one-on-one interviews with AKA women to serve as evidence for the book's arguments.

In my interdisciplinary exploration of the Greek-letter experience for a specific demographic, I am aware of the racial binary it may appear to reproduce, because my case study is on AKA. As much as BGLOs provide an example of social, cultural, and political forms of resistance from the predominantly White ones, BGLOs still fared better in some ways than other racial-ethnic fraternal groups. Latino Greek-letter organizations are a more recent phenomenon and continue to lack the resources enabled by legacies and established alumni from which Black and White organizations benefit.[8] Historical accounts of Latino and Asian American Greek-letter organizations are not explored here, although in some chapters, I discuss the work of other ethnic groups in women's clubs and in BGLOs.[9] White fraternals' history of appropriating American Indian rituals and culture and indigenous organizations with philanthropic, social, and cultural elements is another study altogether.[10] To expand the area covered here, future work should consider the precarious position of sexual minorities in all existing fraternals and the ways the newly forming queer fraternals resist and have different social and political agendas from the hetero-dominant ones. Sexuality's relationship to the normative structure of Black sororities and fraternities is explored here in brief, yet a thorough explication of sexuality in the larger Greek fraternal formation is a subject taken up aptly in two anthologies by the founders of the gay, lesbian, and bisexual national fraternal alliance, Lambda 10.[11] Gregory Parks and Craig Torbenson's anthology on diversity in college fraternities and sororities, *Brothers and Sisters*, also accomplishes the difficult task of representing a good number of the aforementioned identity categories.[12]

Although I am not a sorority member, my position as an outsider and insider in the organization does award me insight into the subculture I describe in the book. I am an insider insofar as I have had a great amount of exposure to BGLO culture, and I am a Black female public intellectual, like the women I write of here. Yet I remain an outsider as a nonsorority member. This *intersubjective* space, which signifies the interplay between the two identities of insider and outsider, allows me to partially enter into the cultural space of the sorority and to critique it from the outside and inside. Many Black sorority women and intellectuals in general helped this project along and made the intersubjective struggle of toeing the line between cultural critic and friend or relative a pleasant one. Some women in AKA, however, may find disappointing my discussion of elements of sorority life that stand in opposition to the organization's public persona. In response to this, I can only say that it is not my intent to analyze Black sorority life as the answer for Black women and political culture but, rather, as an example of the grounds upon which seeds of cultural and political transformation might germinate.

Situating AKA as a Counterfraternal and Black Counterpublic Movement

The core of my argument in *Disciplining Women* relies on understanding the permeability of the public sphere for political action among social groups, the interrelationship of culture and politics, and the maintenance of power in society through disciplining practices and hegemonic control. Hegemony is the process in which a dominant group gains consent from its constituents to determine the cultural, political, and ideological character of the nation-state. In opposition to hegemony, counterhegemony is the process in which a different and hopefully progressive balance of power begins to take hold. The facilitation of this process is possible owing to the struggle of counterhegemonic movements and social bodies to form a power bloc to the existing, and often oppressive, dominant hegemonic structure.[13] Counterfraternal movements are by their very formation counterhegemonic; they account for Greek-letter organizations that exist in contestation with or that arose in response to the dominant culture. *Disciplining Women* maps this hegemonic struggle within the Black and larger public spheres by showing how AKA women regulate their subculture while utilizing the space of a Greek-letter sorority for a multitude of purposes.

Chapter 1 introduces two popular films about BGLO life, *Stomp the Yard* and *School Daze*, to demonstrate how the films present masculinist and contradictory signifiers of Blackness. *Stomp the Yard* promotes male BGLO life through an aesthetic mixture of hip-hop culture and modern Black dance, and *School Daze* promotes the idea of male BGLO life as counterproductive, elitist sites of cultural mayhem. Both films point to problems within these organizations, but neither does so with historical complexity and cultural nuance, and neither film seriously considers Black sororities, thereby increasing the empty space of sorority representation for Black women in the popular imagination. The ramification of the popular representation of BGLO life as male centered in the two films, I argue, is its propagation of the idea—through the absence of or caricature of Black women and their organizations—that the Black sorority is an unimaginable site of progressive cultural politics.

I move from a narrative analysis of representational politics in film to the racial, ethnic, gender, class, and sexual dimensions implicated, created, and fostered in BGLOs in everyday life. In so doing, I reveal how BGLOs act as a means to acculturate individual men and women into the dominant societal structure, which in earlier decades of their formation caused intracultural discrimination. Yet BGLOs simultaneously resisted normative structures through strategic social and cultural practices in the name of creating a counterfraternal bloc. Chapter 1 provides a historical and cultural foundation to understand AKA as a part and an extension of this counterfraternal bloc and history. Further, it situates how the gender, race, sexuality, and class of AKA women shaped their person and their activist strategies for operating within the public sphere as sorority women and as Black women.

In chapter 2, I introduce the idea of AKA as inhabiting many of the characteristics of a Black counterpublic, that is, as a site that converges cultural and social spaces with political platforms. For AKA, their multiple origins affected how they constituted their counterpublic formation, and their cultural, social, and political consciousness affected how they would transform and use the space of a Greek-letter organization for insurgent and conservative purposes. I describe the sorority as a social and political space that performs work in the dominant and Black public spheres. My analysis of AKA's counterpublic-sphere work shows how the women created a theory of social justice and acted upon their consciousness for change through the sorority affiliation. The chapter draws from sorority and historical archives to chart AKA's activities during turn-of-the-century suffrage and reform movements; twentieth-century anti-lynching activism; World War II political activities; 1950s and 1960s civil rights activism; 1970s chapter expansion into Europe, Asia, the Caribbean, and Africa; 1980s transnational political programs in Africa; 1990s AIDS activism; and current efforts for political voice and social relevance. Insofar as this chapter charts the longevity of AKA as a group engaged in various forms of activism, it is able to provide an example of an ongoing social movement among younger and older Black women in the organization. Although I acknowledge their good deeds and work toward social justice throughout the twentieth and twenty-first centuries, this chapter also argues that AKA's politics of respectability and reform ventures may have adverse consequences for the masses of Black Americans that their counterpublic-sphere work aims to help.

The subject of chapter 3 concerns the way that AKA undergraduate sorority women create and negotiate their identities through symbolic behavior and cultural practices. Drawing on African diaspora and performance theory, I describe AKA undergraduate women as reproducing and recreating gender, sexual, and ethnic identities through stepping. I begin with a history of stepping in BGLOs and proceed to focus on the polyvalent and ritualistic properties of Black sorority step shows, drawing on ethnography, video footage, and secondary sources on dance and performance and on etymology studies. In being openly sexual at times in their language and movements during a step performance, AKA women resist, contradict, and recycle twentieth-century politics of respectability as mandated by their foremothers in the Black intelligentsia. By conducting a close reading of AKA sorority and other Black American sorority step performances, I reveal the diverse ways in which one constitutes culture and how it transforms over time based on a particular historical moment and cultural practice. *Stomp the Yard*, a few articles, and one book have taken up the subject of stepping as a primary focus, but this chapter adds to the literature by expanding on how Black women's contributions to stepping relate to discourses of sexuality and femininity across generations.

Ritual and cultural practices are a central force of AKA identity. AKA women's former and sometimes current pledge activities create a rite of passage, which stems from a long-standing cultural tradition among Black Americans to patrol and redraw the boundaries of Black respectability. Black sorority pledge activities, including rites that one might construe as hazing, have received popular media attention, but no serious scholarly attention. Chapter 4 thus begins with a brief history of hazing in BGLOs and then focuses on two hazing cases involving AKA sorority. Guided by the theoretical work on violence and power, critical legal studies, and critical race feminism, this chapter reveals the contradictions and multiple meanings of respectability, femininity, violence, power, and the law for AKA undergraduate and graduate women. Although some of these rites contradict the notions of respectability among Black American women I introduce in chapters 2 and 3, they also socialize women into commonly held characteristics—parables of character that I outline throughout the chapter as reminiscent of nineteenth-century and early twentieth-century respectability politics. The paradox here lies within the use of coercive, anti-respectable behavior by members to transform sorority hopefuls into their ideal of a sorority sister. I argue that the contradictory and dangerous rites of hazing act as a private way to resist the constraining politics of respectability that these women are expected to embrace and embody in the public sphere, as mandated by older women in the sorority.

Using the possible cultural meanings of AKA's 2008 centennial convention and the controversy concerning the induction of First Lady Michelle Obama into AKA as a starting place, chapter 5 paces through challenges of Black counterpublics by addressing pressing issues AKA women face in academic, public, and social life. I bring together the voices and experiences of younger, middle-age, and more senior women to offer a generational trajectory of becoming, being, and reflecting on AKA's role as professional women, sorors, and community activists. At the time of the interviews, the women's ages ranged from eighteen to sixty-two. Many women were in their early twenties and mid-thirties, one was in her forties, and three women interviewed were in their late fifties to early sixties. I interviewed twenty women total, from nearly every region in the United States. States represented in this chapter include California, Kansas, Illinois, Ohio, Georgia, Pennsylvania, Virginia, and Arizona. A few of the women described their class background as working class, yet many AKA women interviewed claimed a middle-class background. Most of the women crossed over into membership at a predominantly White college, with the exception of two who did their undergraduate training at a historically Black college; one at Spelman College and another who began a pledgeship at Hampton Institute. AKA interviewees represented here are working students or those who hold a variety of positions in business, law, computer technology, public relations, education, and psychology; one interviewee does unwaged work in the home.

AKA voices appear throughout the study, but the design of chapter 5 is to create a space where their voices converge to bring my discussion of sorority membership not to a close but, rather, to a space where others might enter. In particular, the women address three core themes of concern to Black women and their sorority: class, gender, and racial struggle, regrets and mistakes pertaining to pledging and hazing, and maintaining hope through action in the Black public sphere. Their voices emerge as vital to understanding Black sorority life within a contemporary context, and they reveal larger cultural problems and political struggles that Black counterpublics face today. Some AKA women took great pains to protect the organization and to create a positive image of AKA during our conversations; others expressed misgivings and personal tragedies experienced as sorority members. In all, their voices show that AKA's cultural and counterpublic-sphere work is pregnant with possibilities and contradictions. By including the voice of women within the organization as the last chapter, the reader has a unique opportunity to draw parallels between AKA's responses and the previous historical and cultural discussion present in this book.

At the book's conclusion, I draw from popular fiction, that is, T. J. Butler's novel *Sorority Sisters*, and from ideas about the role of the public intellectual to argue that no social-political space is perfect or wholly transformative, but that does not mean such formations cannot provide insights for change and reflection. As cultural critic George Lipsitz writes, "Scholarship connecting academic research to the work of social movements holds great promise for the generation of new knowledge, as well as for the development of resistance against the increasingly indecent global social order." It is not only the politically and culturally constructive components of AKA that may provide the form of critique and resistance of which Lipsitz writes, it is also AKA's problematic aspects that should provide insight into areas in Black communities that require transformation. Historian Robin Kelley reminds us of this when he writes: "Too often, our standards for evaluating social movements pivot around whether they succeeded in realizing their visions rather than on the merits or power of the visions themselves. By such a measure, virtually every . . . movement failed because the basic power relations they sought to change [or question] remain pretty much in tact. [Yet] it is precisely these alternative visions and dreams that inspire new generations to continue to struggle for change."[14] The AKA sorority, I argue, is an example of the ethnic struggle and political articulation that Kelley and Lipsitz describe, existing as a social body that struggles between being absorbed and influenced by the dominant cultural hegemonic process and resisting it by its mere social existence, cultural and ethnic composition, and different and often transformative political goals. Black sororities as a whole are a part of a larger cultural phenomenon where Black

Americans invent spaces to engage in cultural expression and enact social and political practice.

That the Black sorority functions as a social movement has been established by historical scholarship, but an interdisciplinary and a scholarly examination of the specificity of Black sorority life via a case study on AKA provides two additional intellectual interventions. One, it provides a much-needed look into an unexamined subculture among Black women through the practices and problems of everyday life, as seen in their process of distinction, sorority stepping, pledging, and hazing. Two, juxtapositions between popular culture, history, and the circulation of AKA voices help in the accounting for history and contemporary lived social relations. AKA entails a set of complex experiences that reveals the contradictions in cultural formations necessary of theoretical analysis, critical evaluation, and cultural interrogation. More than a venture in the critical critique of a subculture, my intent is to ensure that the many years of labor it took to bring to fruition *Disciplining Women: Alpha Kappa Alpha, Black Counterpublics, and the Cultural Politics of Black Sororities* are worthy for author and reader alike.

1

Stomp the Yard, *School Daze*, and the Cultural Politics of Black Greek-Letter Organizations

> Theta represents the elite of every aspect of Black life. We are only as strong as our weakest link. A fraternity is a major, life-long bond.
>
> —Big Brother Sylvester, *Stomp the Yard*

> All this talk about tradition means you cannot keep up with the present.
>
> —DJ, Theta pledge, *Stomp the Yard*

> Being in a fraternity is about more than just stepping.
>
> —April, DJ's "object" of desire and campus socialite, *Stomp the Yard*

Sony Pictures, in 2007, released the first film of the twenty-first century to employ the cultural practices of Black Greek-letter organizations (BGLOs) as an example of how the hip-hop generation negotiates college life, socioeconomic class, and cultural meanings. The film's title, *Stomp the Yard*, presents one of the principal practices of BLGOs—stepping—as a metaphor for the struggle over the meaning of Blackness. Stepping is a form of dance that relies on a mixture of African aesthetics, vernacular language systems, and intricate body movements; it is an example of Black Americans' distinct and transformed cultural practices. *Stomp the Yard's* protagonist and soon-to-be-stepper-extraordinaire, DJ Williams, is a working-class, first-year college student, and a skilled street dancer from an urban environment. Still scarred by the recent and brutal death of his brother after a dance-off competition gone wrong, DJ cultivates a guarded persona and guarded heart, while remaining skeptical of one of the primary social aspects of Black college life: BGLOs. His skepticism strengthens once he recognizes that the object of his affection, a female student named April, is also the girlfriend of a pompous and irrationally jealous fraternity brother. After he is coaxed into pledging Theta Nu Theta fraternity because his dance skills are expected to help the Thetas win a step competition, however, DJ slowly begins to realize that the skills that once brought him monetary gain on the streets, that is, improvisational dance, had the ability to serve other purposes. The film's romantic heroine, April, adds to DJ's change of heart about fraternity life when she informs him that being in a BGLO entails *more* than stepping. *Stomp the Yard* is successful in its presentation of stepping as a cultural, social, and political sign of Blackness for BGLOs. However, the totality of *Stomp the Yard's* narrative does not assert April's claim.

Stomp the Yard is a coming-of-age story, urban drama, and romantic tryst all in one, which exposes mainstream America to the microcosmic world of the Black public sphere as envisaged through Black college life. Not unlike Spike Lee's film *School Daze* (1988), released nineteen years earlier, director Sylvain White's *Stomp the Yard* is less a thorough examination of BGLOs than a film that uses the organizations as an opportunity to show how African American men define and struggle over the meaning of Blackness, class, and sexuality on college campuses. For DJ and the rival Mu Gamma Xi fraternity member Grant (who is April's current boyfriend), stepping is the site where Black men work through and negotiate this struggle, and April is the prize of successful masculinity. As I have written elsewhere in my cinematic analysis of the film *School Daze*, the latter film also presents a similar troubling scenario to spectators through its *mise en scene* and narrative.[1]

Stomp the Yard therefore shows stepping and BGLO life as a masculine terrain where women are objects for ownership or commodities to buy and fight over. Given this masculine framework and oversight, the Black sorority may appear as an unimaginable site to articulate similar shifts and cleavages in the understandings of culture, class, and gender. *Stomp the Yard* and *School Daze* fail to provide a visual or narrative window into how one might situate sorority life for Black women within these discourses, but both films offer an opportunity, through their exposure of BGLO life to a mass audience, for such a conversation to begin.

This book argues through a case study on Alpha Kappa Alpha that the sorority's work in the Black public sphere illuminates the specificity, complexity, and diversity of Black cultural practices, and that their ongoing efforts toward political mobilization and social change in the Black public sphere represent a vital political practice. Its arguments are in part a response and challenge to BGLO presentation in *Stomp the Yard* and the type of caricatures in Lee's *School Daze*. Lee, in his representation of Black Greek life, presents two diametrically opposed views on Black culture and perceptions of self in *School Daze:* the haves and the have-nots. The haves are the Wannabe characters, beige to light-brown-hued men and women who are members of two fictional organizations: the Gammites (fraternity) and the Gamma Rays (little sister sorority). The Gammites and Gamma Rays are color conscious, flaunt crass materialism, are politically (a)pathetic, are presented as a mimicry of White fraternal members, and spend the majority of their time engaging in unproductive hazing and pledging rituals. Lee calls the have-nots the Jigaboos. These dark-brown-hued college students are Afrocentric and politically focused; they commit their energy and activities to demanding that their college, the fictitious and historically Black Mission College, financially divest itself from South Africa. *School Daze* explores the following question: In what ways do BGLOs, which claim to uplift their communities, find themselves trapped within their own color biases and class elitism, where the masses of Black Americans suffer as a result?

If *Stomp the Yard* is the hip-hop generation's version of Black life in the twenty-first century, then *School Daze* is the epitome of the narcissistic and materially motivated generation often associated with the Reagan-Bush years of the late twentieth century. One of the actors in the film, Roger Smith, who played one of the Gammite roles, comments about *Schools Daze*'s documentation of BGLOs in the 1980s: "I have this great theory that *School Daze*, the film, will prove to be a very interesting comment on culture. Here's the example: The Gammites, the pledges who are supposedly Wannabes, are perhaps the most African men on campus, culturally that is; their sense of kinship, bonding, their sense of movement, rhythm, the chants, call and response, addressing the elders. It's all very African. They've got all this happening, but they see themselves as Greeks."[2]

Smith focuses on the fraternity men representing contradictory forms of ethnic identity. For Smith, to inhabit the space of a Greek-letter organization mutes the diasporic element of BGLOs' cultural formation. A Greek letter identity is incommensurate with a Black ethnic identity—the two cannot coexist without one having to give—something implied when he says that the organizations "are the most African" but "see themselves as Greek." This position on culture denies the power and prevalence of cultural hybridity, but it also romanticizes what the actor praises as essentially cultural/African (written as masculine) while remaining detached from the reality of the historical formation of identity and cultural change. However, my research reveals that for AKA, a Greek-letter sorority is a site where African diasporic identities are created, negotiated, performed, transformed, and lived through everyday life experiences, not one where cultural identity is relinquished, lost, and assimilated. *Stomp the Yard* and *School Daze* are refractive illustrations of modern-day BGLOs, but little scholarship to date explores how the participation in these groups grew out of a complex set of color, class, culture, sexual, and gender arrangements.

The Process of Distinction: Color, Class, and Sexualities in Black Greek-Letter Organizations

Given the historical relevancy and relational aspects of culture, any analysis of a particular subculture should ideally begin by establishing the cultural formations and movements that took part in shaping its emergence. Although Spike Lee's *School Daze* insinuates that BGLOs are mimics of their white counterparts, Greek-letter organizations represented the most visible social option available to the large majority of college students throughout the twentieth century. Participation in the Greek system for Black Americans allowed them to function, in the eyes of White college administrators, as legitimate and recognizable college organizations.

Legitimization was not the sole reason for their formation. BGLOs are an example of a body of women and men who utilized an existing social space and skillfully transformed it for their own political purposes. Inasmuch as the newly forming BGLOs are a part of a historical movement among Black Americans of cultural and political work through social institutions, fraternals, and secret societies, these organizations were akin to the well-formed cultural fraternals that existed throughout the African diaspora. Today, these fraternals fall under the historically Black, collegiate, umbrella organization the National Pan-Hellenic Council (NPHC). The organizations are as follows: Alpha Phi Alpha (fraternity founded in 1906), Alpha Kappa Alpha (sorority founded in 1908), Kappa Alpha Psi (fraternity founded in 1911), Omega Psi Phi (fraternity founded in 1911), Delta Sigma Theta (sorority founded in 1913), Phi Beta Sigma (fraternity founded in 1914), Zeta Phi Beta (sorority founded in 1920), Sigma Gamma Rho (sorority founded in 1922), and Iota Phi Theta (fraternity founded in 1963).

The development of BGLOs was a product of the diverse social and cultural circumstances that each group faced. While Alpha Phi Alpha's, Kappa Alpha Psi's, and Sigma Gamma Rho's formation took place at predominately White colleges (Cornell, Indiana, and Butler universities, respectively,) AKA's, Omega Psi Phi's, Delta Sigma Theta's, Phi Beta Sigma's, and Zeta Phi Beta's formation took place at the historically Black college Howard University. The site of their emergence had a direct bearing upon their organizational structure and the ensuing cultural, social, and political consciousness each developed independently, and later collectively, when the NPHC formed in 1929.[3] Predominantly White and historically Black colleges had different educational goals. Indeed, historical developments and social structures shaped their organizational character. Historically Black colleges provided Black American students with the opportunity to attain a higher education, because many White colleges would not admit Black American students due to segregation in the United States and discriminatory admissions policies solely on the basis of race. Historically Black colleges were more often than not the only choice for people of African descent in the late nineteenth and early twentieth centuries.[4] White college institutions were used as an apparatus to perpetuate White and, often, male privilege (White women, ethno-religious groups, and other people of color, too, faced barriers to university admission in the nineteenth and early twentieth centuries). In contrast, historically Black colleges opened up educational opportunity structures previously closed to Black American women and men.

At the turn of the twentieth century, both college formations encapsulated political ideologies that leaned toward forms of liberal democracy and conservative accommodation. At the historically Black colleges such as Howard, where the president was White until the early mid-twentieth century, these institutions were hardly bastions of radical politics open to the culture and presence of the masses of Black Americans. An example of this was in 1922, when the White president of Howard University, J. Stanley Durkee, proclaimed that the Black American theater productions students hoped to bring to campus were culturally inappropriate because of their focus on African folk cultural idioms. Black conservative administrators and professors at Howard shared this sentiment, too, until the mid-1950s.[5] Howard University, founded a few years after the end of the American shame of slavery, began to serve the growing Black American middle- to upper-middle classes. Further, until the 1920s, reportedly 80 percent of the student population at Howard and many other historically Black colleges, including Wilberforce University (Ohio), Spelman College, and Fisk University (Tennessee), and Hampton Institute (Virginia), were allegedly of a light-skin complexion. The color makeup of some historically Black colleges, at least in the first part of the twentieth century, suggested a dependent relationship between light skin color, class advantage, and higher education.[6]

Entanglements of Distinction: Elitism, Colorism, and Fraternal Formations

Colorism—the counterproductive practice of skin color bias practiced by the broad and full spectrum of skin gradations in African American, White, and all communities of color—is a specter that haunts BGLOs. In addition, an obsessive discourse propagated in BGLO history books about members constituting the "first" among those within African America to achieve doctorates, political office, and majority representation in regarded professions reads as elitist rhetoric. In their defense, BGLOs insist that only the most academically sound- and leadership-minded individuals gain membership, and that hue was never a criterion. As one member responded to the accusation of elitism and exclusion in the educational publication, the *Black Collegian*, "We are elitist in that we strive for academic achievement. We are exclusionary in that our membership is limited to those matriculated in a four-year university."[7] AKA member Ellen mirrored this stance during an interview session for this book; she compares BGLO selection to the criterion used in society at large concerning social and organizational "fit." She defends BGLOs in their insular practices as being congruent with the protection of family units, and she insists that their self-discipline and exclusion is in the name of investing in their organization and communities:

> To attend a top university you are evaluated heavily, to get a promotion at work you are put to the test. These things are done to separate the weak from the strong. To me sororities are the same. Just like in a family unit, when you have invested so much time and dedication into a child's future, you refuse to let outside entities tear it apart. The sorority is the same way. We take care of our own. We teach our own. We refuse to settle for anything less than the goals we have set out to accomplish. So if we are misinterpreted for defending our investments in ourselves, our families, or communities, then several professional institutions need to reevaluate their own guidelines and regulations before commenting on ours.[8]

Nonfraternal members, however, argue that in the past, BGLOs' selection process for members was indeed color coded and similar to the social fraternals, such as the Links, Girl Friends, and the Boulé.[9] At the turn of the century, social fraternals among Black Americans, sometimes benevolent but not formed with the sole intent of providing mutual aid for members or their communities, emerged within middle- to upper-middle-class enclaves in the East and Midwest regions of the United States. One generation removed from slavery, the social fraternals represented and created a space for the emerging Black professional class to socialize. The most popular and well known were the sororal groups the Links and the Girl Friends (1945, 1927), the fraternal groups the Boulé (also known as Sigma Pi Phi) and Guardsmen (1904, 1933), and the adolescent social club Jack and Jill (1938), all of which remain active today.[10] The controversy over the early- to mid-twentieth-century social fraternal and sororal groups within the Black American community was rooted in membership barriers based on color and class. In the first half of the twentieth century, physical attributes and class position were important criteria for entrance into the chapters of many of these groups.

Allegations of colorism among social fraternities and sororities, especially the aforementioned five, are widespread. Accusations exist that many of these organizations administered "paper bag tests," whereby members could not have skin darker than the color of a beige paper bag. Black social fraternals thus operated much like the blue vein secret societies among Black Americans that were prominent in the South and Eastern regions of the United States, where the veins of potential members had to show through their skin and a comb had to glide through their hair without snarling in order to qualify for membership. These markers of whiteness—fair skin and straight or loosely curled hair—held great aesthetic capital for a number of members and chapters, thus adding another layer of exclusivity for the organizations.[11]

One might explain colorism, classism, and other forms of intracultural prejudice among these groups as internal oppression, where the hailing of an individual into ideologies of self-perception and worth is antithetical to the growth and nurture of the racial, ethnic, gender, and sexual identities they inhabit. The fraternals among Black Americans that engaged in the practices of color prejudice and other intracultural prejudices might very well exist as products of false consciousness that arise out of subconsciously accepting and acting out the dominant culture's belief system of the inferiority of Black Americans. Nevertheless, the reality that one may resist and counteract these ideas and actions requires accountability, rather than merely apologia, by and for social fraternal members who engaged in colorism. BGLOs cultivated and faced similar cultural politics as their foremothers and forefathers in social fraternals. Large numbers of fairer-skinned members in a few of the Black American Greek societies at Howard in particular, at least until World War I, left them vulnerable to accusations of colorism.[12]

Historically Black colleges such as Bethune-Cookman College (Florida) and Tuskegee Institute (Alabama) did not appear to represent this color and class stigma or stereotype. However, they did prescribe conservative approaches to racism, economic advancement, and cultural politics.[13] The latter colleges encouraged students to succeed in ways and areas that would not threaten or make waves in the chokehold of racism and segregation in the United States. In contrast, the former college insisted students succeed and surpass what their White counterparts thought they could accomplish academically and monetarily, yet they too did not prescribe radical means to achieve the ends of racial and economic equality. Indeed, political, color, and class divisions in historically Black colleges were microcosmic examples of the larger cultural politics within and between assimilation and accommodation, within which Black America found itself encroached from the late nineteenth to early twentieth centuries.[14] The two competing prescriptions of accommodation and assimilation in social relations were not exact polar opposites in practice. There were in-between positions for Black Americans, characterized by fluctuating and shifting perceptions of what it meant to occupy the subject position of being educated, socially alienated, a racial-ethnic minority, and a part of a diverse culture of people.

For BGLOs, to create a formation radical in its approach to social and cultural discrimination with visible Black American cultural elements would prove to be a challenge at predominantly White *and* Black American institutions. Generational schisms would exist at Howard in particular, where five of the eight BGLOs formed, particularly among older White college administrators, the Black American professorate, and the emerging social and cultural consciousness of younger students. BGLOs experienced the contradiction of many counterformations that emerged in opposition to the dominant: while trying to break apart and distinguish themselves from the prevailing, hegemonic oppressive social and political structures of the larger culture, they too became susceptible to encapsulating the very ideologies they claimed in a collective struggle to resist. The Greek-letter organizations formed at Howard toed the line between conservative liberalism and insurgent activism. By contrast, the groups formed at predominantly White institutions would use the seemingly neutral space of the Greek-letter fraternal to carry on, in secret, bonding, social, and cultural work in an environment that was antithetical to the affirmation of their culture and the cultivation of their intellectual pursuits and development. Still, the complex intertwine of color, class, politics, and education—at least historically—existed within historically Black and predominantly White institutions.

To what degree a large color spectrum was representative of past student populations as a whole is difficult to ascertain, although photos of BGLO chapters in the early twentieth century are found in most university archives and special collections. As with many student organizations and individuals, the aesthetic, political work, and experiences of BGLOs changed over time; no single policy or approach existed, and different historical moments and college affiliations provided different opportunities and visions. The extent to which arbitrary and counterproductive distinctions took place among members of yesteryear lies with an unreachable population, that is, the deceased founders of the organizations. In spite of this, additional oral testimony of members and their collective memories, secondary sources, and hypotheses help put together this color, class, and sexual puzzle.

Norma Boyd, one of the founders of the AKA sorority, claimed that her role and the role of others like her—fair skinned, educated, and wealthy—allowed for a foot in both worlds, Black and White. Boyd considered herself a spy in the world of Whites, who often passed to "come back and report just how the other half does" so that the "darker people of the race" could strategize with them against the perceived enemy within the dominant culture.[15] Historian Deborah Gray White argues that Boyd and other fairer-skinned activists used their position not over, but in solidarity with, their Black brothers and sisters. Nonetheless, Boyd and others who shared her perception on color advantage heightened the criticism of fraternal members.[16] Boyd's comment may not have been intended as condescending, but it did seem to imply an underlying subtext, that is, that they were inherently special and worthy of praise and celebration for their education, accomplishments, and, sometimes, their color.

In a contemporary context, members of the AKA sorority revealed to me how historical ideas about color, class, and distinction in an era of assumed postsegregation remains. AKA member Pamela, who pledged at a predominantly White institution in the 1990s, points to the various ways these issues are present depending on the college institution, and she sees Spike Lee's *School Daze* as an exaggeration of these issues. Unlike her sorority sisters of yesteryear, and as a woman who identifies as darker skinned, she feels the sorority is less dependent on using color as distinction or color as a social device. She argues of Black sororities and AKA that

> there is the perception that we are elitist—that all of us come from the "right" families and that there is a lot of colorism. However, I think darker women are more represented now and there are women in AKA who look a lot of different ways. The African American sororities today examine their values more closely. Black colleges perhaps participate more in colorism and *School Daze* was an exaggeration to make a point. Today, there is not the paper bag test, but colorism overall is not finished. I, as a dark-skinned woman, probably would not have been accepted into the sorority back in the day.[17]

Pamela's self-reflection is not necessarily widely held, but she does account for historical change without concluding that colorism does not exist in BGLOs. Similarly, AKA member Candice, who pledged at one of the University of California college campuses, insinuates that the civil rights movement may have alleviated counterproductive modes of distinction such as color and class, but she is quick to remind that there is a kernel of truth in what she defines as the stereotype of BGLOs. Unlike Pamela, she sees *School Daze* as more than an exaggeration, citing the film as an irresponsible portrayal. In reference to the perception of BGLOs and the film's impact, she proclaims: "People always think we're elitist, color conscious, and bourgeois. I am definitely not like that, nor is our organization. But like all stereotypes there is truth. I think we're beyond that mostly, especially after the civil rights movement. I think the Spike Lee movie [*School Daze*] was irresponsible. There are more pressing issues in the Black community to talk about, we do not need to sit around and worry about skin color. It was definitely a wrong portrayal for this day and age."[18]

Candice's point is earnest, but of course, silence about colorism within BGLOs and in existing scholarship about BGLOs does not silence their critics. BGLOs at predominantly White and historically Black institutions may enact various forms of distinction contingent on historical moment and their locations, but both are culpable for enacting transformation in contemporary times. One might argue, therefore, that worrying about and alleviating counterproductive distinction are precisely what all Black organizations must do, in public and in private, in order to make the standard of Black public service and their workers who serve anew.

BGLOs and the Cultural Politics of Class and Sexuality(ies)

Former president of Zeta Phi Beta, Sojourner Jackson, admitted that in the 1930s, when she graduated from a historically Black college, fraternity and sorority membership meant "you were supposed to be above other people . . . at that time if you didn't have the money—if your parents didn't give it to you—you couldn't get into the organizations."[19] William C. Brown, who is a member of Omega Psi Phi, said that when he pledged in 1939, acceptance into his fraternal meant that he "would be a part of a group of men who were going someplace."[20] Agreeing with Brown, Ozell Sutton, former president of Alpha Phi Alpha, claims that even contemporarily, the Black Greek system is "a network that cannot be matched anywhere in the black community."[21] Brown's and Sutton's statements show a linkage between the past and present and infer an unapologetic sentiment of social and class distinction. In this social context, BGLOs, like White and Black American social fraternals, represent who has cultural capital and social, political, and economic power in their communities. Networking opportunities are surely helpful for members, but for every social circle, those on the margins of that circle exist without access to the professional networking intrinsic to BGLOs. Deborah Gray White describes the double-bind and double-work of Black middle-class formations, observing that since the turn of the twentieth century "classism was inherent in the networking strategy that made the [Black American] middle class the conduit through which resources flowed *into* black communities."[22]

Members of these BGLOs may appear at times to succumb to the dominant conceptualization of aesthetics and the capitalist-driven ethos of what sociologist E. Franklin Frazier called their "conspicuous consumption."[23] Frazier noted that the first eight of NPHC BGLOs spent a total of $2,225,000 in 1952 on cotillions and other social parties. In response, the organizations argue that their lavish parties fund their core civic and community development programs.[24] Few members and chapters hold enough independent wealth to fund their local and national community work without fund-raisers, thus the reality of their social aspect and their avowed selfless benevolence no doubt lies somewhere in the middle of both positions. For example, a member of Kappa Alpha Psi noted that he became skeptical of fraternity participation in the late 1970s. After he asked his fraternity chapter to donate money to a scholarship program for Black American students at his university, where he was an athletic coach, the national fraternity granted him $100 out of a substantial treasury of millions.[25] Kappa Alpha Psi's discretionary funding in this case did little to refute Frazier's claims. More pointedly, such examples reveal the slippery distinction between being conscious of the needs of those who are disadvantaged because of class and having a class conscience.

To reach beyond Frazier's description and move toward prescribing a cultural politics of action, cultural critic bell hooks offers a useful outlook and practice for those Black Americans privileged by education and class. Hooks's arguments are useful in reconsidering the role of the class privileged in the nation's past and present for BGLOs and African America. She contends that it is "possible to gain class power without betraying our solidarity toward those without class privilege, by living simply, sharing our resources, and refusing to engage in hedonistic consumerism and the politics of greed."[26] Hooks asserts that wealthy Black Americans can reframe their class advantage in solidarity with, rather than at the expense of, other Black Americans. The possibilities and limitations of BGLOs may thus hold lessons for social and cultural formations that fail to merge their rhetoric of class consciousness with personal choices of consumerism and tangible civic work in their communities. A reasonable percentage of AKAs fall within a middle-class socioeconomic bracket; however, their community development work, as shown throughout the remainder of this study, often speaks as loud as their words.

A growing amount of scholarship on the nine BGLOs chronicles their civic engagement work in detail, including my own explication of their activism during the past two centuries published elsewhere, but lesser discussed is the relationship between these organizations and sexual identifications.[27] Race work, academic excellence, and community development did not mean that members would overcome other forms of prejudice besides colorism and classism, such as heterosexism. Proclaimed solidarity based on the idea that all Black Americans are in the same social predicament because of racism alone is problematic and elides other forms of discrimination. Cornell West, cultural critic and member of the Alpha Phi Alpha fraternity, argues that for Black Americans, "Racist treatment vastly differs owing to class, gender, sexual orientation, nation, region, hue, and age."[28] AKA member and children's book author Jacqueline Woodson explained this in an introspective autobiographical essay in a

1999 issue of *Essence* magazine. Woodson wrote that she will always defend and affiliate with her sorority and remains close to her sorority sisters, but as an "out" lesbian, she often finds the sorority's emphasis on femininity and, by association, heterosexuality, difficult and privileged criteria. Woodson writes that she and other nonheterosexual women "often feel stereotyped and misunderstood."[29] Fraternals are a social form predominantly characterized by single-sex socialization and organization, but there is a dominant ethos of heteronormativity and heterosexual courtship encouraged within the fraternal framework as a whole. As a result, the possible role of non-normative sexualities as they intersect with racial identity in BGLOs reveals the limitations and commonalities upon which Black Americans identify.

Woodson's commentary is descriptive of how the large majority of sororities and fraternities ascribe to normative sexual codes. To understand this, one might consider the racial and class context in which sexualities emerge. In explaining Black American middle-class patrolling of sexuality in general, cultural critic Kobena Mercer writes that rigid sexual morals and conservative attitudes about sexuality among Black people exist in a large part to compensate for racist myths that present Blackness and Black people as sexually and morally depraved.[30] Feminist and cultural critic Patricia Hill Collins argues that in a racist and sexist society, heterosexuality, and class advantage for those who identify as heterosexual and economically wealthy, remains one of the few areas to acquire power and retain privilege.[31] Nonheterosexual fraternal members may find themselves in a precarious position in relation to the performance of gender and sex in these organizations—a performance that remains safely situated within heterosexual frameworks. Thus the fraternal apparatus distinguishes itself in other ways beyond the barriers of class and hue.

Conclusion

BGLOs' problematic position within the structures of sexual, color, and class domination may call into question the possibilities of seeing AKA as a counterfraternal or counterpublic movement. I argue, however, that such groups can exist as productive and counterproductive at the same time. When one peels back the mask of propriety that members find necessary, an "innocent Black subject," to borrow phrasing from sociologist Stuart Hall, is unlikely to live underneath the surface skin.[32] There is credence to the accusation of colorism, classism, heteronormativity, and the overall elitism of BGLOs; nonetheless, there were and are differences in how these variables of distinction work within the organizations. Therefore, one can draw careful conclusions about the specificity of BGLOs' practices. At predominantly White universities, the color and class diversity among members was more apparent, whereas at historically Black colleges, class and color in a seemingly homogenous environment, at least in terms of race, became the way in which they could, and sometimes did, create distinction. On the basis of perceived and material differences of gender, class, sexualities, and color, BGLOs held and exercised various amounts privilege in relation to these shifting identity contexts.

Stuart Hall writes that identity does not exist outside of representation.[33] That is, visual media and views of society may impact how people form and understand their individual and group identities. This crucial idea seems to shape how BGLOs perceive and excuse the limitations of BGLO life, thus in turn shaping how they present and understand their own experiences and cultural politics. The most cursory observation of BGLO chapters in the twenty-first century demonstrates a range of hues; BGLOs claim to embrace nontraditional student participation in the organizations, but they remain largely silent on the issue of sexuality. As the oldest Greek-letter sorority created among Black women, AKA and its social, cultural, and political practices remain at the heart of these discourses of distinction, identity, and power. AKA is not immune to the problems of everyday life hitherto explained. Still, their community development work advocated cultural and political change in the Black public sphere. AKA's ability to realize counterpublic-sphere work through their actions shows an ongoing commitment to provide clarity between BGLOs' image in popular culture, as seen in *Stomp the Yard* and *School Daze*, their own past and current self-representation through cultural practices and politics, and representative action in the Black public sphere.

2

Alpha Kappa Alpha, Black Counterpublics, and the Ambiguity of Social Reform

> Through the political agitation of those such as antilynching leader Ida B. Wells and the protests of organizations such as the NAACP, African Americans used a variety of tactics and approaches in the struggle to reinsert themselves into the channels of public discourse. Simultaneously, an active counterpublic was continued through organizations such as the Negro Women's Club Movement.
>
> —Michael C. Dawson, "A Black Counterpublic?"[1]

In 1997, four Black Greek-letter sororities—Alpha Kappa Alpha, Delta Sigma Theta, Zeta Phi Beta, and Sigma Gamma Rho—joined C. Delores Tucker, the chair of the National Political Congress of Black Women, in the Black Women's Sojourner Truth Monument Crusade. Tucker and her supporters fought to prevent a congressional resolution, which called for moving a statue of three White leaders of the women's suffrage movement from the basement of the Capitol to the Rotunda, unless there was an addition of an image of the Black feminist, abolitionist, suffragist, and human rights advocate Sojourner Truth. On April 22, 1997, Congresswoman Cynthia McKinney, a Democrat from Georgia, introduced legislation to put the sorority women's and other civil rights groups' request into action. The federal government suggested a separate statue of Sojourner Truth, but Black women activists refused to compromise.

Tucker remarked pointedly, "Black women are sick and tired of being left out of the history of this nation."[2] The Sojourner Truth Monument Crusade is one example of the way Black American sororities act to address the absence of scholarly attention to, and public knowledge of, the participation of Black American women in public life and politics.

AKA's counterpublic-sphere efforts from 1908 through the late twentieth century mirror the activist pro-action demonstrated in the Sojourner Truth Monument Crusade. The sorority's work oscillates from benevolence and reform to radical political interventions, and much of AKA's political strategizing and activism is tantamount to tangible, counterpublic-sphere work. There is a generous body of intellectual work on the conservative and radical components of counterpublics, yet for the purpose of my arguments here, I draw from the Black Public Sphere Collective's (BPSC) theorization of Black counterpublics to define AKA's various roles in public life. The BPSC is a critical mass of Black intellectuals who write about and hold commitments to working toward the betterment of Black people's lives on a large-scale and grassroots level.

For this insurgent group of intellectuals, Black counterpublics entail "the critical practice and visionary politics, in which [Black] intellectuals can join with the energies of the street, the school, the church, and the city to constitute and challenge the exclusionary violence of much public space in the United States."[3] Given AKA's efforts in the Sojourner Truth Monument Crusade and their initiative in similar as well as more radical collective efforts for an entire century, the women's activism demonstrates the BPSC's definition of counterpublic-sphere work. Counterpublic-sphere work has increased subversive possibilities to existing forms of race, gender, and sex domination in universities, where the production and maintenance of ideologies take place, and in social formations that may appear insignificant on the surface.

The arguments offered here grapple with the ways AKA sorority struggles with class bias and conservative cultural politics, and how these shortcomings collide with their counterpublic efforts, explications that are absent in existing literature on Black sororities.[4] I further provide a comparison between AKA and other racial-ethnic women's social and political organizations to assert that AKA, like their Chicana, Asian American, Indigenous Nations, and White ethnic sisters, took on activist work out of necessity owing to their subordinated position as sexualized, gender, ethnic, or racial minorities. Thus what follows is a brief comparative history of AKA's historical formation and ideological stance vis-à-vis White and racial-ethnic women's clubs, a theoretical discussion of the contradictions and merits of their reform and counterpublic-sphere work, and political prescriptions for this and similar organizations concerned with addressing the life conditions for people of African descent. My comparative history and explication of AKA counterpublic-sphere work maintains that the sorority is more than a social organization dabbling in benevolence and reform. AKA exhibits an ethnic center that draws in a significant amount of college-educated Black women in the name of collective support, academic excellence, and commitment to change in their local and global communities.

Comparative and Diverse Formations: Women's Clubs as Social-Political Centers

Black sororities are sister organizations to women's clubs and other civil rights organizations of the nineteenth and twentieth centuries. In the nineteenth and twentieth centuries, women's clubs provided a gender-exclusive arena for self-actualization through involvement in political and social reform. These groups emerged at a critical historical moment when White women and women of color began to organize for enfranchisement and create reform movements to address issues such as health care for poor and working-class families, child welfare, temperance, and literacy. White and Protestant middle-class women, Catholic, Mormon, Jewish, Black, Asian American, Chicana, and working-class White women all created religious, social, benevolent, and literary groups to prove that education and political work were neither trivial nor impractical for women. Organizations such as the National Council for Jewish Women, the Mormon Cleophan Club of Salt Lake City, the

General Federation of Women's Clubs, the National Association of Colored Women, and the Black Christian Women's Association performed benevolent work within, and sometimes outside, their communities.[5] White and Black women's clubs continue to receive the most scholarly recognition, but such groups are a cross-cultural phenomenon.

Cultural critic Cynthia Orozco writes that, since 1870, Chicanas have organized their own women's organizations, including *Sociedad Beneficiencia*, founded in Texas to supply relief to soldiers; Chicana clubs in Los Angeles, California, which emerged in the 1920s; and Chicanas' work with settlement houses and the YWCA at the turn of the twentieth century. Since the nineteenth century, Asian American women have formed alliances to resist the forces that excluded them from American citizenship, and they have worked within domestic, professional, and working-class-based organizations to counter their exploitation in the labor market and their lack of access to American publics. Their organizations—from Chinese women's immigrant groups, those related to professional nursing and physician interests, to the more recent Asian Immigrant Women Advocates (AIWA)—address their precarious position and experiences regarding barriers to U.S. citizenship and their exploitation in garment, domestic, and middle-class work environments. For some women's political organizations, their activism has upset the very idea of what citizenship means for sovereignty and cultural autonomy from mainstream society. Adherents to Women of All Red Nations (WARN), an intertribal cluster of Indigenous Nations activist women, made goals of cultural and political sovereignty a primary concern from the 1970s to today.[6]

As women autonomously formed ethnic-based alliances in response to their exclusion and their urgency to help their communities, White working-class women's clubs also emerged to resist White middle-class women's settlement efforts that were at times patronizing and Anglocentric. White working-class women's clubs, such as the Daughters of Labor, provided a space for women to speak about their labor woes and exploitation in factory work. Their club doubled as an organizing body to disrupt and challenge their lives as workers, and as a social base for recreation.[7] Many historians of women's cultures argue that these groups represented the yearning for sisterhood with other women and the necessity for members to express their identities as women and as responsible citizens. Although at times political in their practices, women's clubs facilitated social interaction and self-affirmation between and for women. Interwoven into clubwomen's everyday lives were the threads of race, ethnicity, national belonging, and class. Clubs of women of color also shared and faced what cultural and feminist critic Chandra Talpade Mohanty calls "a common context of racial struggle," which politicized their efforts on the basis of gender, ethnic, and racial identities.[8]

Benign or Malign Benevolence?
Black Women's Clubs and the Politics of Respectability

Segregation policies in the United States and racism within White women's social and political organizations continued to encourage Black women and other women of color to form ethnically centered clubs that served their communities, interests, and needs. In particular, many Black women held multiple memberships in benevolent, civil rights, women's, and sororal organizations. Black activists Mary McLeod Bethune and Mary Church Terrell of Delta Sigma Theta, Norma Boyd, Rosa Parks, and Coretta Scott King of AKA, and Ida B. Wells, who started the Alpha Suffrage Club, belonged to civil rights and sororal organizations and used both for activist work. Ida B. Wells started the Ida B. Wells Club in 1894. This organization sought to draw attention to the lynching of Black women and men. Later, many Black women's clubs emerged that tried to change existing negative perceptions of Black womanhood held by the dominant society. The sexual image of Black women in the White popular imagination, for example, was that of culturally, socially, and morally depraved persons. In response, Black clubwomen had a pressing need to defend and refine their womanhood. Similar to the aims of the ideologies of Republican Motherhood and the cult of true womanhood espoused by White women's clubs, those of Black women's clubs focused on upholding Christian values, becoming productive citizens, and cultivating and rearing families with similar values.[9] Ultimately, these women began to cultivate and embrace what many historians coined *the politics of respectability*.[10]

Although members of White women's social, political, and literary clubs and White reformers also subscribed to the politics of respectability, for Black Americans, particularly those of the Black intelligentsia, these ideas had particular sexual, ethnic, and political meanings, as well as social and cultural consequences. The racial caste system at this time influenced Black Americans' desire for others to see them as respectable. They thus used moral strategies to combat racial attitudes about their communities and about Blackness. Historian Stephanie Shaw observes that many Black Americans, particularly of the middle classes, "hoped that extremely upright behavior would ward off dangerous attention and counteract the negative stereotypes of African Americans that were common throughout white America."[11] Cultural critic and labor historian David Roediger argues that White Americans still conflate Blackness and hypersexuality, which in the past cost many Black American women and men their lives through rape and lynching.[12] For Black American women in particular, the rhetoric of noble womanhood and the insistence on respectable practices aimed to discourage sexual assault by White and Black men, for which there was little recourse during the era of slavery and well into the twentieth century.

The rhetoric of respectability that Black American women and men espoused, however, had intra-ethnic consequences. Historian and cultural critic Kevin Gaines argues that many early twentieth-century Black activists and intellectuals used the rhetoric of respectability, which contradicted and ignored the complexity of Black life and often circumvented class struggle.[13] Class, the historical phenomenon constituted in and through social relations that, according to theorist E. P. Thompson, "happens . . . as a result of common experiences, inherited, and shared," does not wholly reflect the Black middle class at the turn of the century.[14] There was no unified thought for those involved in race work; some were sensitive to class, and others, in their pursuit to uplift and reform, publicly vilified poorer

Black Americans. The perceived articulateness and education of the Black intelligentsia, argues Gaines, made their political efforts more palatable to the Whites who controlled the political power structure. This perception allowed these activists to do cultural work in the Black and dominant public sphere.

Early Black activists' claim to respectable practices set them apart and made class-disadvantaged Black Americans appear "shiftless and lazy"—the categorization reserved for Black Americans that early black activists were vehemently trying to disprove. The politics of respectability, intended as a subversive practice, often had adverse ideological and material consequences for the Black American community. Nevertheless, many of these men and women realized that disenfranchisement and racist attacks against one Black person, regardless of class, kept all Black Americans subordinate. A materially based middle-class standing, they came to realize, would not act as a buffer against White racism. Although some of the twentieth-century activists belonged to the emerging Black professional managerial class (BPMC), earning middle-to-upper-middle-class wages, they knew they would never acquire the material wealth enjoyed by their White counterparts in the professional managerial class, nor the psychological "wages of whiteness."[15]

Black women's clubs and the Black sororities of the BPMC became a dual sphere where private-sphere interests intersected with public action. Women of many ethnic, class, and religious persuasions in the nineteenth and twentieth centuries used the space of either a literary, religious, benevolent, or social club to transcend what early women's history scholars call the private (conjugal home) and public (political sphere of citizenry) spheres. The work of these organizations in the public sphere reflected their interest in transforming the racist and sexist society that kept their communities subordinate. Clearly distinguishable from White women's clubs, which expressed concern about slavery, lynching, and racism, Black women's clubs made their crusades personal and contingent upon their survival as a gender and as a people. One may recall the suffragists Elizabeth Cady Stanton and Susan B. Anthony infamously adopting the slogan "Woman first, Negro last" after dropping the abolitionist crusade in favor of White female suffrage. Their choice is an example of the contribution of White reformers to civil rights movements, as opposed to the commitment of Black clubwomen.[16]

Cultural critic Anne Ruggles Gere argues that there was a decrease in White upper-middle-class and working-class women's clubs by the First World War and after realizing their dream of enfranchisement in 1921.[17] However, voting rights for the masses of Black men and women did not exist until the later twentieth century, therefore, Black women's clubs and other ethnically centered political formations continued to address their denied access to the vote. The work of White twentieth-century reformers sometimes generated suspicion and contempt from those they wished to help. This was a stark contradiction to the mostly positive reception of the work of Black women's clubs. In racial and ethnic communities, particularly in immigrant and migrant urban areas, these women's clubs and benevolent groups operated as cultural and political foundations for their people. Cultural critic and activist Angela Davis writes that what set White and Black women's clubs apart was Black women's "consciousness of the need to challenge racism in support of men and women of African descent whose lives had been transformed by their shared history of slavery, racism, sexual exploitation, and colonization."[18] Certainly, racism and sexism left the work of Black women's clubs unfinished.

More than a Social Group and beyond a Reform Movement: The Historical Roots and Political Routes of Alpha Kappa Alpha Sorority, Inc.

Compared with the work of Black women's clubs, the work of the Black sorority provides another example of the way that Black American women use social space to act politically in the public sphere. Sprung from service-oriented social organizations, the AKA sorority emerged as a response to the reality of racism and sexism, and to demonstrate the intellectual capabilities of Black women. In general, despite Blacks' academic record, they did not have access to honorary Greek societies such as Phi Beta Kappa, founded at the College of William and

Mary in 1776. Membership invitations from White social sororities to Black women were nonexistent because of segregation policies in the United States. According to Benjamin Hooks, a former president of the NAACP and member of the Black fraternity Omega Psi Phi, "Before the days of racial integration, White sororities and fraternities simply did not invite Blacks. In 1942, I may as well have considered joining the Ku Klux Klan."[19] Because of the social relations that held Black American women socially and politically subordinate, the Black sorority in general, and AKA in particular, emerged as a service organization. The Black sorority therefore sought to assert Black women's academic excellence and to create social bonds, professional networks, and activist outlets.

The AKA sorority was the idea of Howard University student Ethel Hedgeman Lyle, as well as eight other Howard women who shared her vision: Anna Easter Brown, Beulah Burke, Lillie Burke, Marjorie Hill, Margaret Flagg Holmes, Lavinia Norman, Lucy Slowe, and Marie Woolfolk Taylor. Currently, the sorority has a membership of more than 200,000 in almost every part of the world, including the United States, the United Kingdom, the Bahamas, the Virgin Islands, Korea, and Germany. Hedgeman, born in St. Louis, Missouri, received an academic scholarship to attend Howard University in 1906. She was an active member of the Young Women's Christian Association, the Christian Endeavor, and church choir, affiliations that shaped her community-based activities once she organized the sorority. Given that the idea to form a sorority at Howard was hers, the first eight members wanted to elect Hedgeman as the chapter president of AKA. Yet, because Hedgeman was still a sophomore, the women felt it was best to select Lucy Slowe, a senior, an innovator, and a recorder of how the organization's internal structure would operate. At the turn of the century, when BGLOs were forming, it was important for these men and women to prove their academic capabilities. It was also a priority of BGLOs to respond politically to their oppression as women and men of African descent and to create a network of friends during and after college.[20] Indeed, according to Paula Giddings, their "development was more than an imitation of White Greek-letter groups that excluded them. Even the Greek appellations were, in part, a defiant response to the notion that a 'Negro would never learn to parse a Greek verb or solve a problem in Euclid,' as former Vice-President and states' righter John C. Calhoun once opinioned."[21]

The AKA's goals went beyond nebulous ideas of sisterhood and individual achievement; these women sought to transform the society in which they lived. Incorporated in 1913, the sorority operates as a business organization, Ivy Center, with a national headquarters in Chicago. Their national headquarters acts as a structural base for the creation and deployment of their political work and ideology. The sorority's incorporation resulted from the first leadership rupture in AKA, which was a reflection of the competitive aspects and internal struggle that social-political formations experience. In 1912, according to AKA historian Marjorie Parker, some members of the sorority wanted to vote for a new motto, name, symbol, and colors to represent the organization. One of the former presidents of AKA, Nellie Quander, resisted the proposed changes, as did other sorority members. Quander argued that the proposed changes would dishonor the founders of the sorority; she thus immediately moved toward incorporation, which was a legal action that would ensure that the sorority's foundation would remain intact as the original founders had conceived.[22] As a result, the women who suggested the changes left the organization and formed the second Black sorority at Howard University, Delta Sigma Theta. Delta member Paula Giddings presents a different version of the discontent among the sorority women in 1912. Giddings, voicing the views of Delta Sigma Theta members, writes, "We wanted to be more than just a social group. We wanted to do more, when we graduated, for the community in which we were going. . . . We wanted to change some ideas, we were more oriented to serve than to socialize."[23]

Beyond the desire of some members to change the "motto and sorority colors," as AKA historian Marjorie Parker has contended, Giddings implicitly suggests that AKA's scope was not political, and the discontented members left to form Delta Sigma Theta. Another version of the breakup, disseminated throughout BGLO life, comes from sorority rumor and lore. Through interviews with AKA women conducted over several years, I learned there were personal differences between the women in 1912. Many informants claimed these differences were the result of competition over the male partners of the sorority members. Whether one prefers the folklore version, AKA's version, or Delta Sigma Theta's version, AKA women were definitely involved in cultural work at the time the internal rupture occurred in the organization. The AKA sorority remained leaders in the YWCA and the NAACP and continued to rally for civil rights and suffrage after the organizational split. Nonetheless, the rupture between the sorority women should call into question romantic notions of sisterhood, upon which sororities and women's clubs base their identity.

AKA's breakup shows that the process of sisterhood does not happen easily or in a vacuum, even for women who share a racial bond and, seemingly, a similar socioeconomic class. Yet the benefit of their split came about through the changing demographics of their membership and the addition of other Black American sororities, such as Delta Sigma Theta, which would continue cultural and public work in their own way, based on their own vision. The incorporation of AKA allowed the sorority to become national as the following chapters emerged in the Midwest and beyond: Beta Chapter in Chicago, Illinois; Gamma Chapter in Urbana, Illinois; Delta Chapter in Lawrence, Kansas; Zeta Chapter in Wilberforce, Ohio; and Eta Chapter in Cleveland, Ohio. As AKA chapters spread throughout the United States and beyond, the composition of the organization changed from women with similar socioeconomic backgrounds and experiences to a more diversified group of women who were beyond their college years and who were acculturated within different regional environments.

Integrating Theory with Practice: The Public Sphere, Counterpublics, and Black Counterpublic-Sphere Work

In many social, cultural, and political movements, change is most recognizable when public life and politics coalesce. Cultural critic Jürgen Habermas argues that participation in the public sphere allowed Anglo-American male bourgeois society in the nineteenth century to evaluate and resist the state of social and political life through the dissemination of discourses and by gaining access to specific social apparatuses (media, meetinghouses, etc.) as a means of deploying their political ideas.[24] Habermas's work presents a critical framework in which to view political participation in public life. However, feminist scholarship has revamped Habermas's explication of public life and politics by asserting that an extension of his theory may benefit additional organizations and historical moments. Cultural critic Nancy Fraser, for example, extends Habermas's argument by describing the ways historically marginalized groups gain access to the public sphere and realize social and political transformation through what she theorizes as *counterpublics*.[25] Counterpublics, Fraser argues, are "discursive arenas" where historically marginalized groups "present counter discourses of their identities, interests, and lives"; they act as competing publics to the dominant society and emerge as a response to particular social conditions at specific historical moments. Counterpublic formation draws on cultural workers, often uses the apparatus of the media, and mobilizes for a specific issue or agenda.

Cultural critics Houston Baker, Mary P. Ryan, and Ellen Messer-Davidow cite movements in which counterpublic groups conceptualized new social relations and disseminated their concepts through various media apparatuses, which resulted in transformation. Black male activists and orators transformed the American public sphere, argues Baker, by working to change the existing American arrangements in the 1960s for the masses of Black Americans. Ryan outlines how White women activists in the nineteenth century participated effectively in public politics despite patriarchal constraints. Messer-Davidow reveals the political Right's success in maneuvering within the public sphere to make their conservative ideas more popular to a substantial portion of mass society, and argues that leftist groups would benefit from similar organization.[26] All theorists provide examples of counterpublics, which help explain the various ways groups access public spaces for insurgent and conservative political ends. AKA's various forms of counterpublic-sphere work have relevance beyond the historical reminiscences of Habermas, Baker, and Ryan, as well as Fraser's carefully constructed theoretical rearticulation of Habermasian concepts.

Recall that Black counterpublics engage in practices and politics where Black intellectuals, in coalition with foundational Black organizations in urban communities, including schools, churches, Black businesses, and social organizations, challenge and work to transform the oppression and exclusion that Black Americans face in the United States. In the same vein, AKA continues to accomplish counterpublic work for Black people living throughout the African Diaspora. AKA is a material example of counterpublic formation and work, as they used direct action, deployed counterdiscourses, proposed anti-racist legislation, and encouraged and ensured higher education for Black women and men. Unlike their White sorority counterparts who engaged in benevolent work, the agenda of AKA was far-reaching and socially responsible because of the racial injustices that Black women faced in the public sphere.[27] Whereas the mission statement of the first White sorority, Kappa Alpha Theta, formed in 1870, avows to create and promote sisterhood, AKA's counterpublic work moves beyond creating sisterhood in a gender and race-biased institution (i.e., the college university). In comparison, AKA's organizational mandate aims to "cultivate and encourage high scholastic and ethical standards, to promote unity and friendship among college women, to study and help alleviate problems concerning girls and women, and to be of service to all [hu]mankind."[28] Like their sisters in the Black women's club movement and benevolent societies, the Black sorority responded to the specific social inequities between the races. Exploring AKA as an effective counterpublic lays the groundwork to understand how social-political organizations may sustain activism over an extended period. A systematic explanation of their counterpublic-sphere work in the twentieth and twenty-first centuries shows a transformation from benevolence and reform work to the calculated political interventions that brought about significant change.

The Politicization of a College Sorority: The Counterpublic-Sphere Work of Alpha Kappa Alpha Sorority, Inc.

AKA's counterpublic-sphere work has consistently been in alignment with the BPSC's goal to increase race consciousness and interrupt discrimination as experienced by Black women and men. Between 1908 and 1913, AKA's primary agenda consisted of maintaining academic excellence by example; involvement in national suffrage, the YWCA, and civil rights; and engaging in cultural practices through same race and social interaction. The women in AKA had clear goals when serving their communities. AKA's early counterpublic-sphere work began with conducting demographic studies to determine need in Black communities in their immediate environment. Each sorority chapter was encouraged by its national headquarters to perform "at least one piece of Christian, social or civic service for its community."[29] These attributes influenced the women to establish a strong political formation. To borrow phrasing from cultural theorist, psychiatrist, and activist Frantz Fanon on insurgent intellectual practices in general, AKA women began "to organize coherent action, to communicate among groups, to formulate political theory and policy, to write and teach and . . . perform and invent" as a way to immerse themselves, "body and soul, into the national struggle."[30]

Chief goals for AKA were programs that would better the cultural, economic, social, and educational levels of Black women and men. Programs adopted by the various sorority chapters ranged from helping communities attain civil rights (direct activism) to increasing access to adequate health care (reform work). As the sorority spread to other university campuses, graduate chapters of AKA emerged within Black communities, allowing alumnae to continue sorority affiliation, social interaction, and political action through the name of the organization. The graduate chapters had the opportunity to induct women who may not have had the opportunity to attend a college university but were interested in being involved in community action. As stated earlier, as the membership of AKA grew within and outside the United States, it became more demographically diverse than in its earlier years. Part of this diversification came about through economic class standing and nationality. While undergraduate chapters initiate women who are matriculated in a four-year college university and have a "B" academic average, graduate chapters claim to select women who are already involved in community service and politics, and who desire to create social bonds with other Black women outside of the university setting.

Many of the chapters formed outside the United States were composed of existing members who moved due to military relocation or studies abroad. Other women who were not initially members of AKA created chapters abroad because of the influence of AKA's social and political reputation. AKA spoke to its sorority sisters through its national magazine, the *Ivy Leaf*, about experiences of attending universities abroad, being in the armed services, and doing activist work in Germany, Japan, and England.[31] As the women approached the mid-twentieth century, sorority members resembled not the elite Black intelligentsia of yesteryear nor the product of family legacies at historically Black colleges such as Howard. Rather, some were the first in their family to affiliate with a BGLO and attain a college education.

Between 1913 and 1920, AKA women were involved in national suffrage and reform movements. In 1913, AKA sponsored a lecture by its first White and honorary member, Jane Addams, at the University of Chicago. At the lecture, Addams stressed the benefits of social and community work, and the social work courses she developed at the university.[32] Addams worked closely with Black clubwomen and the AKA sorority in Chicago to improve life for urban Black Americans. Although reform work might appear problematic in view of today's efforts for adequate inclusion, Addams is one of the few White reformers who adopted a traditionally pluralist approach by including a significant number of Black Americans in her settlement houses.[33] Upon Addams's passing, an editorial in AKA's magazine proclaimed that through Addams's work, one might see how "ideals are colorless. This we see again in the life, labors, and achievements of Jane Addams."[34] Addams was the first, but not the last, White woman made an honorary member. In 1949, AKA invited and inducted the activist and former First Lady of the United States, Eleanor Roosevelt, into membership.

In 1921, the sorority's national headquarters required every chapter to set aside a week in January to commemorate the founding of the sorority and develop activities that promoted "Negro history, literature, music, and art in order to promote an increase in 'race consciousness' among Negroes."[35] The *Ivy Leaf* published members' poetry, short stories, and artwork, as well as reprinted material that promoted the arts. AKA women participated in the Traveler's Aid Society, which helped Black Americans who migrated to the North from the South to adjust to their new environment. Ida Jackson created in 1934 AKA's most recognized project, the Mississippi Health Project. Jackson, who had already organized sorority members to train Black American teachers in their "Rural Negro Teachers Program"—a program where AKA women spent their summers training Southern Black women to acquire state accreditation—began a similar uplift program that would concentrate on providing health care to rural Blacks in Mississippi.[36] Writing about the Health Project, Jackson stated that AKA women "had a duty to change things, or how can we face a new day?"[37]

The project brought together medically trained AKA members, teachers, the U.S. Public Health Service, and Mississippi's Holmes County Health Department to serve Blacks in the rural areas of Holmes County. Jackson chose the community because of the oppression and obstacles that Blacks faced in rural areas of Holmes County and the failure of many New Deal relief policies to adequately aid Southern Black American communities.[38] Jackson was concerned about the federal government not providing medication and health services to Black Americans in general, and the Health Project, in part, became an answer to this problem. AKA member and medical doctor Dorothy Boulding Ferebee was director of the program, as well as director and founder of the Southeast Settlement House and Prenated Clinician at a Black hospital, the Freedman's Hospital. Her work with the Mississippi Health Project called upon other AKA members to set up free, often mobile, health clinics, to serve tenant farmers and their families on location. Jackson found that the White farmers feared and purposely tried to hinder their tenants from receiving medical care in Mississippi. Drawing from his mother's personal letters, Jackson's son and biographer writes: "When they went to Mississippi, they found that the plantation owners were not too keen on their labor force being exposed to this new relationship with the Northern Negro Medical People. Ida and her people were puzzled as to what was going on. . . . After a short while, she went to the plantation owners and it was at that time she realized they did not want their people to leave the land for fear they might not come home. Ida thought the best way to solve the problem would be to take the [medical] unit to the plantations."[39]

For the Negro Teachers Program and the Mississippi Health Project, Ida Jackson insisted that women have versatility, educational training, knowledge about and experiences with the South, the ability to understand Southern Whites and Negroes, and close proximity to Lexington, Mississippi. As Jackson describes, AKA internally funded the Mississippi Health Project: "They had not asked for [monetary] outside help; they received funds from their own membership."[40] Although a criterion for participating in their programs in the South was knowledge of the region and cultural climate, this did not impede the rhetoric of malign benevolence from rearing its ugly head. Dr. Ferebee explained that the health care initiatives taken up by the sorority in Mississippi were also a corrective to some of the "rural South's ignorance, crudeness, superstitions, hostility, and prejudice, among both Negroes and whites."[41] The words of Dr. Ferebee—for example, references to Southern Whites and Blacks as being crude, superstitious, and ignorant—point to the reality of being unable to purge biases based on class, and, in this case, regional bias as well. After the Mississippi Health Project attained its goals in the Black Mississippian community, AKA made the decision to open a National Health Office in New York City to continue to study and meet Black health care needs.

In addition to providing health services to Black Americans, AKA made the end to lynching a primary concern. The sorority began a national anti-lynching campaign organized by AKA member Norma Boyd, who was involved in national suffrage campaigns in the 1920s and the president of AKA in 1941. In the 1940s, Boyd gave public lectures to educate and spread support for AKA's anti-lynching campaign and wrote the first anti-lynching legislation for the U.S. Congress. Boyd's house served as the headquarters for the sorority's crusade; her chapter sold anti-lynching buttons, designed and distributed Christmas cards to raise money, printed newsletters about the bill's progress, and remained active in lobbying until 1948, well beyond the NAACP's involvement in anti-lynching legislation.[42]

As AKA spread to other college campuses and communities, each chapter adopted its own political agenda, in addition to upholding the national goals of the organization. The national goals were a way to direct each chapter in alleviating problems in the national social structure, so that chapter-specific activism became a microcosmic reflection of its headquarters' political priorities. Although nearing the mid-century, AKA's practices continued to mirror the politics of respectability and the reform programs of earlier decades. Throughout the 1940s, AKA women sponsored programs such as "finer womanhood week" and created a reform project, Project Family.[43] Project Family was a coalition between AKA members and social workers that adopted twenty families and administered adult education, providing advice on birth control, budgeting, and career opportunities.[44] Whether families construed AKA's benevolent acts as helpful, a condescending interference in their lives, or a mixture of both remains a significant question. Whatever the answer, it does seem that White reformers' somewhat patronizing settlement efforts had an influence on AKA's early contributions in Black communities.

Race and gender identification among Black sorority women did not erase class differences and social condescension. Yet their common context of racial and gender struggle with those with whom they worked seems to have been a stronger bind than that experienced between their White sisters in social-political formations. Recall that White working-class women's clubs formed to express and alleviate their exploitation in low-wage and at times dangerous factory work.[45] Many middle- and upper-middle-class White women's clubs sponsored their younger counterparts in "working class girls clubs," as they referred to them, but despite the rhetoric of sisterhood that such groups proclaimed to foster, class-based problems did exist between their contingent coalitions. Although middle-class White women's clubs and working-class women's clubs worked together and befriended each other, class divided them in subtle and sometimes not so subtle ways. Middle-class women's club members were willing to come to working-class girls' club meetings "and be pleasant and friendly," as a Boston working-class club member wrote in 1891, but they did not treat the working-class club women as equals and never invited them to their homes.[46] It seems, then, that class continued to wedge divisions between women in their activist efforts, and these divisions manifested differently for White and racial-ethnic women's club formations.

In the late 1930s and early 1940s, AKA activism continued to focus on disenfranchised members of their own and other communities, which led them to respond to the turmoil brought on by World War II and its discriminatory precedents. In 1943 in St. Louis, Missouri, Norma Boyd, the Supreme Basileus of AKA, addressed her sorority sisters at a gathering of the women, proclaiming that the women must recognize that while "many individual sorors and chapters [were] already engaged in a variety of wartime services," it was essential that "planning and organization [take place in their] period of emergency to be organized into a program of [national] conscious effort."[47] Their conscious effort for citizenship, in what the AKA women felt was a moment of emergency, metamorphosed into AKA's National Non-Partisan Council on Public Affairs.

Established by Boyd in 1938, the National Non-Partisan Council on Public Affairs comprised sorority women and other civil rights organizations that lobbied politicians. During wartime, the council was part of a three-prong program that provided direct war services, supported victory among the Allies, and constructed post-reconstruction war efforts. AKA, through this lobbying body, pushed through legislation on April 28, 1944, that helped integrate Black women in the navy, and in the aftermath of their admission, AKA commented on discriminatory practices that the Black American navy women experienced. The AKA women found it objectionable that Black women in general were admitted to the navy, but they were not considered for promotion to officer. Instead, they only replaced Black men who could not work (thereby keeping the numbers of Black Americans serving stagnate), and they were trained in segregated schools. As a response to this injustice and segregation, AKA disseminated news releases about the navy women's experience, thereby marshaling public opinion on the matter, began an extensive interventionist campaign in Congress, and corralled the support of other national organizations to correct the injustice. This counterpublic-sphere work resulted in the admittance of Black women as officers and enlistees. The council also introduced bills to Congress for federal aid in education, to abort poll tax bills, to make federal funds available to urban areas such as the District of Columbia to ensure equal distribution to cover Black populated areas, and to create employment opportunities for Black veterans after the war. The National Non-Partisan Council's lobbying and success represented core elements in the creation of a counterpublic, inasmuch as the sorority had accomplished, by 1945, the following:

1. the planning and sponsorship of conferences on race and gender issues;
2. the dissemination of information about Black disenfranchisement, including speeches given on radio programs;
3. the cooperation with other women's and civil rights organizations;
4. the funding of education and encouragement of Black activity in public politics;
5. the use of civic, political, economic, and educational activities on behalf of racial integration in all phases of public life in the United States;
6. the planning and work that helped improve life for Black men and women in the armed forces; and
7. the stimulation of thought and planning for the adequate solution of problems in peace and in anticipation of the postwar era.[48]

AKA women worked for and toward civil rights from their inception in 1908, but the 1950s and 1960s civil unrest brought new challenges for the sorority women, which influenced their approach to political activism. The AKA sorority continued their activities in public demonstrations, as seen during the women's suffrage efforts at the turn of the twentieth century. The sorority women participated in, along with other civil rights organizations, the March on Washington, and they boycotted segregation in public accommodations. In 1962, they opened the first Job Corps Center for women in Cleveland,

Ohio, which "assisted the government in preparing women and girls for economic independence" through vocational and job training.[49] Their national headquarters' commitment to civil rights influenced the efforts of individual chapters and their members. AKA created a resolution on civil rights in 1969 for their chapters to adopt, which mirrored the insurgent as well as the conservative practices of the organization. The resolution is worth quoting in its entirety:

> Alpha Kappa Alpha is militant and determined to improve and advance the conditions of all people. We have consecrated our first effort toward the improvement of our own understanding of the possibilities for action in our local situations. We hold further that orderly protest is a part of the constitutional right of each individual, and we will participate in movements, which advance our goals, but we cannot condone, participate, or give support to violence. We believe that social change is inevitable, yet we do not believe in change for the sake of change. We, therefore, will support clearly conceived and well-directed programs, which promote human dignity. Alpha Kappa Alpha pledges to share her resources of time, skills, and finances to advance these goals for all people.[50]

The sorority's resolution slides backward toward the politics of respectability and conservative visions of change, despite rhetorical commitments to militancy. When the women write, "We believe that social change is inevitable, yet we do not believe in change for the sake of change," they may appear to imply little more than a call for well-planned programs with structure. "By any means necessary," the quoted motto of Malcolm X, was far from AKA's agenda. Still, their programmatic planning, conceptions of redistributing power, and commitment to opening up access to public life for Black Americans materialized in financial forms. During the period 1961–1962, the sorority promoted a national fund-raiser for college students who participated in sit-in activities in North Carolina, and AKA paid the college tuition for the first Black women who desegregated the University of Georgia.[51]

The late 1960s transformed the sorority nationally as its counterpublic-sphere work, already significant in its political programs and strategies, increased its focus on conventional civil rights ventures. "The important thing to do," as the 1960s came to an end, a writer in the *Ivy Leaf* insisted, was "to take a stand and to not allow Martin Luther King Jr. to have lived and died in vain. We must call the nation's attention to the fact that Dr. King lived for all people and that something is required of us rather than [an] eye for an eye and [a] tooth for a tooth of justice."[52] In 1976, there was a national mandate from AKA headquarters for the sorority women to involve themselves locally in the fight for human rights, first-class citizenship for Black Americans, and women's rights.[53] By the mid-1970s, then, the sorority's political programs remained consistent, and their Cleveland Job Corps center became a central site of their work. From the time of the center's opening in the 1960s to the mid-1980s, more than 19,000 students received job training and education, which resulted in a 95 percent rate of long-term job placement.[54]

Perhaps one of the sorority's most unacknowledged efforts was a lobbying and letter-writing campaign, reminiscent of their earlier years with the National Non-Partisan Council on Public Affairs, which led to the nationally recognized Martin Luther King holiday. In 1983, in coalition with other BGLOs and civil rights organizations, AKA initiated a writing campaign resulting in more than a half-million letters sent to congressional offices in Washington, along with petitions amounting to 4.5 million signatures. In 1986, President Ronald Reagan signed House Bill HR 3706, which was the bill AKA member Katie Hall introduced to Congress that would make Martin Luther King's birthday a holiday.[55] In 1964, the sorority awarded Martin Luther King with a plaque acknowledging his efforts in human rights, and the Martin Luther King Holiday campaign, more than twenty years later, showed linkages between past to present activism and civil rights concerns.

In the winter of 1986, AKA took on service with a global perspective as its focus. Sixty AKA members of the Xi Omega Chapter demonstrated in Washington against apartheid with the organization Transafrica. There was an arrest of Xi Omega's Genelle Fry, Phyllis Young, and Lela Moore, because of their protest and activist efforts in ending South African apartheid. AKA's protest of South African apartheid spread throughout the United States, as the AKA Chapter Kappa Omega conducted a prayer vigil to protest apartheid at the Richard Russell Federal Building in Atlanta in conjunction with the Women's Division of the Southern Christian Leadership Conference. In addition, the Pi AKA Chapter at Fisk led anti-apartheid marches at both Tennessee State and Vanderbilt universities. AKA's demonstrations show the raised consciousness of members beyond benevolence and reform and to direct action that put aside self-interest for the benefit of a global Black community.

AKA women continued to reach beyond the borders of the United States through their African Village Development Program. Although various chapters had been involved in hunger relief efforts for Ethiopia, AKA realized that in conjunction with Africare, their efforts could enable direct relief to a number of African villages. In 1986, national headquarters encouraged each graduate chapter to provide relief to an African village. The AKA sorority assigned each graduate chapter a village, and each was to contribute from $250 to $5,000 toward women's labor-saving devices (such as grain mills), livestock, poultry, child nutrition, food trees, health care, firewood, and educational training. A number of chapters visited the villages they sponsored, such as the Tau Omega Chapter of AKA, which helped plant gardens in the Sam N' Jaay village and whose funds enabled the building of a water well. In 1985, the Seta Nu Omega Chapter of AKA gathered school supplies for the Gorée Island Primary School in Senegal, West Africa, and a member of the chapter went on a pilgrimage to Senegal to deliver the supplies on Christmas Eve. Africare reported in 1987 that 158 chapters participated in the program, representing four AKA sorority regions: Mid-Atlantic, North Atlantic, Western, and Southeastern.[56]

AKA provides an example of long-term counterpublic-sphere work that penetrated the larger public sphere and, at particular moments, transformed social relations (e.g., anti-lynching legislation, the Mississippi Health Project, the National Non-Partisan Council on Public Affairs, and the Martin Luther King holiday). AKA challenged, as did White women, women-of-color club movements, and other early feminists of the nineteenth and twentieth centuries in general, the doctrines of public and private, as these women engaged in cultural work at a time when great limitations were being placed on all women. As the last chapter in this study will demonstrate, the sorority's goals and political programs have and will mostly likely continue to change over time. While AKA member Norma Boyd led the sorority in the quest for the eradication of lynching at the beginning of the twentieth century, sorority chapters today are responding to social problems of their own times. Current undergraduate and graduate chapters name AIDS education, working with the Red Cross and battered women's shelters, programs geared toward increased literacy in the community, voter registration, and scholarships as local chapter agendas. In addition, AKA graduate chapters work to carry out the yearly programs designated by national headquarters. National goals for the period 1994–1998 included increasing momentum to implement mathematics and science literacy, funding senior residence centers, securing their presence in politics in Washington, D.C., and partnering with local and national Red Cross branches. The regional chapters in 2000 reported that they accomplished the following work that year:

1. $40,000 collected for their membership-sponsored elementary school, IVY AKAdemy School, in the rural part of Swazi Zulu, near Durbin in South Africa
2. $125,000 given in scholarships for higher education from their Educational Endowment Fund
3. Further nurture of their ONTRACK program, a youth program designed to promote citizenship among African Americans, which has served 6,000 youths
4. $25,000 to the United Negro College Fund
5. $10,000 to the National Council of Negro Women
6. $10,000 to the National Urban League
7. $7,600 to a Dallas, Texas, organization that aids the children of battered women

In addition to the aforementioned work, AKA's Supreme Basileus called for a national voter registration and voter drive.

In response, each chapter worked with Black-voter precincts in its respective community to register voters living in the city and suburbs. The women also worked to register close friends and relatives and to place flyers in churches and other locations Black Americans frequent to stress the importance of voting and to move toward electing a president who shares the legislative values of the sorority.[57]

Conclusion

The complicated nature of the AKA sorority rearticulates "the social" and "the political" in profound ways. AKA's multiple origins affected how they constituted their collective identity as an educational, social, and political one, and how this consciousness facilitated how they transformed and used the space of a college sorority for Black counterpublic-sphere work and reform purposes. In the context of a Black women's organization in a racist and sexist society, "the social," and "the political" are almost impossible to disentangle. An analysis of their activism shows how the women created a theory of social justice and acted upon their consciousness for change through the sorority affiliation. Their chapters' suffrage campaigns, Negro Teachers Program, health care interventions, anti-lynching legislation, political participation during World War II, 1960s and 1970s civil rights activism, 1980s anti-apartheid demonstrations, transnational hunger relief, and African development programs in the twenty-first century mark this work as more than typical forms of benevolence, or individual, random good deeds.

AKA's conservative components, commitment over time, and the breadth of its hands-on activism across chapters provide a nuanced way of seeing the possibilities of a Black collegiate sorority. AKA's Black counterpublic-sphere work also serves as an example of the ground upon which seeds of transformation might germinate in new times, for new identities, and with a renewed vision of change. AKA's social aspects, as seen in their split in 1912, intentions for reform, and current activism are not without contradictions. Such conflicting political practices are present in their cultural practices as well. As with their counterpublic-sphere work, AKA's performance of sexuality, gender, and class in the public sphere sheds light on the difficulty of forming an autonomous Black female identity that can at once acquiesce, negotiate, and subvert the pulls of normative feminine practice.

FIGURE 1. Delta Chapter, Alpha Kappa Alpha, The Jayhawker, 1921. p. 178. *Courtesy of the Spencer Research Library, Kansas Collection, University of Kansas.*

FIGURE 2. Delta Chapter, Alpha Kappa Alpha, 1930, women in front of AKA house in Lawrence, Kansas (Dorothy Hodge Johnson Collection). *Courtesy of the Spencer Research Library, Kansas Collection, University of Kansas.*

FIGURE 3. Alpha Kappa Alpha house, 1011 Indiana Street, Lawrence, Kansas, 1940. *Courtesy of the Spencer Research Library, Kansas Collection, University of Kansas.*

FIGURE 4. Delegates to Tri-annual YWCA Conference, including AKA members Dorothy Hodge Johnson and Maxine Jackson, who aided in the adoption of the YWCA to end its policy of racial segregation, 1946. *Courtesy of the Spencer Research Library, Kansas Collection, University of Kansas.*

FIGURE 5. AKA Rushees paying pledge fees, Kansas City, Kansas, 1955. *Courtesy of the Spencer Research Library, Kansas Collection, University of Kansas.*

FIGURE 6. AKA Delta Chapter, University of Kansas from The Jayhawker, 1959, p. 118. *Courtesy of the Spencer Research Library, Kansas Collection, University of Kansas.*

FIGURE 7. AKA Delta Chapter, University of Kansas from The Jayhawker, 1963, p. 166. *Courtesy of the Spencer Research Library, Kansas Collection, University of Kansas.*

3

Stepping into the African Diaspora

Alpha Kappa Alpha and the Production of Sexuality and Femininity in Sorority Step Performance

> The black public sphere—as a critical imaginary—does not centrally rely on the world of magazines and coffee shops, salons and highbrow tracts. It draws energy from vernacular practices.
>
> —The Black Public Sphere Collective[1]

In a large auditorium, four groups of sorority women, Alpha Kappa Alpha (AKA), Delta Sigma Theta, Zeta Phi Beta, and Sigma Gamma Rho, emerge from their seats to "walk," otherwise known to BGLOs as step dancing in-line. In unison, each sorority performs its stylized, signature dance movement, exchanges its verbal code, and displays its hand signal. The AKAs raise their pinky and screech *Skkkkeeeeeeeee Weeeeeeee.* The Deltas form a pyramid with their thumbs and index fingers and snap, yelling *Oo-oooop.* The Zetas shout *ZZZEEEeeeeee PHHiiiii,* while pressing both thumbs together to replicate the letter "z." In addition, members of SGRho extend three fingers while pressing their thumb and pinky together as they call out *Yeeeeeoooooop Eeeeee-Yiiiiipp.* Wearing Greek-letter paraphernalia in pink and green, crimson and cream, blue and white, and gold and royal blue, the women set the thematic stage for what a diverse mix of college students, Greeks, community members, and judges eagerly anticipates. All have come to see what the four groups of sorority women deliver each time they perform: a mélange of sorority history, avowed commitment to benevolence and respectability, sexual braggadocio, unapologetic confidence, stomping, slapping, clapping, tapping, jumping, and modern hip-hop dancing.

The lights in the auditorium dim as half of the line dancers disappear behind a stage to await their entrance and others take their seats in the audience. A sorority sister or fraternity brother belts out a soulful rendition of James Weldon Johnson's "Lift Every Voice and Sing," the Black national anthem written to celebrate Black American emancipation, while audience members rise to place their right hand across their heart. Following the performance of the Black national anthem, a group of sorority women wearing identical clothing lockstep on the stage and introduce themselves to a participatory audience, which rambunctiously shouts:

I see you soror!
I see you!
Be out!
You go girl!
Yeeeeeoooooppp!!
Eeeeee-Yiiiiipp!!
ZZZEEEeeeeee PHHiiii!!
Oo-oooop!!
Skkkkeeeeeeeee Weeeeeeee!!

Newcomers to Black sorority step shows may think they have just entered the twilight zone, but learned participants in this event ready themselves to experience the deep play of the "Delta Zone," "AKAtude," Zeta women who say they are "So fine," and Sigma Gamma Rhos who claim they are "the Sexy Ladies of SGRho."[2]

Black sorority step shows illuminate the performance of gender, sexual, and ethnic identity. Sorority women's performances also represent a social space where the intersections of multiple identities convene to form a meticulously crafted public persona. Numerous articles on Black fraternity stepping exist, yet no study to date focuses solely on sorority stepping and its production of Black sexuality and femininity.[3] The focus here on AKA sorority step performance is therefore a strategic intervention to provide an analysis of stepping as an example of the struggle to reclaim Black womanhood, create a sexual identity, and revitalize Black cultural forms. The gender and sexual identities produced and negotiated are the focus here, but the dance aesthetic and cultural work that are the outcome of these shows are equally fundamental to understanding sorority step performance. Stepping ritualizes Black expressive culture, communicates the contradictory norms of its participants through verbal signifying, and links a transformed African diasporic aesthetic to a specific dance tradition.[4]

My frame for analysis—cultural theory, performance, and dance studies—helps explain the ways Black women act as innovators and historical agents in the creation and transformation of Black dance. I begin by providing a brief history of the origins of stepping in sororities and the composition of the performance, and I then proceed to use ethnographic field notes, interviews, and video performance to draw out the contradictory, gendered, and sexualized meanings present in this performance as enunciated in dancers' verbal chants and as seen in their precise body movements. I conclude with a discussion that points to the larger implications and relevance of sorority step performance. In so doing, I address, to borrow phrasing from cultural critic Stuart Hall, the following question: "What is 'Black' about Black sorority social and cultural practices?"[5]

Historical Foundations of Black Sorority Step Shows and Performance

Black sorority step shows are events where members of historically Black sororities raise money for their community service programs and national public sphere and political work. Step shows are often the main attraction during Black History Month events, on Juneteenth, homecomings at historically Black colleges, and the African World Festival.[6] Step shows generally have fraternity and sorority step teams performing, however, organizations compete segregated by gender. Criteria for judging include technical ability and skill, appearance, and originality. Culturally diverse college students and members of the surrounding Black community pay to attend step shows, which produce anywhere from $200 to $2,500 for a given show.[7] Well over 5,000 chapters with more than a half million members in the United States participate in stepping in-line, step shows, and yard shows.[8] Most members of Black sororities learn and perform in step shows, yet step show participants are often new initiates, otherwise known as neophytes. For these young women, step performance is a way for neophytes to "come out," as it is often said in the Black Greek-letter vernacular, to the wider college community as proud members of their respective organizations. The current components of the step show, though, owe their existence to the creative ways in which people of African descent use dance as a tool for political self-expression, pleasure, and survival.

The origins of stepping in sororities do not generate from one particular historical moment or dance practice. Competitive skits and talent shows were already a component of Black sorority practices at their inception in 1908. Members of BGLOs recall that stepping in-line in the 1940s and 1950s was quite common, and that this practice continued to evolve from a pledge activity to nonprofit fund-raisers in the 1960s and 1970s. Dancer and cultural critic Jacqui Malone, in describing what she calls "the visible rhythms of African American dance," notes that as early as 1877 there were forms of step dance in Black dance troupes, which influenced sororities and fraternities. These groups sponsored dance and other Black performing arts events, allowing the opportunity to view, learn, and adapt this practice to their own cultural performances.[9]

Stepping was one of many practices that mirrored the cultural shift toward integrating visible signifiers of ethnicity into Black social institutions at the turn of the twentieth century. Of course, such signifiers had always been present. Cultural critic Annemarie Bean, for example, writes that the African elements of African American performance are a continuum of practices from slavery to the present.[10] These transformed and transplanted Africanisms by Black Americans throughout history and at events of cultural and political celebration show the longevity, rather than the nostalgic moments, of culturally specific aesthetics in everyday life. The integration of stepping into sorority social practices is one example of this cultural continuum. "The performance of stepping," notes a member of the AKA sorority, "is a way to keep alive what makes us different as people of African descent."[11]

The performance of stepping at Black sorority step shows encompasses complex body movements and verbal play that incorporate West and South African dance movements, military drilling, modern dance, acrobatics, and martial arts choreography. Stepping consists of heavy and buoyant steps, swaying motions, and syncopated, intricate hamboning.[12] Stepping is aesthetically similar to the South African gumboot dance, where sounds generate from hand and foot movements. In addition to these precise and improvised body movements, performers of stepping use wooden canes to create a different intensity of sounds, where each sound in the performance is a drumbeat. Sorority members organize the beats in a uniform manner, and the beats complement the meter of the rhythmic chants repeated during the step process. The body thus replicates an instrument during the performance, transforming it into an animated, anatomical drum. Folklorist Elizabeth Fine, drawing from interviews with members of Black sororities and fraternities, isolates four main characteristics of step performance: stepping, or the actual body performance; saluting, where the respective performing sorority salutes other members of its organization or "founders"; cracking; and freaking: "In the crack or cut, one group makes fun of another group, either verbally, nonverbally, or both. 'Freaking' refers to a member who breaks the norm of synchronization and unity, in an attempt to get greater audience response. The freaker . . . is a crowd pleaser."[13]

The formal components of sorority stepping, and its similarity to dance and improvisation in slave communities, place it as a Black American vernacular creation, yet the African elements of this performance are abundant. In his analysis of African dance, historian Robert Farris Thompson outlines five key elements of West African dance performance that are applicable to Black sorority stepping: (1) the concept of performance—movement, interaction, masquerade; (2) multiple meter—when two or more sounds or movements are being performed simultaneously; (3) apart playing and dancing—a leader or crowd pleaser moves within and outside of the organized and improvised choreographed performance; (4) call-and-response—vocal interaction; and (5) songs of allusion and dances of derision—the use of innuendo and metaphor, verbal or nonverbal, to conceal and reveal meaning.[14] In the following AKA step performances, the aesthetics described by folklorist Elizabeth Fine, cultural critic Jacqui Malone, and historian Robert Farris Thompson are apparent, thus revealing what is African, or African American, about Black sorority social and cultural practices.

Reclaiming and Rethinking an Aesthetic and a Cultural Form: AKA Stepping and Cultural Signification

During a 1998 AKA step performance at Stanford University in Palo Alto, California, the women bow their heads and stand in a symmetrical lineup, while the leader of the group paces around the women. All performing participants wear close-fitting black pants, loose black vests, pink satin Lycra shirts, and black high-heeled boots. The leader begins:

> LEADER: Nabisco gots the crackers . . .
> AUDIENCE: Uh huh!
> LEADER: And Campbell's got the soup . . .
> AUDIENCE: That's right!
> LEADER: But the Alpha's (meaning AKAs) got the Sigmas, the Omegas, the Alphas, and the Nupes (nicknames for all Black fraternities). That's right. Gonna take your man!
>
> The leader then raises her right hand in the air, snaps her fingers, and says, "Heeey!" She joins the group in line, and all shout "*Skkkkeeeeeeeee Weeeeeeee*" as they move their hips around and teeter side to side. Next, the women, in complete unison, clap underneath their knees and behind their backs, stomp their feet, and leap into the air with acrobatic ease. Throughout the performance, the leader steps in unison with the other women and then "freaks," or improvises, altering the movements the other women

perform. The AKA women stomp, clap, dance, and leap as they chant:

STEP TEAM: We are the ladies, of pink and green. We are the finest, you've ever seen. We're gonna thrill the house tonight, and when we're done, you'll see the light!

The competitive language the women use may seem problematic in the larger context of gender and sexual relations, which is a topic I take up later. For now, I connect the body movement to African aesthetics and signifying practices. When the leader begins the performance and midway improvises step movements, and when the other women make a mixture of sounds with their hands, vocal chords, and feet, Thompson's criteria of multiple meter and apart playing and dancing are present. As their feet touch the ground, they make a reverberated pounding sound, and that, along with the clapping, creates a multiple drumbeat sound. Further, when the leader calls out to the women to respond to her taunting and sexual braggadocio (e.g., "Nabisco has the crackers, and Campbell's got the soup, but the Alpha's got the Sigmas . . .") and the step team responds "*Skkkkeeeeeeeee Weeeeeeee! Skkkkeeeeeeeee Weeeeeeee!*" they are enacting call-and-response rituals. The audience members, who interject with an attitudinal tone "Uh huh—that's right" add another layer to the call-and-response pattern, making it a dynamic three-way performance of communication. Unpacking the presence of songs of allusion, and dances of derision, requires knowledge of sororal organizations and what cultural and literary critic Henry Louis Gates has written about extensively, that is, *signifying practices.*

Gates employs several topological and theoretical approaches to outline the use of a trickster figure in Black American cultural practices that utilize signifying and rely on repetition, representation, intertextuality, and vernacular language. As folklorist Claudia Mitchell-Kernan explains in her analysis of Black vernacular language, signifying is "a tactic employed in verbal dueling. . . . [It] refers to a way of encoding messages or meanings which involves, in most cases, an element of indirection."[15] Step chants also work as intertextual texts, insofar as step chants are interrelated texts with common elements and narrative devices. Step performers utilize stylistic devices to draw upon their shared and divergent histories as Black women, or their shared context of cultural struggle. All of these elements are present in stepping through the women's body movements and the addition of vocal arrangements. To explore this further, I rethink folklorist Elizabeth Fine's analysis of an AKA step routine at a 1985 step show.

Fine explains that AKA initiated the step show to raise scholarship funds for Black students and proceeds to describe the sorority women's performance. She includes a transcription of the women's step chant:

> STEP TEAM: I was walking cross the yard just as happy as can be when a confused little pyramid approached me.
> I said, "Are you all right, can I give you a hand?"
> She said, "Stop DST."
> I said, "Don't understand."
> I said, "Let me tell you something 'bout my sorority."
> She said, "Is it anything like DST?"
> I said, "Me, a D a S a T?"
> [. . .]
> I said, "You steal too much
> Oh Sigma Gamma Alpha
> You know it's hard for you to do that
> Because you're nothing but a copycat
> But what can we expect from DS Thieves?"
> The Delta story has now been told
> That your new colors are red and gold
> They even had to change their name
> I said we're laughing at you
> This is a serious matter.[16]

Fine presents a strong interpretation of the main AKA cultural meanings articulated in this chant. For example, she writes that the comment about Delta colors being red and gold is likely a "crack" about Delta choosing red and gold for their sorority colors, and then later having to change to red and white because a White fraternity sued them for having the same Greek colors and name as theirs. Fine misses another level of signification, however, as crimson and cream, or red and white, are also the colors of the Black fraternity Kappa Alpha Psi. This suggests that the Deltas are, as perceived by AKA, copycats in many ways, and their calling DST "Oh Sigma, Gamma, Alpha," wherein Sigma is part of the DST name, Gamma is the White fraternity that sued them, and Alpha is part of Kappa Alpha Psi's name, is an example. Fine notes that the pyramid is the Delta symbol, and thus the AKA women use the word pyramid as a symbol to represent a Delta in the chant, as articulated when the women chant, "I was walking cross the yard just as happy as can be when a confused little pyramid approached me." Yet this chant must also refer to the sorority's history, when in 1913 the women split into two different sororities. To say the Deltas are confused pyramids is a common trope in AKA step performance. The Deltas, the AKAs implicitly suggest in this chant, are disloyal. This is seen in many of AKA's cracks toward the Deltas during step performance, one of the most popular being "*Oooo-Weee*" ("Oooo" being the phonetic spelling for half of the DST signature call, and "Weee" being the last part of the AKA verbal call) you went the wrong way, 'cause all of your founders are AKAs!"

There is an intertextual and a dialogic conversation present in the "it's a serious matter" signifying chant, as the conversation carries the most meaning for those two sororal groups. However, the audience will typically respond to such remarks, or what sounds like or appears as a signifying statement, during the performance. The AKA narrative strategy positions the women as modern-day trickster figures: AKA encodes meaning that the audience or cultural critics might inadvertently miss if they are unknowledgeable about AKA, DST, sorority history in general, and the roots of signifying in Black cultural expression. Their performance becomes a song of allusion and resembles a dance of derision, as the women use their voices and bodies to convey a multiplicity of meanings unknown to those who are not members of BGLOs.

When AKA composes chants that are specific to the organization, it allows the public display of stepping to serve private functions, too, where the women are revealing and concealing their identity and history at the same time. The sororal calls that each respective group uses to salute each other during step performance, *Yeeeeeoooooooppp!! Eeeeee-Yiiiiipp!!* (SGRho), *ZZZEEE-eeeeee PHHiiii!!* (Zetas), *Oo-oooop!!* (Deltas), *Skkkkeeeeeeeee Weeeeeeee!!* (AKAs), carry meanings that are known only to members, are aesthetically African in their tonal structure, and are an example of the use of sororal-specific vernacular language that become songs of allusion to outsiders. Yet through the repetition of the performance, audience members notice signature calls and hand movements that allow them to participate in the decoding of the performance. After attending several step shows, the audience learns portions of Black Greek-letter organizational culture and is able to participate in the dialogic performance.[17] When a given audience views a group of Zetas making a pyramid with their hands and then manipulating their fingers to form the letter "z," which happened at a University of California at Riverside (UCR) Step Show in the spring of 2000, it knows that the Zetas are signifying on the Deltas. The manipulation of the hand gesture from the pyramid to the letter "z" acts as a symbolic way for the Zetas to say anyone who pledged Delta went the wrong way in choosing sorority membership. When this signifying performance at UCR occurred, the audience roared with laughter and cheers, and even members of Delta Sigma Theta, who were in the audience, stood and clapped. The latter reveals the participatory nature of step performance among audience members and among other Black sorority members not performing.

Intertextuality, apart playing and dancing, and call-and-response are also seen in an AKA chant performed in their signature "it's a serious matter" hook line:

LEADER: Question . . . I said what, what, it's a serious matter—

STEP TEAM: What, what, it's a serious matter. In 1908 was our founding date. In '74 we did it once more.

LEADER: Tell me!

STEP TEAM: What, what, it's a serious matter.

LEADER: Tell me . . .

STEP TEAM: Nine fine founders at Howard's Minor Hall, twelve charter members and that's not all.[18]

The AKA women show the diversity of the performance from cracking or marking to sharing coded knowledge, in a public forum, about the founding and history of their organization. Lines such as "nine fine founders at Howard Minor's Hall" might puzzle those who do not know that the AKA sorority began at Howard University, and that the nine women who initiated the sorority lived at Minor Hall, a dorm for women at Howard. "It's a serious matter" might gain recognition from audience members, as it is a familiar line in an AKA step performance, but some might not know that this is a multilayered statement. It refers to the nature of Black sororal organizations having deep meaning for its members, and the commitment the women have to the organization. At times, the women will explicitly explain their history, and at other times, they abbreviate, code, and place it within signifying discourses. Step chants, then, are identity signs that connote and denote conflicting and competing meanings. These subtleties are absent in the early and groundbreaking work of folklorist Elizabeth Fine on stepping, but, more importantly, my interpretation points to the many layers of meaning and signifying specific to AKA sorority step chants.

"AKAtude," the Delta Zone, the Sexy Women of SGRho, and Zetas Who "Gots" to be Fine: The Performance of Gender and Sexuality in Black Sorority Step Shows

I turn now to a comparison of sorority step performances in general to explore their negotiation of Blackness, sexuality, and femininity, beginning with a 1995 step performance of Delta Sigma Theta at Alabama A&M University. DST's performance illustrates the transgressions of what Mikhail Bakhtin theorizes as a carnivalesque, theatrical stage, where, as Stuart Hall writes, "the forms, tropes, and effects in which symbolic categories of hierarchy and value are inverted."[19]

The women perform a military-inspired step routine in beige jumpsuits with their sorority emblem and founding date appliquéd on the side in red. The DST step team presents a standardized appearance: they all wear identical short black wigs and combat boots. Through body movements and the lyrical prose of their step chants, the women transform prototypical gender presuppositions by the use of androgynous stylization, while performing the cut or cutting, also known in the Black vernacular as playing the dozens, marking, or loud talking on other sororal organizations. The women clap in synchronization behind their legs, reach across symmetrical lines of performers, and press their hands together to form a pyramid, as they chant:

> ANNOUNCER: Ladies and gentleman, for your safety, we ask that you do not try these steps at home.
>
> STEP TEAM: Now I don't want to hear about the pink and green, because it's all about the women in the crimson and cream. I don't want to hear about the blue and white, because I am a Delta Diva for the rest of my life. And no I don't wear blue and gold, because I belong in the Delta Zone. To pledge DST you have to give your soul . . .
>
> FREAKER: Someone wants to know what it takes to be in the Delta Zone?[20]

The women's performance displays incredible synchronization and skill, as their lyrical chanting coincides with the meter of their body movement. Each beat made through their stomping, clapping, and body slapping matches the rhythmic aesthetic of their voiced chants. The chant lines about preferring the colors crimson and cream over others signify that pink and green (AKA colors), blue and white (Zeta Phi Beta colors), and gold and royal blue (SGRho colors) represent sorority women who do not "give their heart and soul" to sorority membership. The Delta performance inverts known signs to the audience and sororal and fraternal groups, as it closes with the women dancing off stage to "Atomic Dog" by George Clinton, which is one of the signature step songs of the Black fraternity Omega Psi Phi. DST's performance blurs the line between feminine and masculine performance; the women appear to reject common standards of femininity through their clothing, and through their performative tribute to Omega Psi Phi. A closer examination of Omega Psi Phi fraternity's step performance illustrates this point.

The Omega Psi Phi signature step style includes acrobatic, hard stomp movements and hypermasculine elements by which members make claims to being strong, muscular, and sexually competent. The Omegas usually end their routine with the song "Atomic Dog," which is a rap and funk song that boasts about male sexual prowess. Contemporary step performance allows for sexual expression not possible in 1911, when the Omegas formed, because of the politics of respectability. Recall that Black sororities' and fraternities' commitment to upright behavior in the public sphere meant to contradict stereotypes of Blacks. The Deltas refashion this song and the Omega movements to pay tribute to the fraternity. After the Deltas stepped in-line to "Atomic Dog" at the Alabama A&M University step show and left the stage, the Omegas shouted out dog-barking sounds and yelled, "Q Phi! You go!" (The Omega nickname is "Q" Dogs). This is one of the defining characteristics of sorority step performance: when some sororities step, as seen in this DST performance, they pay tribute to Black male fraternities and their historical founding, which fraternities *do not* reciprocate. In an interview with the author, a member of Kappa Alpha Psi, Conroy, opines, "Fraternity stepping is more so geared toward displaying the prominent aspects of the individual organization than sorority stepping. Sororities will tend to do tributes to the fraternities in some fashion, whereas fraternities will rarely reciprocate such actions in their shows."[21]

In explaining the differences between male and female stepping, a member of AKA argues, "We give tribute and praise, we want to lyrically express our chapter history. We are complementing fraternity stepping from a female perspective."[22] A member of Zeta Phi Beta adds, "Sometimes we borrow each other's steps. Since Zeta Phi Beta is the sister organization to Phi Beta Sigma, we sometimes give tribute to the Sigmas."[23] An example of a Zeta tribute to the Sigmas was illustrated in a 2000 step show at San Jose State University, where Zeta women informed the audience during a step routine, "Whether Sigma, or Zeta, it's all Phi Beta baby!" The Sigmas in the audience yelled back, "Z Phi! You go!" The expression "Sigma or Zeta" that the Zetas use suggests that whether it is the women or the men of Phi Beta, they recognize the historical and cultural connection, which they believe unifies the two BGLOs.

During the 1995 Alabama A&M step show, where members of DST performed, AKA signifies on DST during their own step performance. AKA members wear outfits similar to those worn by DST members: white, androgynous-looking jumpsuits. The AKA women wear sunglasses and bandanas over their face and hold toy guns in their hands pointed in divergent directions. An announcer explains over an intercom AKA's historical founding and legacy, and that the audience must help AKA stop the violence in Black communities (the show was performed to raise money for anti-violence programs that the major nine BGLOs support in Alabama). Next, the AKA women throw down their guns and remove their jumpsuits, bandanas, and sunglasses to reveal the hyperfeminized clothing they wear underneath: form-fitting white blazers that zip up the front; straight, styled, and flipped hair with barrettes positioned neatly on each side; green satin pants; and white, high-heeled, buckle-tap shoes. The AKAs then launch into a robotic, highly acrobatic, soft-step performance. The women make use of wooden canes to create multiple meter and rhythmic beats as they tap their canes on the ground and slide them through their legs and around their bodies. Several women, while standing in a line, leap over a parallel line of their sisters while they frog-jump over one another's heads. Next, the women sit on top of one another's shoulders and form a two-person, cheerleader-type pyramid. The bottom stepper, standing, moves her arms from front to back while softly tapping her feet. After the pyramid and cane movement, the women integrate modern hip-hop dance. Sorority history, pride in their organization, and rhetorical claims to unity among all sorority women act as the backdrop for their verbal performance of the crack, or cut, targeted toward DST:

> STEP TEAM: The ladies in the pink and green have the prettiest stuff you've ever seen. It started back in 1908, when sixteen supreme women had a vision so great. You may turn your head, or roll your eyes, but we know you're

jealous, it's no surprise. But we don't have to brag, and we don't have to boast, 'cause it's plain to see who has it going on the most!

ANNOUNCER: The women of Alpha Kappa Alpha sorority would like to promote unity among all African American Greek-letter organizations!

STEP TEAM: AKAs are always imitated, but never duplicated . . .

This performance makes use of commonly understood feminine aesthetics, that is, through their disrobed, hyperfeminine appearance. AKA dance moves, however, and the opening act, when the women were dressed in androgynous clothing are contradictory to the feminized attire the women later reveal. When the women chanted that AKA is "always imitated but never duplicated," they made a cutting remark directed at DST, whom they taunted as being replicas of their organization. AKA works in coalition with other BGLOs on a variety of public sphere and community projects, and the announcer's rhetorical intrusion of AKA "promoting unity across BGLOs" is a signifying practice to soften the "bite" of their accusatory conceit.

The AKA women, at a University of Southern California (USC) yard step show in the spring of 2000, perform a step routine that also emphasizes conceit and rigid conceptions of femininity. The step team enters the stage to a rhythm and blues song. The women then halt, and the leader of the step team approaches each step team member. The leader stands in front of each stepper and pretends to fix her hair and makeup through arm gestures. All women wear high-placed ponytails, Lycra pantsuits, dance boots, and pink chiffon scarves. The step routine displays technical ability in the performance, while the women salute their "respectable" founders and engage in beauty-aesthetic bragging:

AUDIENCE: Be out Ladies! Set it out! I see you! Be out sorors—tell them who we are.

STEP TEAM: We are the first—08, 08! Alpha Kappa Alpha, we thought you knew, so many funky beats, we don't know what to do. It's all in our hands, and all in our feet, so listen to this rhythm of the funky beat— *Skkkkee-eeeeeee Weeeeeeee!!*

FREAKER: (Slowly talking while gesturing to the step line) Now break it down

S-O-R-O-R-S!

STEP TEAM: AKA baby! Alpha-Kappa-Alpha!

FREAKER: Sorors, we need to give them something to think about.

ANNOUNCER: Alpha Kappa Alpha Sorority was founded in 1908 by sixteen phenomenal women, whose sole purpose was to create unity among college-trained women.

STEP TEAM: 08, 08! We see you trying so hard, but yet we are cute, you're looking all crazy 'cause you know it's true. And when we step out into the yard, you wonder why, all the men just look, and pass you by. I say is it you, or is it me? I bet you wish you could wear the pink and green. So, so pretty!

AUDIENCE: Be out Kelly! Get it girl!

STEP TEAM: Alpha Kappa Alpha: *Baby*. Alpha Kappa Alpha: *Breathe*. Alpha Kappa Alpha: *Stop*. *Skkkkeeeeeeeee Weeeeeeee, Skkkkeeeeeeeee Weeeeeeee*![24]

The AKA women use comedic parody, and the pre-step primping amazes the audience, as in "I can't believe they did that!" responses. The audience always appears to relish the braggadocio of sorority step performance, as they repeatedly tell the women to "be out," meaning, again, be confident in who you are, when the sorority women engage in such performative conceit and shenanigans.

At the very same USC step show, the sorority Sigma Gamma Rho also taunts the audience with braggadocio and sexual innuendo. The women, wearing black T-shirts, black jeans, and black boots, chant:

AUDIENCE: Be out sorors!

STEP TEAM: Break it down! *Yeeeeeoooooppp! Yeeeee-oooooppp!* Switch.

FREAKER: Did somebody say switch? Freak it! Ahhh

AUDIENCE: Where you at Allison? Come on, set it out!

FREAKER: Are you ready? I'm ready. But you all aren't ready for SGRho!

Sigma Gamma Rho Sorority Incorporated was founded at Butler University on November 12, 1922, in Indianapolis, Indiana, by seven, dynamic, beautiful teachers. Here, standing before you today, are the 1999 initiated members striving to uphold our sorority motto: Better Service, Better Progress. And yet, we are the sexy ladies of that royal blue and gold. We are the no half-stepping sisters of SGRho. But there are some things we just won't do! (The leader lies down with back on the ground.)

MALE AUDIENCE MEMBER: What is that? What won't you do?

FREAKER: There are some things we don't do. Man, there are some things that we just can't do! That's right. And we're going to tell you what these things are (the leader leaps up and takes her place in the step line).

STEP TEAM: Ah, if it isn't blue, then you have nothing to say, and if it isn't gold, don't be mad cause you went the wrong way! *Yeeeeeoooooooppp!* [25]

SGRho creates tension and excitement among audience members by lingering around the question of what the women will and will not do, which, given the response of the male audience, general claps, yells, and cheers, is interpreted as sexual in nature. The women begin and then retract from this sexual verbiage by immediately launching into the end part of the step routine where they begin a performance of rhetorical signifying. At this juncture, the women invert and then call upon the politics of respectability, a recurring trope of step performance.

Zeta Phi Beta, during a step show at University of California, Riverside, in 2000, shows their commitment to social responsibility, respectability, and religiosity, yet the women also engage in sexual braggadocio. Wearing Zeta Phi Beta T-shirts and tight blue jeans, the women enter the stage singing the Zeta hymn in a gospel tonality while clapping their hands. They take the stage and digress from the song into chanting and hard stomping, acrobatic leaping, and clapping. The women stomp each foot in synchronization, pivot from side to side while tightly jerking their heads, and clap their hands together, underneath their knees, and on their thighs in a hamboning fashion:

> FREAKER: I said my sorors?
>
> STEP TEAM: Yah!
>
> FREAKER: We are the illustrious sisters of Zeta Phi Beta Sorority Incorporated. We are locked up, prayed up, and are of one soul, one mind, and one love, and that love is Zeta.
>
> FREAKER: I heard some of you in the audience want to be a Zeta?
>
> STEP TEAM: What? What?
>
> FREAKER: Well, let's tell them what they have to be:
>
> STEP TEAM: You know you gots to be smooth. And you gots to be sexy (steppers place their hands underneath their breasts and lift them up). And you know you got to be fine . . . so fine . . .[26]

At first listen, sorority step chants, as recorded above from the Zeta performance, may seem like nothing more than child-like rhymes, which acquiesce to gender and sexual stereotypes. In their explanation of gender styles in sorority and fraternity stepping, one member of AKA remarks: "The goal in AKA stepping is to step as hard as we can and be as feminine as possible, to incorporate the skill of fraternities and still look feminine while doing it."[27] When AKA members say they want to ensure that their "appearance is feminine," when Zeta Phi Beta loops the line "you gots to be sexy, fine, and smooth to be a member," and when members of Sigma Gamma Rho insist they are "the sexy ladies of SGRho," they do appear to reproduce debilitating and rigid standards of femininity. Yet the women's performance may also suggest that they are trying to carve out a public gender and sexual identity on their own terms. During a step show at San Jose State University in the spring of 2000, members of Zeta Phi Beta sorority shared the following: "We see stepping as getting back to African roots, where you're making beats with your whole entire body, instead of using actual instruments. It's a way for collegiate women to compete in a positive environment.

When we step we like to put a feminine spin to the performance, because we want to be sophisticated, classy, sassy, and sexy, but we are not like other [Black] sororities. We are not afraid to break a sweat when we step, because when we break a sweat it shows that we are out there working hard for the sorority."[28]

Cultural critic Hazel Carby describes how the sexual and gender positioning of Black women within dominant cultural discourses throughout history shapes the construction of Black female femininity and sexuality, particularly for activists and literary authors in the nineteenth century and later. The sorority's emphasis on femininity is not unlike their ancestors in the Black intelligentsia, such as Mary Church Terrell, Ida B. Wells, and Anna Julia Cooper. It was established in the previous chapter that the rhetoric of and emphasis on femininity attempted to counterbalance the history and materiality of Black women being hypersexualized and masculinized in order to exploit them sexually and economically during and after slavery. Yet although the created feminine aesthetic defines a respectable womanhood, in modern-day Black sorority step performance, the sexual connotations of step performance undermine and resist this connotation. In this way, women today are redefining a public sexual confidence not available to Black women in the nineteenth and early twentieth centuries. For Black female activists in the nineteenth century, "In order to qualify for a paragon of virtue it was necessary to repress all overt sexuality."[29] It is likely that contemporary sorority women perform their identities in step performance based upon specific historical and cultural contexts, thus adopting and inverting nineteenth-century sexual politics to make stepping relevant to modern Black female sexuality and femininity.

Beyond Resistance and Containment to Transgression and Transformation: The Deep Play and Carnival of Sorority Step Performance

Several conclusions may be drawn from sorority stepping, but two likely responses seem most pressing to entertain because both represent how one might misunderstand sorority step performance. On the one hand, one might view sorority performance as sexual and cultural *containment*, where the women recreate malignant perceptions of gender and sexuality through social and cultural practices. Their performances, then, may seem to lead to the women participating in their own gender and sexual oppression. One might very well argue that sorority stepping is solely counterproductive. The view of stepping as an example of containment is worthy of exploring, as it has the possibility to raise valid questions about the effects of social practices. The containment position might therefore argue the following:

1. The beauty aesthetic boasting and competitive language are debilitating for women in a culture where appearance and physio-anatomy often become the locus of female oppression.
2. Step performance places women as adversaries, thereby fueling patriarchal and heteronormative conceptions of gender and sexuality.
3. Step performance in sororities constructs gender and sexual ideologies in counterproductive ways that are not too different from the various technologies of gender that stereotype them in the public sphere and in White supremacist minds.
4. The repeated sororal rhetorical claim of being "sexy" in step chants places Black women in a hypersexualized space. This was the ideology that their foremothers in the Black intelligentsia resisted, and that was originally and malignly conceived out of the White supremacist imagination.

Yet to counter containment stances, one might also view sorority stepping as *resistance*. A counterargument concerning sorority stepping might entertain the following:

1. In the context of the Black sorority step show, performers assert themselves as confident, and their performance responds to society's devaluation of Black women's beauty in the public sphere.

2. Black sorority step performance increases unity among its members and acts as an example for other women to visualize how they may proudly keep alive cultural traditions in public.
3. The women are controlling the image, taking on the mask of femininity and at times dislodging it; some performers ridicule femininity, while others use it as a rhetorical device to demand gender recognition, or womanhood.
4. Stepping is a performative device to articulate and practice sexual freedom in public.

Viewing step performance through social and historical constructs affects the meaning of this practice. In addition, race and history should change how we see feminism, social life, and what constitutes feminist work. I thus want to take time here to return to my discussion of accessing public space and the work of counterpublics in order to trouble the aforementioned binary interpretations of this practice.

Scholarship in cultural and social history has established that the dominant culture often viewed the showcase of ethnic rites and symbols by Black women and men from the onset of slavery to after emancipation in a negative light, especially if this performance was autonomous and not for the entertainment of White Americans. As David Roediger explains, "White vigilantes, who rioted and disrupted [ethnic rites and symbols of] Blacks in the nineteenth century, did place a limit on Black expression in the public sphere."[30] Contemporarily, it is common to hear in the conservative commonsense rhetoric, and within neoliberal and neoconservative discourses, that racial and ethnic groups should observe their cultural rituals privately, as opposed to publicly. Debates concerning bilingual education, English-only corporate policies, and the containment of the public attire and hairstyles of Black athletes in the NBA in the early twenty-first century are examples of the disjuncture between practices viewed as safe multiculturalism and practices and signs of difference viewed as threatening to the dominant ethos of acceptable language systems, appearance, and citizenry.[31]

For women, the public celebration of identity, particularly one that allows the articulation of a self-defined sexual identity, is a vital step in achieving gender autonomy. Throughout history, Black women in particular have faced additional struggles in attaining sexual autonomy and gaining equal access to public space. As writings about the struggle for everyday Black female sexual autonomy by feminist, activist, and AKA member Anna Julia Cooper suggest, asserting a radical sexual politics was not possible for Black women in the nineteenth century because of the historical legacy of racism and sexism.[32] In addition, cultural critic Jayna Brown demonstrates in her book about Black female performance in the first part of the twentieth century that Black female stage performers were able to produce moments of agency and reconceive ideas about the modern woman through dance innovation. However, Brown argues that their performances were not free from the constraints of prescribed norms of dominant feminine identity, the sexualization of Black female bodies, and the racial exoticism propagated by the spectacularization of the white gaze.[33] Contemporary step performance is a contradictory practice that comes out of the specific racial, gender, sexual, and historical experiences revealed by Cooper's writings and Brown's astute cultural criticism. Sorority women use the platform of step shows to celebrate cultural difference on their own terms, to display sexual confidence, and to perform gender parody. The use of gender and sexual verbal play heard in step routines is thus more complex than narcissistic boasting; it is neither containment nor resistance, nor is it only containment *and* resistance. Rather, it is the stage where Black women perform the contradictions of femininity, sexuality, and diasporic identities as historical actors in everyday life.[34]

Common threads in step performance include each sorority bragging that its organization is more academically sound, with sorority members wearing colors of great symbolic importance, honoring their supreme founders, and boasting that they are the most skilled steppers.[35] This works as an additional way in which the women differentiate themselves from other sororities by operating within what they already know culturally, that is, signifying practices. Surprisingly, the step show audience does not appear to mind. On the contrary, audience members will yell the loudest and respond positively to the most confident, innovative, and stylized performance and to the group that signifies, loud talks, or marks on another group with unmatched wit. Audience members, whether male or female, sorority or fraternity member, student or nonstudent, encourage the women. The repeated phrases "I see you," "be out," and "set it out" are symbolic, verbal gestures of acknowledgment and support from the audience that solidify the women's rites of passage into the sorority and their newfound public identity.

To provide another illustration of this stepper-audience interaction, I return to the theoretical paradigm of cultural theorist Mikhail Bakhtin and his discussion of carnival. As Stuart Hall explains in his employment of Bakhtin's theory of carnival, for Bakhtin, popular expressions can work as

> a metaphor of cultural and symbolic transformation . . . it is *not* simply a metaphor of inversion. . . . In Bakhtin's "carnival," it is . . . the purity of this binary distinction, which is *transgressed* . . . [revealing the] mixed and ambivalent nature of all cultural life, the reversibility of cultural forms, symbols, language and meaning; and exposing the arbitrary exercise of cultural power, simplification, and exclusion which are the mechanisms upon which the construction of every limit, tradition . . . formation, and the operation of every hierarchical principle of culture closure, is founded.[36]

The "multiple meanings and potentialities" in sorority step performance "that would not manifest themselves in normal conditions [or in mainstream and unitary interpretations] reveal themselves [in new ways]" in stepping.[37] That is, stepping is a site of performative cultural contradiction, and sorority step performance comes from a multitude of Black American racial and gendered experiences. The women's masquerade and performance of gender and sexuality, the body movement of the "freaker" as the perpetuator of spectacle in this performance, and the comedic signifying in step chants attest to this contradictory aesthetic. Further, the howling laughter, clapping, and cheering during the performance by the audience are all characteristic of a carnivalesque reaction. There are no angry audience members, male or female, waiting to confront the women about their braggadocio after the step event. On the contrary, braggadocio, verbal dueling, and masquerade are the elements that they pay to see, and even perhaps vicariously imagine acting out. Step performance displays a confident identity and technical dance skill that the audience appears to admire. Their participation in the performance through call-and-response rituals solidifies stepping as a shared, folk, cultural phenomenon. It is also the carnivalesque experience that Black sorority women create and share, thereby producing a vernacular community between one another and their audience.[38]

The AKA sorority views the cultural practice of stepping, the fund-raising it leads to, and the honoring of their founders as a serious matter, but sorority women and their audiences also view step show performance as pleasurable and fun. The social and personal transformation that stepping allows includes the importance of learning a dance tied to cultural heritage, and the personal confidence that results from this process. Janet, an AKA member I interviewed about step performance, confirms the multiple aspects of step shows, and she highlights with enthusiasm the meanings that stepping holds for the performer: "Although many non-Greeks come and look and support these step shows, I think the experience inside is far different from that on the outside. I loved the friendly competition, the sisterhood, being in a room full of ladies in pink and green, not knowing a single name, yet not feeling alone. It was awesome, and although the year I competed did not result in victory for my chapter, I felt victorious in that I actually learned how to step—that I did it!"[39]

Conclusion

The gender, culture, and sexual implications of stepping and the chants that complement them suggest that stepping is more than social folly. Indeed, the social is profoundly political and infused with cultural meanings by people in everyday life. The meanings injected into this cultural practice by sorority women draw on their experiences as women of African descent and the collective memory of their organization's contributions to Black American life. Stepping, then, serves the multiple functions of being a cultural practice that accomplishes tangible cultural work. Sorority stepping allows the women to perform as cultural workers in their communities through the monetary gains derived from and used for their counterpublic-sphere work. This point is worth emphasizing, as sororities raise thousands of dollars each year through the showcase of their stepping performances, money that flows directly *back into* the Black community. Further, the sorority step show keeps alive a folk and diasporic tradition while constructing a public identity to the larger campus culture. In sorority step performance, the women are empowered to express and control their image in this public space in order to assert themselves as sexually confident women.

The realization of how culture transforms over time helps one visualize sorority stepping not as an African tradition, although the African elements are certainly present. Nor is it only an American vernacular practice particular to peoples of African descent living in America. As historian Lawrence Levine writes, "Culture is not a fixed condition but a process: [it is] the product of interaction between the past and present. Its toughness and resiliency are determined not by a culture's ability to withstand change . . . but by its ability to react creatively and responsively to the realities of a new situation. [It is not a question] of survivals, but of transformations."[40]

Step performance is more accurately, then, the transplanted component of culture influenced by various cultural forms that find their roots within and outside the nation-state of America. Step performance bridges cultural practices across geographical locations, while highlighting cultural forms crucial in propagating from one generation to the next. This is the key to understanding the larger implications of Black sorority step performance for the analysis of culture, as it is an example of how groups affect cultural formation through what they choose to keep alive. Black sorority stepping represents the diversity and specificity of American cultural practices. The Black American sorority experience, in addition to and beyond the practice of step performance, allows one to see how American experiences and identities are gendered, dependent on historical sexual positioning, and always, as cultural critic Stuart Hall writes of identity, "In the process of change and transformation." Black identity is not a fixed or an essentialized entity, writes Hall, as power, historical, and cultural forms shape identity, and identity allows one to act as a political agent.[41]

A large majority of step shows will have at least one White, Asian American, or Latino member who knows about and performs stepping quite skillfully. I have yet to see stepping in White Greek sororities and fraternities materialize en masse, but as the former academic advisor for a multicultural Greek-letter organization that uses step dance as the core of its identity and step shows to earn money for its counterpublic-sphere work, I witnessed firsthand the potential of stepping across racial-ethnic communities to incite change. If the increased diversification of stepping tells us anything, it might be that Black cultural institutions have had a large impact on other cultures throughout history, and that this impact continues to gain momentum in the twenty-first century.

As Black culture changes, so too do the performers in step shows as they incorporate new aesthetics and integrate the cultural influences that come from the multiple experiences of the Black Atlantic and African diaspora. In this way, Black sorority step shows reveal culture as multiply constructed, complex, and in its historic mutability. It is this element of step performance that should invite a critical examination of the diversity of American culture and why and what cultures choose to transfer is important. Black women's innovation in dance and performance is a pedagogical device in exploring these crucial avenues of investigation. One of the main lessons in cultural analysis that sorority step performance teaches, then, is that what often seems culturally peripheral to the dominant culture, as theorists Stallybrass and White reveal more generally, may just be culturally central to those relegated to the margins.[42] To write about the multi-accentuality and intertextuality of step performance, and to assert its cultural relevance for Black women, is not only a process in intervening in epistemological constructs that use White culture as the benchmark to compare Black Americans, it is also a process of signifying in itself. Nowhere is the question of culture and signification as it collides with the production of Black feminine identities more contested than in AKA women's employment of ethnic rites and at times risky rites used to induct women into the sisterhood.

4

Disciplining Women, Respectable Pledges, and the Meaning of a Soror

Alpha Kappa Alpha and the Transformation of the Pledge Process

> The idea of a [. . .] public sphere highlights the problem of understanding how specific power arrangements shape and reshape the discursive spaces within which social groups interpret their needs, invent their identities and collectively formulate their political commitments. Put another way, the presence of a counterpublic can direct attention to the public arenas where microlevel discursive interactions are shaped by wider institutional power arrangements and discourses.
>
> —Steven Gregory, "Race, Identity, and Political Activism"[1]

During a four-week period in the spring of 1991, the Epsilon Gamma Chapter of Alpha Kappa Alpha (AKA) sorority at Kent State University conducted an underground pledge process for new initiates, without permission from their national headquarters. Sorority members transported pledges by car from Kent to Cleveland, Ohio, where they engaged in unofficial pledge rites and activities in both cities. Because of the incidents that occurred while pledging a group of Black women, a twenty-six-year-old alumna of Kent State and graduate student at another university in the Ohio area and current Kent State students were tried in a Portage County court. According to the transcription of the court case, pledges experienced three phases during the unofficial pledge line: the pre-pledge stage (four days), the ivy stage (sixteen days), and the goddess stage (eight days). Each stage consisted of different tests of endurance among the pledges, including history lessons about the sorority's activism and accomplishments, performance and dance-routine lessons, undisclosed miscellaneous tasks, and sisterhood or trustworthy tests.[2]

Unsatisfactory progress by pledges during each aforementioned stage was met with an increase in physical discipline for noncompliance. The goddess stage consisted of the most intense physical violence, where open-handed slaps to the face, pushing, punching, and wood paddling took place. Pledges testified in court to having nosebleeds from being required to stand on their heads for prolonged periods of time, to having discolored or blackened eyes from being hit in the face, to losing consciousness as a result of bleeding and blows to the face and head, and to having bruised, scarred, and bleeding buttocks from being beaten with a wooden paddle wrapped with silver duct tape, which sorority members referred to as "the enforcer."[3] Two pledges were permanently scarred from the beatings. Some pledges were warned by sorority members not to seek medical assistance because medical personnel would have to report the beatings to the police. Pledges were also warned that if they dropped out of the pledge process, otherwise known in the Black Greek-letter vernacular as "dropping line," they would, according to pledges' testimony, "get hurt."

Despite pledges' testimony about their extreme maltreatment by sorority members, the chief defendant in the Ohio case pleaded innocent to charges of hazing. The woman in question appealed her subsequent conviction on the charge of hazing and assault, arguing that she and other sorority members had not meant to seriously injure the pledges and were carrying out time-honored traditions, which she herself had experienced during her own pledgeship. She went on to say during the court proceedings that "surviving this process is the only way for a Black woman to gain *respect* among her peers in the [Black Greek] community." As a result of the incident, nine AKA women faced charges, and the chief defendant was tried, convicted, and sentenced to 108 days of imprisonment for assault and thirty days for hazing, and she received a $250 fine. The presiding judge suspended her sentence to 250 hours of community service, a mental health evaluation and psychiatric visits, and sixty days of homebound incarceration. The chief defendant appealed the conviction, but the sentence was subsequently upheld in an appeals trial.[4]

The pledge process, hazing, and the new membership intake policy, adopted by the nine major BGLOs, which compose the National Pan-Hellenic Council (NPHC), have affected AKA as a counterpublic formation in significant ways.[5] Black sorority women's former and current pledge activities create a rite of passage that stems from a long-standing cultural tradition among Black Americans to patrol and redraw the boundaries of Black respectability. The contradictory rites of pledging and hazing function as a private way for Black sorority women to resist the constraining politics of respectability that they are expected to embrace and embody in the public sphere, as mandated by their national sorority headquarters' characterology. The private tests that pledges endure from sorority members during their pledgeship appear to socialize them into parables of character reminiscent of nineteenth-century and early twentieth-century respectability politics forayed by their foremothers in the Black intelligentsia. The paradox here lies within the use of coercive, anti-respectable behavior by members to transform sorority hopefuls into what I call "respectable pledges."

Black sorority pledge processes, including rites that one might construe as hazing, have received popular press but no serious scholarly attention. An examination of the psychological reasoning behind pledging and hazing rites in Black sororities allows the opportunity to analyze the interplay between violence, culture, power, and the production of Black femininity. An examination of pledge processes and specific hazing incidents points to sites where Black sorority women are creating and maintaining cultural identity and power within the crucible of the fraternal apparatus. I argue that Black sorority women use ethnic-specific rites to redistribute cultural flows of power within their subculture, and in so doing, they produce new registers for understanding the complex social function of violence and the cultural politics of Black feminine identities. This work thus relies upon and adds to the work coming out of critical race feminist studies and critical legal studies, which aims to expose the historical and current implications of how the legal apparatus upholds White supremacy and hierarchies of gender and race as it pertains to Black female subjects.[6]

The pledge process and hazing in Black sororities is not only a process during which sorority members who hold power over pledges exercise that power in detrimental ways at the expense of the emotional and physical health of subordinate(d) pledges. Thus far, pledge processes and hazing rituals are placed within discourses that see these rites as representative of immature and inhumane rites that pledges endure to belong to a transparent social collective. To dismiss and relegate pledging or hazing in BGLOs simply as an abuse of power—which has been the prevailing attitude of universities, law enforcement, the U.S. court system, and most scholarship on the topic to date—ignores two main components specific to BGLOs' pledge rites: the cultural necessity of and meanings attached to these rites of passage for this subgroup's survival, and the agency of pledges and ensuing cultural and subgroup knowledge gained about BGLO life during and after pledges are made members. I tease out these ethnic and cultural nuances of the pledge process practiced by Black women to make sense of the ideological contradictions of the pledge process, hazing, and the construction of, and meanings inflected into, sisterhood and femininity for the AKA sorority. I follow this path to the ends of penetrating through, explaining, and therefore mapping the underlying cultural, political, ethnic, and gendered meanings of pledging and hazing practices from the benign and routine to the most malign and potentially dangerous. I argue that even in the most extreme violent cases of physical hazing, there is still much to learn from the pledges' and existing members' willing participation in the cultural and historical specificity of the social drama of the act.

Faithful to Ivy: Pledging and Hazing in the AKA Sorority

All eight major BGLOs' headquarters and the NPHC that governs them agreed upon and mandated in 1990 a ban on the pledge process because of hazing incidents that occurred during each organization's respective pledgeships.[7] For the AKA sorority, this meant the public death of their Ivy Pledge Club, through which sorority hopefuls pledged their loyalty to the organization in a rite of passage based on a recycling of Africanisms; a continuum of self- and group-inflected pain, regulation, and spatialization; detailed and shifting hierarchies; calculated and arbitrary reward systems; and symbolic sisterhood tests co-designed by pledges and chapter sorority leadership. Members of the sorority nominate and vote on postgraduate candidates for sorority membership after candidates establish a record of community service. In contrast, undergraduate members often undergo prolonged rites to prepare for and prove themselves worthy of becoming a sister. Former pledge processes for undergraduates ranged from weeks to months—opening up the possibility of what most Greek-letter organizations define as hazing. Hazing, in its universal and legal definition, involves requiring pledges to engage in conduct or endure excessive mental, physical, and verbal treatment that does not have direct bearing upon their role as potential members.[8]

The AKA sorority's governing body sought to make the following distinction between pledging and hazing for their members and sorority hopefuls: pledging would involve getting to know current sorority members and sister initiates, maintaining scholastic achievement during the application or pledge process, showing respectable character traits in public, accepting and promptly carrying out community service by a designated dean of pledges in a timely manner, cooperating with big sisters and their fellow pledge sisters, and learning sorority history in order to gain knowledge about the philosophy, aims, objectives, and political programs of the sorority. In contrast, the sorority denounced and defined hazing as performing personal tasks for big sisters that did not coincide with the larger good of the organization, excessive deprivation of sleep to carry out superfluous activities, difficult and unnecessary physical labor, and mental harassment and ludicrous treatment—for example, immature horseplay and practical jokes. Underscoring the two slippery definitions of each was a suggested agreement that pledges and existing members use their own good judgment and discretion during the pledge process to help them distinguish between pledging and hazing. Gray areas in the intended distinction between pledging and hazing blurred lines for members and pledges. This allowed for slippage in the interpretation and practice of pledging that, when not carried out properly, often led to hazing. In the former pledge process and in continued pledge activities, or unofficial pledging, the line between pledging and hazing remains unresolved and indistinct, especially regarding existing sorority women and sorority hopefuls.

The early 1990s was a period of internal rupture in the organization, as the pledge ban affected sorority rites of induction and caused an increase in the hierarchal restructuring of the organization. As a result of the 1990 ban, according to the national headquarters of the AKA sorority, women are currently initiated through a three-day process, where pledges learn sorority history at a retreat, establish their potential for leadership and community service, and pass a series of interviews conducted by existing members. All four Black sororities approved the new membership intake process more than a decade ago, but legal complaints prove that an underground pledge process in undergraduate chapters remains in at least two of the oldest organizations (i.e., AKA and DST), and that this process often leads to what is commonly accepted in legal discourse and by university officials as hazing. Indeed, the most serious hazing incidents occurred *after* the 1990 ban on the pledge process. Take, for example, the increasingly dangerous hazing incidents involving the AKA and DST sororities:

- In 1978, the Tennessee Supreme Court found three DST members guilty of a hazing incident that occurred in 1975 at Tennessee State University. The DST members were suspended for injuring pledges during a paddling session.[9]
- In 1978, the AKA sorority chapter at the University of Texas at Austin was found guilty of hazing a pledge, who received medical care at the university's health center because of bruises. An investigation found that the sorority required the woman and other AKA

pledges to "ingest unpleasant food, recite sorority history, and perform physical exercises" under duress.[10]

- The national headquarters of AKA and DST investigated their chapters at Howard University in 1988. They suspected that AKA and DST women were hazing pledges, engaging in favoritism in selection, and conducting other undisclosed improper pledge activities.[11]
- Members of the AKA sorority at Jacksonville State University pleaded guilty in a court in 1991 for the physical and mental hazing of six pledges. The AKA women were fined $144. As a result of the incident, the national headquarters temporarily suspended the chapter's activities.[12]
- An AKA pledge at Georgia State University filed a police report with the Atlanta Police Department alleging she was "kicked, punched, choked, and stomped by five fellow AKA pledges" on April 21, 1997, for not attending an unsanctioned pledge recruitment activity (requiring pledges to haze other pledges instead of existing members circumvents the legal responsibility of the national organization and chapter). The national and Georgia regional headquarters of AKA had no record of a planned recruitment activity that weekend.[13]
- A pledge told campus police at Western Illinois University that a predominantly Black sorority hazed her. She claimed that sorority members took a hairpiece from her head and stuffed it into her mouth; struck her while squatting; and required her to eat unusual mixtures of food, including a mixture of onions, vinegar, and hot sauce, resulting in regurgitation on her blouse. After vomiting, the pledge alleges that the sorority members forced her and other pledges to re-swallow the already regurgitated food particles. She also claims they forced her to grind her elbows into cornflake cereal until they bled, and then they forced her to eat the bloody cereal mixture. Sorority members apparently required routine exercise, including sit-ups, until the skin on her and

> other pledges' buttocks cracked, and after failing to recite sorority history in a proper manner, sorority members hit pledges upside the head with a book (most likely the sorority's history book). The pledge alleges to have received treatment at a hospital emergency room twice during the unsanctioned pledge process. The case was tried in a Cook County Circuit Court on December, 19, 1999.[14]

AKA and DST are not alone in their participation in post-1990 underground pledge activities and hazing. Hazing in Black fraternities was the topic of numerous newspaper headlines throughout the 1990s. In 1993, after being body slammed and pushed during a pledge rite, Mike Davis, a Kappa Alpha Psi pledge at Kansas State University, died, and the national fraternity was sentenced to pay $2.25 million in damages. Omega Psi Phi granted pledge hopeful Joseph Snell of the University of Maryland $400,000 in 1995 after enduring a rite designed to make his skin color blacker.[15] Hazing is often thought of as a masculine and largely physical activity. Sorority hazing, in contrast, has received press but no scholarly attention. Recent lawsuits against two of the most prominent sororities—AKA and DST—document that sororities do participate in physical and mental hazing.

According to a study on the changing perceptions of membership intake in BGLOs conducted two years after the pledge ban, 22 percent, or fewer than one-quarter, of Black undergraduates believed the ban on pledging would not end it and would only push such practices underground, resulting in an increase in hazing.[16] Another survey conducted in 1999 by Walter Kimbrough, vice president of student affairs at State University of New York at Albany, found that 53 percent of Black Greek-letter members, out of 200, admitted that they participated in an underground pledge process. Kimbrough argues that his statistics underestimate participation, reflecting respondents' fear rather than candid responses. He felt that many were too afraid to admit they engaged in pledge activities that university officials and the penal and judicial system might construe as, and therefore might indict as, hazing.[17] Unofficial pledge processes in Black sororities, including the more extreme behavior of hazing, reveal a web of contested meanings wherein loyalty, authenticity, group survival, and obedience become signs of subgroup identity for members and pledges alike during post-1990, underground pledge processes.

The statistics and hazing incidents present several challenges in arguing for the deeper meanings about the pledge process and for understanding the social function of violence within Black sorority culture. How does becoming a respectable pledge collide with what many might deem an unrespectable pledgeship? Sorority women rationalize pledge rites as a means to revitalize culture and to gain, show, and perform respect. The Ohio State case that began this chapter may seem similar to the rampant hazing among all Greek-letter organizations by all racial and ethnic groups, however, pledging in Black sororities has particular cultural elements that emanate out of and resist the historical formation of Black feminine identity.[18] Swahili names for pledges and pledge lines, learning South and West African dance, and other secret, ethnic specific rituals are a part of the former, and underground, pledge process. AKA hazing during pledgeships adds another layer of meaning and complexity into how the sorority women use the process as a cultural, psychological, and physical mechanism to induct members to the ends of creating transformed feminine identities and respectable pledges. In my examination of these rites, I reveal the ways in which the women resist the mandate of respectability through the means used to acquire their goal, which is, paradoxically, the central contradiction of those rites.

Field interviews, court cases involving hazing, and recent surveys confirm that unofficial hazing remains after the 1990 ban on the pledge process, and that it is not likely to disappear anytime soon. Unofficial hazing is intended to create differentiated meanings for members and sorors within the realm of feminine interrelationships. For AKA, this has at times meant that before the potential initiates arrive at the stage of the official three-day process to become a member, undergraduates sometimes endure a series of rites in an unofficial, pledge-type process in order to also become a soror. Sorority women interpret "soror" as representing a true sister and the term *member* to denote a woman who was read in at the sorority headquarters' retreat without having to endure pre-retreat rites and without having to undergo the "old" pledge experience to emotionally bond with her sister-initiates. Although soror is the Latin root of the word sister, it is specifically rearticulated within Black sororities to describe a sister within the context of an extended Black Greek-letter feminine kinship system.[19]

Understanding the significance of soror as a Black feminine identity in relation to the creation of a Black Greek-letter vernacular community is helped by realizing the weight that language has in the formation of subgroup identity in general. As Stuart Hall explains, language is a prime factor in Black identity formation and acts as a means to "build up a culture of shared understandings."[20] Women who choose induction at the retreat without going through a pre-retreat process retain a lower status in the sorority, and, in the minds of some, they are ideologically and socially set apart from the "Old School Pledgers" (OSPs) in the sorority, and thus, by extension, are not true sorors. The sorority thus faces a current moment of identity fragmentation on the basis of a struggle between AKA headquarters inducting *members* through their formal three-day retreat and OSPs initiating *sorors* via an underground pledge process.

The NPHC, AKA sorority headquarters, and its postgraduate regional leadership appear at odds with the OSPs and their practice of unofficial pledging, primarily because of the lawsuits that result from underground pledge practices that cross over the line to hazing. Hazing lawsuits increase the ability for the state to bankrupt BGLOs, thereby threatening their reputations, credibility, and monetary ability to carry out their extensive national and chapter service programs in the Black community. Herein lies a core contradiction of becoming a soror using hazing and underground pledging: hazing is antithetical to the sorority's public persona and has the capability to impede its ability to carry out counterpublic-sphere work. Nonetheless, pledge rites, whether benign or malevolent, remain essential for many OSPs, because sorors view these rites as an effective means for acculturation into the sorority and into a specific kind of Black feminine identity capable of fulfilling service requirements. If 1990 reflects a coming apart for the sorority insofar as membership status is concerned, then exploring the evolution of pledging and hazing in AKA in a historical context provides a shifting conceptual trajectory in which to further understand the current crisis the ban has caused for members and potential members.

Practices that accompany becoming a soror remain a point of contest and contention for the sorority. By the 1960s, incidents of hazing during pledgeships in BGLOs became public, and AKA was a part of this trend. This is not to say that hazing did not go on before the 1960s, but it is to say that reports emerged in larger numbers and became a rite of passage that caused disruption and acculturation. In the sorority's internal news periodical, the *Ivy Leaf*, the Supreme Basileus (president of AKA) Julia Purnell wrote about the conflation between pledging and hazing in 1964, when she made a formal statement about the mistreatment of AKA pledges in the organization. Purnell wrote:

> Whenever we pledge women by their clothes and appearance, whenever we attempt to build unity by hazing and by force, whenever we value social reputation more than academic standing, we tear down the structure from which we have benefited the most. But when we treat our pledges with respect and consideration, when we emphasize the ways in which we can help women make a better adjustment to academic responsibilities, then we are building on the unity of purpose of the sorority and the unity as education [oriented] institutions.[21]

Purnell's statement goes beyond warnings about the ramifications of injury during pledge rites and hazing; it illuminates other problems within the realm of culture and everyday life of which the Black sorority pledge process refracts. Her counsel that chapters not choose members on the basis of materialism and beauty aesthetics is a clear indicator of perceptions of class and its intersection with the construction of femininity as shifting and unstable criteria. Similarly, Purnell's statement about maintaining unity by force denotes an already formed cultural politics of induction and conception of identity with which the organization was struggling at the time. That the AKA president found it necessary to speak on the matter of hazing in its internal publication without naming chapters or a particular individual's mistreatment of pledges indicates that members commonly knew of and practiced these rites. In 1962, two years before Purnell's statement in the *Ivy Leaf*, AKA at Howard University was suspended until 1966 because of inappropriate initiation rites.[22] Purnell's statement is thus fourfold in understanding how Black sorority women are rearticulating femininity through the pledge process, as her commentary aids in seeing the pledge process as a site where class, culture, femininity, and violence intertwine and are performed, taking form on the bodies of Black sorority women during and after their pledgeship.

Research and field informants for this study substantiate that the 1960s were particularly prone to an increase in hazing, which many believe has a causal relationship to the overall cultural and racial turmoil of the mid-twentieth-century civil rights era. Members say this moment has intensified the necessity to put pledges through rites that would aid them in the hostile racial environment they inhabited. One of the foremost writers on hazing, Hank Nuwer, states that "little hazing took place in Black sororities before the 1960s," which coincides with historian Paula Giddings's brief treatment of the subject in her work on DST, where she also marks this particular decade of civil rights activism as a moment of increased hazing during pledgeships.[23] Prominent politician and civil rights activist Andrew Young commented in a 1990 *New York Times* article that in 1949, his pledge process with the fraternity Alpha Phi Alpha, which he claims consisted of mental challenges and not physical abuse, was good training that helped him and others face the violence of the Ku Klux Klan.[24] Yet there has always been, and likely always will be, a period of turmoil for Black Americans. Young refers to a strenuous pledge period in 1949, indicating a struggle over civil rights for Black Americans before the 1960s. His statement incites conjecture as to whether there was an increase in strenuous pledgeships and hazing in the 1960s, as Giddings, Nuwer, and my informants suggest, or if pledges and universities felt freer to report and act upon the incidents.

It is more likely, I argue, that although pledging practices may have intensified during the 1960s because of the racially *in-*

tense environment that surrounded Black American men and women, the opportunity and ability to report such incidents increased too, making it impossible to equate reported incidents with the actual history and practice of hazing. The first reported incident of hazing was in 1961 for Black fraternities and in 1962 for Black sororities.[25] Are we to believe that hazing in Black American fraternities did not occur before 1961, and that no hazing in Black American sororities took place before 1962? The testimony of members and the documentation of hazing require more intellectual probing. Hazing is very likely as old of a tradition as the organizations themselves. It is quite probable that the politics of respectability discouraged public complaints or exposure of impropriety among the groups to outsiders in the early part of the twentieth century. Organizations would likely take care of serious infractions during pledge periods, particularly during their early formation. This process would coincide with a conservative Black cultural politics in which leaders would take on the responsibility to regulate improper behavior among their brothers and sisters, for fear that one Black person's mistake would reflect the race. In 1963, dynamic activist Malcolm X spoke about the necessity to take care of disputes internally within the Black community. Although not all agreed with X's position on how to seize cultural and economic power in the United States for Black Americans, his commentary on how to deal with internal grievances within the Black American community echoed the politics of respectability shared by many of his dissenters and supporters. X felt that

> instead of airing our differences in public, we have to realize we're all in the same family. And when you have a family squabble, you don't get it out on the sidewalk. If you do, everybody calls you uncouth, unrefined, uncivilized, and savage. If you make it at home, you settle it at home; you get in the closet, you argue it out behind closed doors, and then you come out on the street and you pose a common front, a united front.[26]

By the mid-1970s, Black American fraternal pledges were more apt to speak out against hazing because of legal (even if not always material) desegregation among the races, which caused the lifting of social sanctions in the post-segregation era. Close protection of a respectable, Black public persona, which was either unknown or ignored by the dominant culture during segregation, became slightly less important in an era when racial integration would make respectable character traits of Black Americans more visible. This changing cultural reality lessened but did not end the need for a rhetorical reiteration of respectability and material social containment for some, which ironically strengthened the need to continue to instill respectable traits within pledges. BGLOs became a site where the politics of respectability continued to have salience and therefore continued to exist as a tradition cultivated by fraternal leadership. As complaints of hazing and subsequent court cases of indictable hazing increased in the United States in the post-1960s era, the disjuncture between the public position on, and description of, pledging and the ways respectability would be instilled in members became a core tension between older fraternal leadership and younger members. These generational and leadership struggles within BGLOs in the past continue to hold relevance and shape the ideological positions and practices of sorors in the post-1990 pledgeship era.

Disturbing Rites and Distributive Rights: Sorority Culture, Hazing, and the Discourse of Legal Sanction

The incident at Kent State, as well as the numerous hazing infractions in Black sororities that took place during underground pledge processes, anticipates the following question: What do OSPs *and* sorority hopefuls gain psychologically and materially from the social drama of the unofficial pledge process? A closer examination of the defense attorney's arguments in the Kent State case begins the work of providing an answer to this difficult question. It also reveals how the state adheres to and produces racial inequities in the legal and larger social and cultural spheres and relies on race-neutral and colorblind policy. According to Dea Floyd, the defendant's lawyer in the Ohio case, pledging is an old-school tradition in BGLOs, and excessive treatment is sometimes an unfortunate, but culturally useful, by-product of that tradition. The court's and state's prosecuting attorney treated as absurd and ruled inadmissible Floyd's position that pledging is a cultural practice stemming from African rites of passage, and that hazing is a tool to teach modes of Black survival in society. That it is irrational to think and argue that the three stages of pledging are a useful rite of African and Black rites of passage was the unstated, yet implicit, position of the state, if we are to go by the presiding judge's agreement of its inadmissibility into evidence. Portage County Court's presiding judge and the prosecuting attorney concentrated on the violence the women carried out, not the overall cultural performance of rites specific to this group and each stage of its pledge process. OSP's lawyer did not attempt to dismiss the violence carried out that night in the women's defense, but she did attempt to change the discourse so that the court could view the totality of the women's actions in order to affect and lessen the women's sentencing. Culture and law, in this case, were polar opposites, and as the court proceedings reflect, the prosecution metaphorically put Black culture on trial too.

Floyd attempted to introduce into evidence three primary characteristics that she believed should have bearing upon the court's perception and ruling concerning the women's actions and participation in their underground pledgeship: (1) the African rituals practiced in each respective pledge stage; (2) the intention of and cultural construction of the specific types of discipline, punishment, and reward system co-created, co-inflicted, and co-endured by pledges and sorority members; and (3) the survival mechanisms and life skills that resulted from this mutual process that helped members survive in a racially intolerant and hostile society in the United States. Floyd's three-pronged position statement might seem legally extraneous, but it nonetheless reveals the investment and different meanings that sorors and pledges make of the underground pledge process. AKA headquarters, at least publicly, did not agree with Floyd and OSPs, as they suspended the Kent State AKA Chapter after the incident. Further, the Kent State AKA graduate chapter advisor was quoted in Kent State University's school newspaper as saying that the women had "disgraced themselves and the principles for which, as AKAs, they were supposed to uphold."[27] The conflict between the legal apparatus and its enforcers, OSPs and their means of enforcement, and AKA national headquarters' and their regional leadership's public position on pledging and hazing as an enforcer shows the cultural construction of regimented discipline and violence aimed at producing a particular type of social subject. These different positions concerning the pledge process, what constitutes hazing, and even, as OSPs might argue, that hazing is detrimental were the thorny positions battled out in court and ultimately lost by Kent State OSPs and their lawyer.

Younger AKA members sympathetic to underground pledging insist that it was because of the rigorous principles of the organization and their obsession to live up to that ideal that pledges were disciplined to comply with those norms. As pledges are expected to learn sorority history and stepping, and to prove themselves worthy of being a soror, nearly any means is used by OSPs to ensure pledge compliance. The extent to which women can endure the harshest mental and physical treatment is indicative of how well they will be able to endure and intervene in a society that is antithetical to their survival as a gender and people. Sorors argue that once conferred upon as a soror, the women, despite the severity of the underground pledge process, will become sisters, with all the social, cultural, and political privileges the identity engenders. OSPs argue that the White dominant culture, which might also treat the women harshly and with violence in the public sphere throughout their lives, will never help or accept them as the sorority will. This is the lesson, the OSPs contend, learned once members cross the burning sands and become sorors.

Whether seen as illegal or culturally necessary in a court of law, OSPs' privatized behavior stood on trial not just in the public courts but also by Kent State University's student newspaper. In light of the emphasis on ethical character as a prime component for acceptance to the Ivy Pledge Club and the sorority's cultural and counterpublic-sphere work, the private and underground practice of pledging among the AKA women stood out as a sign of public weakness that Kent State University's newspaper, the *Kent Stater*, pounced on with journalistic fervor.

The AKA hazing case became an excuse to denounce the assumed evil fraternal apparatus and its secrets in a more general sense, and it made the Black women targets of subtle, and at times not so subtle, racially inflected news-media bashing. AKA's hazing infraction was used as proof that BGLOs were the worst rendition of the assumingly despised White fraternals on Kent's campus. Kent's White fraternal members, in order to distance themselves from the presumed "black sheep" of Greek-letter organizations, also publicly vilified AKA's Kent State Chapter. Well before the AKA women had their day in court, the student newspaper and members of the White Greek community repudiated, tried, and convicted the AKA Chapter at Kent State that was accused of hazing.

Several editorials ran in the *Kent Stater*, which one might summarize into one overdetermined statement: secrets and hazing are why Black American fraternals are bad. One student reporter for the *Kent Stater* argued that secrecy was the precursor to hazing, and that if BGLOs would reveal or have their practices out in the open, it would be best for all. "Greek Secrecy Leads to Hazing" read one headline for the *Kent Stater* in response to the AKA hazing case. Its student author wrote in an editorial: "Maybe if the African American Greeks explained to us outsiders what everything stood for, we would understand why you have a convulsion when you recite your cheers, talk about your history, and stomp your steps."[28] The student journalist continued that if she were in a gang, she would be proud to tell everyone what her "letters stood for and what her colors meant." "Secrecy breeds a poor sense of trust and harbors bad feelings," said the author.[29] The student's parallel between secrecy and gang activity, and her further conflation of Black Greek-letter organizational practices such as stepping being the same as hazing, is telling in many ways.

Most obviously, the secret component of fraternities and sororities creates great angst for this particular student. Perhaps not so obvious is that it is the cultural specificity of Black American fraternals—the pronounced ethnic difference as seen in their performance of ritual—that appears to be at the core of the animosity toward them when one unpacks the subconscious fears behind the editorials. In this example, the psychology of anti-fraternalism takes on different dimensions when there is an addition of race to the equation. AKA women stood on trial by the student newspaper because of resentment that emanated from not being able to access the form of historically relevant and culturally inscribed Blackness the sorority represents, or, in the reporter's words, the animosity stemmed from not being able to figure out why the women "go into convulsions when they stomp their steps, tell their history, and recite their cheers."[30] The actual treatment of the pledges became lost in the need to know the secrets of the sorority and to ameliorate AKA's counterpublic-sphere work and credibility on campus. In five editorials printed about the case, not one demonstrated concern about what happened to the pledges. Rather, the editorials focused on the overall danger of secret societies. *Kent Stater*'s editorials and articles did not show compassion for the Black American women allegedly hazed at this moment (again, the case had not gone to court). More exactly, the editorials became an opportunity to release anxiety over the cultural tradition of fraternals and these particular Black American women. On the basis of these editorials and news articles, the AKA hazing case became an excuse to dismiss Black sororities as unproductive and secretive—even more so than their White fraternal counterparts. The *Stater* is not the locus of Kent student opinion, but its content should reveal a pattern of racialist discourse from one institution to another, that is, from the judicial system to the university's media apparatus.

Another editorial that ran in the paper by a member of a White Greek-letter fraternity Delta Upsilon was no exception to this racialist discourse. A White male student argued in response to the earlier editorial that his fraternity was open and not secret, therefore hazing was not a problem. Praising his organization and vilifying AKA, he argued that AKA had, to use his word, "tarnished" the Greek image, and that his fraternity was an example for other Greek-letter organizations to follow.[31] A member of the White fraternity Delta Chi argued similarly in another editorial in the *Kent Stater*, saying that critics of fraternals should not associate all fraternals with the AKA sorority, which was an example of "how bad things had gotten in the

Greek system!"[32] An additional student wrote that the "semi-exclusive, secretive nature of AKA makes the *mud* on the sorority women's faces difficult to wipe off."[33]

In all of these editorials, there is no mention of the actual women who allegedly incurred hazing, the cultural specificity and historical circumstances from which Black American sororities arose, or their continued relevance for Black students in our increasingly less than racially tolerant academies. The entire pledge process in BGLOs, which would include rites, chants, and ethnic performance, was always conflated in the *Stater* with harmful cultural secrets and hazing. AKA was compared to White fraternals by anti-fraternalists, yet they were also simultaneously segregated from the White organizations by White fraternals' use of racialist language to describe the AKA women. *Kent Stater*'s student media coverage focused on secrecy and anti-fraternalism in general as the frame to view AKA women, but the editorials and articles by White fraternal members in the *Kent Stater* showed how very different the women were from the social construction of whiteness, and therefore White fraternals too, by using racially suspect terminology and phraseology. The racial undertones espoused in the editorials and by courts give little doubt as to why BGLOs and other such cultural institutions, despite their problems, continue to exist today. However, pointing out the racial bias in the judicial system and in the university, which in this post-Rodney-King-beating and excessive-school-shooting era even a good portion of society would most likely admit to, still provides no understanding of why the women made the decision to engage in unofficial pledge rites. Although it is important to cite their unequal treatment, it is also vital to grapple with the relationship and use of violence among the Black women involved in underground pledging and the creation and culture of femininity, which for them necessitates the violence.

The previously discussed response to the AKA incident at Kent State is illuminating in its suggestion of how BGLOs and Black culture are viewed or not viewed by the state. Yet to achieve a deeper understanding of the rites of pledging and hazing, the AKA women's voices, particularly those of the OSPs, become increasingly vital in understanding the underlying rationalization of the process. Characteristics sought and cultivated in the women during former and underground pledge periods make for an exhaustive list of respectable traits tested during what sorors call "pledge sessions." These underground pledge sessions, even when they appear to cross over the line to hazing, are designed to follow through with the mandate of the AKA sorority manual, the *Ivy Primer*. During ethnographic fieldwork on AKA sorority pledge practices, OSPs revealed to me consistent viewpoints. After spending intense weeks with OSPs and viewing pledge sessions in a variety of settings, OSPs and pledges described to me their rationale for the underground pledge process, which included well-formed and thoughtful, although often contradictory, positions on gender, race, femininity, and power.[34] In a nutshell, informants' responses reveal that, for them, pledge activities are designed to help sorority hopefuls understand the true meanings of becoming a soror and redefine the meaning of Black femininity, collective responsibility, and emotional maturity.

The Making of a True Soror*: Do the Transformative Ends Justify the Radical Means?*

In describing the criteria for membership and expectations for behavior, the *Ivy Primer* states that the ideal soror should control excessive and public display of emotion; conceal weakness; multitask; never use excuses for failure to perform in life; pronounce and inhabit confidence; have clear expression in vocabulary and speech; be law-abiding, resourceful, tactful; exercise sound judgment; make difficult decisions; assume new, added, and difficult responsibilities; show genuine and boastful interest in AKA; commit to the common good of their communities; be prompt in all economic debts and matters; develop clear community outreach programs; exhibit social balance and composure; remain neatly dressed and poised; and be wide-ranging in conversational ability. This exhaustive list is strongly tied to behavior mandated by the politics of respectability, that is, the ascription to upright and nearly angelic behavior, especially in the public sphere, at all times. Pledge sessions become the privatized stage to instill and test these character traits, where sorors and pledges become willing, even if ambivalent, actors. Respectability is not something inherent or necessarily already there in all members; it is something that is often taught or strengthened through disciplining practices during the pledge process. Some pledges will report behavior that crosses the line for them, as seen in the Ohio case at Kent State University, but most pledges want more than anything to prove they have what it takes to become the type of respectable Black woman the sorority proposes to make and cultivate. OSPs see behavior that would seem physical or emotionally cruel to non-sorority members as an effective mechanism that will provide life skills they will need to deal with the American society, which at almost every juncture, particularly in the academy and larger public sphere, will try to break them down.

One informant suggested as much to me while describing her experience scolding a pledge during a seemingly typical pledge session:

> I told a pledge who snapped and was crying during session the other day that "If I am at work, my boss is yelling at me because he is looking for figures, my staff is out sick, the receptionist is not at the front desk, the phones in the office are ringing off the hook, I haven't looked at my interoffice e-mail yet, should I sit and cry?" Pledging is the same way. I told her, "It doesn't matter if five big sisters are yelling in your face until you get your sorority history right. You have to be able to think quickly and fast. And you have to keep your composure at all times."[35]

This interaction between the soror and pledge, that is, an intense question-and-answer period about the sorority's history, is neither harsh hazing nor indictable but rather a benign form of calculated mental pledging designed to strengthen and hone the pledge's ability to function under pressure. Learning sorority history is, after all, a prerequisite for membership. OSPs' position on pledging and this particular example makes claims to being in alignment with the key characteristics outlined in the

Ivy Primer: multitasking, composure, knowledge of the sorority's history, and activism. So when do such psychological and intellectual exercises cross the line and transform into hazing? One informant recalled that a sorority sister dropped her in a garbage bin on her college campus for not wearing her ivy pledge pin. Another key informant revealed that she required her group of initiates before the ban on pledging in 1990 to do strenuous yard work and exercise for several hours while wearing thickly layered clothing on an excessively hot day. Her reason, allegedly, was to teach pledges the value of hard work and for them to "learn not to be afraid to get their hands dirty." In these examples, it is evident that OSPs are rejecting refined, fragile definitions of womanhood and respectability in private through discipline and assertive behavior. OSPs engage in and enforce discipline to create a hyperfeminine identity in the future and in public.

Although pledge practices differ among chapters, there are patterns concerning expectations of pledges during the underground, and in former pledge processes before the 1990 ban. Pledges must greet big sisters whenever asked to do so or whenever a big sister enters a room; they are to learn every detail about the sorority, particularly its involvement in civil rights, social justice crusades, and their struggle to emerge and remain as autonomous organizations in the face of racial and gender adversity. Pledges are to keep a journal of their pledge activities written in all lower-case letters, where they also keep detailed minutia about the background of each of their big sisters in their respective chapter. Lastly, pledges wear the same clothes—usually loose-fitting black sweats—no makeup, and braided or inconspicuous hairstyles either while they are pledging or during their underground pledge sessions.

After listening to and witnessing a few pledge sessions and being allowed to view selected pages from my informants' pledge books, I had many questions for OSPs: Why do pledges write in lower-case in their pledge books? "Because that is pledge writing," an informant responded in angered frustration. Why do pledges face discipline if they do not know their sorority history? "How can you do well in your history classes if you don't know your own sorority history?" another OSP said with a sly grin. When I asked why pledges are required to formally greet big sisters when they enter a room, an OSP said in a raised voice, "[Pledges] need to learn *respect*!" What, then, was the benefit of pledges being required to wear the same dark clothes every day during their pledgeship, braids or nondescript hairstyles, and no makeup if when once conferred upon as sorors they were expected to dress neatly, would often wear chemically relaxed or at least individualized hairstyles, and were expected to look "feminine" and act perfectly poised? Sorors revealed that pledges are supposed to look nondescript while on their pledge line so that no one pledge stands out as aesthetically more beautiful than another pledge. OSPs explained that the pledges are learning to become "a unit" or "one," and in their view, differing aesthetic qualities and perceived beauty would obstruct this process. My informants insisted that if the women are jealous of one another during their pledgeship, they are less likely to bond. In this way, the pledge process creates an initial leveling for the women to allow the bonding process to take place. After my discussions with the women, it was clear that the underground pledge process runs the gamut from the silly to more serious rites, from the obscure to well-crafted discipline and regimentation done with specific results in mind.

I again return to the Ohio case to provide insight as to why pledges comply with these benign and more dangerous rites. The night of the most extreme hazing during the goddess stage is what many chapters in BGLOs refer to as "turn back night." OSPs' goal on that night was to sift out those who could not take the pressure and to turn them back from finishing the process. On the night in question during the Ohio case, the pledges' job was to, as the civil rights song says, "Not let anything turn us around." Why would a pledge endure these rites? Is the compliance with such behavior only in the name of bonding, learning respectability, wanting to, and dying to belong? I shift gears to a brief discussion of how AKA members bemoan the loss of the pledge process and Black fraternity pledge processes and hazing to begin the work of solving this cultural conundrum.

One Black fraternity member at a predominantly White Southern university told a *Washington Post* reporter who covered the end of the pledge process in 1990 about his pledge process, the function it served for him, and the subgroup knowledge he gained afterward: "I cherish a lot of those memories, because I've never been to a point of physical brokenness like that ever in my life. And I know those other guys [on my line] never have either. We sat around a table and cried together [after it was over], and put bandages on each other. Going through hell does create unity. It's a stupid means of doing it, but it does." OSPs echo this sentiment, as a longtime member of AKA explained to me: "After I pledged, I felt that there wasn't anything that I could not achieve, because my self-determination was heightened." [36]

Power, as it intertwines with violence, must not go unrecognized during the pledgeship and must not be apologized away as only a bonding mechanism, nor be dismissed as a rite endured solely to belong. The aforementioned quotations suggest that OSPs bring pledges to a breaking point, but sorority hopefuls feel empowerment once sorors confer their new status as AKAs. But there is another side to understanding the power relationship during the pledge process. Later in the *Post* article, the same fraternity member reveals that although he says he is now against hazing, he had previously been one of the harshest "hazers" as soon as he was given the opportunity to do so in order to—I would suggest—gain power he did not previously have in the larger public sphere. As power was not accessible to him in other masculine or dominant public spheres as a racialized Black male, his experience seems to illustrate that he was able to temporarily access power within the Black fraternal sphere through the use of hazing. In a particular portion of the article, the *Post* interviewee relayed almost malicious excitement, albeit semi-introspection about his use of hazing:

> This one guy [I hazed], he could have beaten me up. The guy was like 6' 3," and I would still really whale on him. I would just smack him and kick him and do all kinds of crazy stuff. Sometimes I'd do it for no reason. Sometimes I'd just go up to him and smack him in his face. I would just do it. Some people did it to me, and that was the justification—Well, I got smacked in the face for no reason,

> just 'cause somebody had a bad day. So I'd just go up to him and say, "You know, you're ugly today." Whap! [37]

However counterproductive and violent one might view these rites through Western and modern conceptualizations of violence, pledges do gain moments of power during the pledge process.[38] In sororities, pledges' primary responsibility is to not blindly carry out big sisters' requests but, rather, to outsmart them, work around them, and devise plans to get them out of whatever difficult situation they are placed in by current members. In this way, the women are creating continuous flows of power during pledgeships, which are not always "top-to-bottom" flows of power but discursively deployed to and among pledges. To use the term *agency* in this case may expand the term too far, but for pledges, the ends of self-empowerment and self-rationalized subgroup knowledge and membership justify the means of aggressive discipline.[39] Whatever the methods, the result is the creation of a perceived authentic identity—a true soror. In this light, it becomes increasingly difficult to view pledging as only detrimental and increasingly difficult to view hazing in BGLOs within a subordinator/subordinate dichotomy. As theorist Michel Foucault argues, having access to various forms of power within subgroups may produce forms of knowledge and power-knowledge relations that are important for group survival.[40]

The OSPs use psychological and sometimes physical forms of discipline to acculturate pledges into characteristics and ways of being in alignment with a very particular construction of what members deem respectable Black womanhood. Once OSPs "make" pledges into sorors, their new identity outweighs the aggressive means, and they feel empowered by their earned identity as sorors. In interviews, many AKAs spoke fondly about their sisters and feelings of elation that they made it through their pledgeship and crossed the burning sands. The embittered women, who regretted the process, still did not seem to regret becoming an AKA, and many remained active in the sorority. Inasmuch as the pledges are active participants in underground pledging and appear to receive something tangible from the process, I argue that the relationship created between pledges and sorors during and after pledgeships reveals deeper meanings of power particular to this subculture of women. Pledging allows the OSPs to define Black womanhood and how they make a soror (read: Black sorority sister) for the organization.

Underground pledging serves a social function for the OSPs because this process prepares and initiates women, in their estimation, to deal with their racially hostile surroundings and provides a support network after they cross into membership, which members argue will last the rest of their lives. Their justification aside, one of the fascinating components to hazing and pledging in a theoretical sense is the multilayered and contradictory functions that both serve. Hazing, which sometimes happens during pledging, performs another facet of carnival described in chapter 3: a series of reversals, social transgressions, restructured hierarchies, and contradictory practices enacted to access, question, and redistribute authority and power. It is a psychological release of, and resistance to, the burden of the politics of respectability, and at the same time, it breeds respectability into sorority initiates. The underground pledge process is the upside of the down; it brings the bottom eventually up to the top; it levels, it disrupts, it unites, and it pushes pledges to their physical and psychological limit, and then it reels them back in just in time; it is resistance and conformity; it illustrates how history informs sorors' current cultural practices and how modern times connect to their past historical dilemmas.

Conclusion

I want to go beyond the descriptive and analytical lens of an ethnographer and a cultural historian and take a diagnostic, prescriptive leap in order to speak to the consequences and the risky rites of the underground pledge process. The problem with AKA headquarters' public stance on pledging is that it creates confusing doublespeak: the sorority mandates and insists that sorors ascribe to and comply with their strict characterology, yet they have publicly taken away the very means for which that compliance was once taught to potential members. It is because of the slippage in the sorority's definition of hazing and conflicting interpretations of pledging and hazing that the underground pledge process has become OSPs' answer to keeping their organization together. Younger members defy and at times seem to resent the position of the older generation, who may have also been "hazers" while in college, yet expect OSPs to let go of a tradition that they feel is important. OSPs appear determined to take any means to create the next generation of sorors. It should come as no surprise, then, that various forms of pledging in the organizations remain. Not all practices and rites of induction during the underground pledge process are emotionally cruel or physical, but hazing during these pledgeships does have serious consequences and leaves a largely negative impression about Black American fraternals among nonfraternal members. Unless new rites of passage are designed to take the place of membership intake, the yearning to make and become a soror will continue via an underground process, which, based on the increase and severity of hazing incidents, will lead to fatal results. As cultural critic Nada Elia writes about Black American women's participation in violence in general: "If we, [as women of African descent,] are genuinely seeking to move away from the oppressive effects of racism and sexism . . . and other forms of divisive systems of exploitation, . . . we must not allow ourselves to duplicate these systems, just as we refuse to be, and sometimes cannot be, defined through them."[41]

Elia's words and position on violence should act as an urgent cultural warning. Underground pledge processes, designed to prepare women for their role as sorors, are problematic because of the increased use of physical discipline and subsequent hazing charges. Paying homage to ivy plants, the sorority symbol that represents the growth, endurance, and soul of the organization, being given an African goddess name once members cross the sacred ceremony known as the burning sands, learning and performing Black American step dance to raise money and show cultural pride, and sacred rites of passage during pledgeships will surely disappear among the influx of hazing charges. Indeed, in response to BGLOs' promise to end underground pledging in 2000, student advisor Walker Kimbrough writes: "One must believe that there are enough brilliant minds in these organizations to create structured, beneficial pledge programs that limit the opportunities for hazing and provide severe sanctions for deviations. But continuing membership intake as it is guarantees the end of one or more organizations in the very near future. I promise."[42]

Kimbrough's words were nearly prophetic. In September 2002, at Playa del Rey beach, two alleged AKA pledges drowned during an underground pledge session. Kristin High and Kenitha Saafir, along with other pledges, agreed to perform a series of calisthenics exercises. The women then proceeded into shallow waters at the beach to engage in a "Simon Says" game with AKA sorority members. One of the women who could not swim was swept up by waves. The waters also overcame another woman who attempted to save her life, and both women ended up drowning. High's family sued the sorority for $100 million in a wrongful death suit. The two women were students at California State University, Los Angeles, and made claims to their families that they were AKA pledges weeks before their deaths. Apparently, nonactive members of the sorority had led them to the beach that day, thus making the sorority's fault undeterminable. Linda M. White, Supreme Basileus of AKA that year, expressed condolences to the families. White wrote on the sorority's Web site soon after the women's deaths that "While there has been public speculation that the incident involved AKA, I want to remind you that we have no chapter of AKA at California State University, Los Angeles—we suspended the local chapter more than two years ago over minor pledging infractions."[43] White's message has more meaning about the Band-Aid approach to the underground pledge process than she may realize.

Sorority identity exists as a product of historical constructions and modern rearticulations of Black femininity and agency, which are two variables that continue to have meaning in the ways the politics of respectability are created and maintained for these women. The AKA hazing case and informants' reflections show how the women create, use, and maintain cultural power within this subcultural group, and within the context of these sororal interrelationships. Their rationales for pledging and hazing function as truth within their subculture, and these rationales become cultural truisms that sorors draw upon as a template for how to respond to and within difficult circumstances throughout their lives. Whereas the cultural use of pledge rites remains an open and a contested question, the ramifications of the use of hazing in this subculture are much more certain. If negotiation between AKA leadership, OSPs, and members remains unspoken and undone, then it will be the state's legal apparatus, and not the women, who will decide their fate.[44] Ironically, it is this and similar types of outsider intrusion that the pledge process, and the AKA sorority as a whole, is designed to obstruct. One hundred years after AKA's formation, sorors continue to regret hazing and defend underground pledging; they struggle with social issues that underground pledgeships aim to correct; and they maintain an unrelenting focus on their hopes and visions for transformation in the Black public sphere.

5

Voices of Collectivity/ Agents of Change

Alpha Kappa Alpha and the Future of Black Counterpublics

> The public sphere is a historically situated and discursive institutional realm. It mediated between private citizens (civil society) and the state and afforded an arena for the national formation and functioning of information, in other words, public opinion. The . . . public sphere operated as a realm where all citizens interacted in reasoned discourse.
>
> —Evelyn Brooks Higginbotham, *Righteous Discontent*[1]

When 25,000 members of the AKA sorority gathered in Washington, D.C., for their Centennial Boulé on July 11, 2008, they did so to engage in reasoned discourse with one another and with public officials about Black voter registration, economic growth, and health initiatives in Black communities. Notably, their gathering came at a meaningful moment in history, marking their sustainability for 100 years and the outcome of their and others' work for social justice. Their annual Boulé also took place at the heels of a heated and strategically fought campaign for the Democratic nomination for the presidency of the United States in 2008 between a Black male, Senator Barack Obama, and a White woman, Senator Hilary Rodham Clinton. A symbolic representation of what that fight meant for those who are members of a racial and gender minority came on

January 15, 2008, when the lawyer, activist, and wife of President Barack Obama, Michelle Obama, accepted AKA's request to become a honorary member of the sorority. AKA founder Ethel Hedgeman Lyle would likely not have imagined, although she would have likely hoped for, a historic moment where the proverbial glass ceiling for gender and racial-ethnic minorities on Capitol Hill became more transparent and malleable, not to mention the possibilities for an AKA member to bear witness at close proximity to this change.

Soon after Michelle Obama's acceptance of AKA membership, the blogsphere on the Internet erupted with critiques about her decision. Members of Delta Sigma Theta questioned her decision to choose AKA over other organizations. Anti-Greek posts charged Michelle Obama with elitism, citing that her acceptance was a representation of bourgeois attitudes and culture. Not surprisingly, AKA members lauded the decision, pointing to her choice as proof of AKA's political relevance. Others questioned the timing of AKA's offer to Obama, retorting that their request was for organizational aggrandizement. In response to an *Essence* magazine article about Michelle Obama's upcoming induction into AKA, one disgruntled reader wrote that Michelle Obama's decision to choose AKA was "disgraceful," and that sororities have no business interfering with politics or advocating for candidates; "they are suppose[d] to be nonpartisan," wrote the reader.[2]

This discourse shows that little has changed in how many view BGLOs in general and AKA in particular, despite the passing of 100 years of service in the Black Public Sphere. In interviews in major publications and news outlets, including CNN and FOX News, AKA leaders responded to the critiques and used their centennial and the ensuing Michelle Obama induction to refocus the discourse on the actual women within the organization, their ideas for social change, and their cultural and counterpublic sphere work. AKA member Angela White told CNN correspondent Jill Dougherty, for example, that AKA founders "not only came up with the idea to support each other in a university environment but [they also sought] to affect the community."[3] Similarly, the 2008 president of AKA, Barbara A. McKinzie, told FOX News correspondent Shawn Yancey that "for us, [BGLOs] were more than social; it was a survival mechanism and a network that tended to create sisterhood, as well as to serve you throughout your life."[4]

AKA's Boulé week came to a close with a march from Congress to the White House with the other eight BGLOs in the name of their desire to realize their initiatives in Black communities concerning health, education, and economic stability. The current Speaker of the House, Nancy Pelosi, and other members of Congress addressed the marchers in support of their vision. In a *Washington Post* story reflecting upon AKA's Centennial Boulé, commitment to transformation, and change in Black communities over ten decades, *Post* writer and AKA member Lonnae O'Neal Parker included in her exposé a quote by Autumn Saxton-Ross, an AKA and health and wellness coordinator. Parker quoted Saxton-Ross as lamenting, "I worry about what message we are sending in a photo taken in our publication, the *Ivy Leaf*, which showed our [AKA] president [Barbara A. McKinzie and other officials] on Howard's campus in full-length furs . . . I worry about the caste system created by a $1,908 VIP pass for Boulé."[5] Saxton-Ross's self-reflexivity, the Michelle Obama induction controversy, and participation in their event by members of Congress suggest that AKA remains wedged between the prickly branches of public sphere politics, counterpublic sphere responses to the needs of Black Americans, and group and individual class consciousness.

Slightly more than ten years before AKA's centennial, the Black Public Sphere Collective made the argument that to understand the varied aspects of Black public life, community organizing, and political action, there was a need for a rearticulation of traditional notions of the public sphere and politics. In the twenty-first century, the question of cultural politics and its articulation in the public sphere is one of immediacy and urgency for cultural critics, cultural workers, and the academic and social communities they serve. AKA's work in the Black Public Sphere demonstrates a long record of engagement with various aspects of social change and reform. In contrast, stepping, underground pledge processes, hazing, and the performance of socioeconomic class demonstrate uneasy entanglements of private practice and opinions about public display. AKA's story shows actual counterpublics at work, however, as these formations are rarely stories of unencumbered success without having to regroup and rethink strategies and goals. The story of social movements and social action is more often one of struggle, regrets, mistakes, visions for change, and direct action. AKA women's voices are thus integral to understanding how individual women within the organization in contemporary times experience being Black and female (struggle) and pledging and hazing (regrets and mistakes), and how they mobilize collectively to transform social, cultural, and political life in the Black and larger public sphere (maintaining hope through action). Situating how AKA voices relate to the aforementioned core themes reveals the vitality, growth, and sustainability of the Black sorority and of Black counterpublics in the twenty-first century. Their ideas and experiences concerning BGLO life also place them in conversation with the discourse surrounding how others view the sorority in the public sphere, something that the Michelle Obama induction into AKA made increasingly visible.

Between Struggle and a Counterpublic Hard Spot: The Making of a Counterpublic and Voicing the Cultural Conundrum of Class

A primary aspect of counterpublics is the occurrence of struggle, that is, their emergence in opposition to cultural, social, and political constraints in the wider public sphere or the larger society. Given the increase in options available to Black women for social interaction and the abundance of social justice organizations from which Black women may choose, it may seem surprising that women continue to decide to participate in BGLOs at the undergraduate and graduate ranks. Yet it is precisely a sense of common struggle and plight that appears to attract women to Black sororities in the twenty-first century, during and after their college years. For undergraduates, isolation on college campuses and a yearning for sisterhood is a factor that surely attracts most women to Greek-letter sororities, but for Black women, it appears there is an amplification of members' feeling of isolation before their pledge process because of their gender and racial minority status. Other relational aspects of identity affect how subjects experience struggle and isolation, yet interviewees reveal that, in some academic settings, race and gender can act as a recognizable signifier to enact conscious and unconscious discrimination. One particular undergraduate interviewee, Katrina, notes this struggle and possible bias in the classroom setting for Black students, and how being in a BGLO was of assistance in coping with isolation and organizing for social justice. Of her decision to pledge AKA, Katrina reveals:

> [I am pledging] because of the low population of Black students on this campus. There is a definite need for sisterhood for Black women in order to make it through this institution. All of the odds are against us, and nobody wants us to make it through [college]. There are professors on this campus who are racist, and they'll let you know that you will not make it through and that their class is going to be twice as hard for you if you are African American. I wanted to do something for the African American community on campus. For me, it is a way for mobilizing to make us more united.[6]

Katrina argues that some Black students feel a burden to work twice as hard to achieve equality and recognition. Her sense of disenfranchisement from the structure of the academy and its professorate added to her overall sense of social isolation as a Black student. Cultural critic Michael C. Dawson, in his pacing through of current, Black counterpublic formations, asserts that Black student organizations in many ways function as oppositional spaces because of racist incidents perpetuated on college campuses.[7] Black counterpublics, I argue, are more than reactionary safe havens for young and old citizens alike; they are stratagem centers.

Expressing the desire to be a part of such organizations brings to the forefront issues of isolation, prejudice, and the historical significance of gender and race, but it does not address why women choose to pledge AKA vis-à-vis other organizations. Although there are four recognizable Black sororities to choose from, all interviewees I spoke to made mention of only two sororities as possibilities for their needs: AKA and DST. Their responses led me to ask: What is it about the AKA sorority that attracts women? What makes this sorority unique in comparison to other Black Greek-letter sororities? In addition, what is the connection between contemporary sorority membership and the complex structural arrangements of Black counterpublics? Why would the partner of a then-presidential candidate accept an honorary membership into AKA? A spokesperson for Michelle Obama remarked, "Because of [Michelle Obama's] respect for each of the historically black sororities and fraternities, her membership is non-exclusive. She looks forward to working with all of them to help bring change to their communities."[8]

Michelle Obama's public representative stressed the nonexclusive nature of her decision to disarm critiques of elitism and exclusivity, but, in contrast, members of AKA with whom I spoke proudly highlighted the exclusiveness of their decision, associating this decision with activist intents. When explaining why she chose to pledge AKA, Katrina shared that she was originally not attracted to AKA; she initially intended to pledge DST:

> I was attracted to the Deltas only because I read their book [*In Search for Sisterhood: Delta Sigma Theta and the Challenge of the Black Sorority Movement*], which made me really excited about the Deltas and sorority life in general. Yet after I was about to make the step for Delta, I figured I should step back and take a look at my options before I committed myself to one sorority. I then took some time to talk to AKAs on campus and to go to some of their events. I really liked what they were doing. They were actually doing something on campus, and the Deltas so far have done nothing this year. I was looking for a sorority who was doing something right now and was not waiting for their graduation to become politically active. I probably would have been more enthusiastic about AKA in the first place, but I didn't have their book.

Katrina's big sisters from chapters across the nation discussed how decisions for membership for them intersected directly with struggle, a genuine dream for change in Black communities, and leadership. For example, a senior and founder of an undergraduate chapter, Roslyn, said that she was "attracted to Alpha Kappa Alpha because of the women who were in the organization; they were strong leaders in their community." She continued:

> Originally, I thought that I would pledge Delta Sigma Theta because my mother is a Delta, but when I came to college, I did not feel a connection with Delta. I was not impressed by anything they had done on campus; they were not presenting themselves as leaders or role models. I was approached and asked if I wanted to bring AKA to my campus, and the women that approached me I was really impressed with. So I read up on AKA, and it seemed like they had the same mind-set that I did in terms of wanting to help the community and wanting to be leaders. I also liked the fact that AKA was the first African American sorority; they set the stage for what sororities should be. It seemed like they had a real commitment to sisterhood and helping other African American women whether they were college educated or not.

Candice, an AKA in her second year as a soror, had similar sentiments concerning sorority membership as a launching to on-campus community mobilization:

> At first I was not really interested. But one day I talked to my aunt who crossed in 1952 about Alpha Kappa Alpha and what her experience was like. She admitted there were problems, but it was worthwhile because it taught her restraint. She knew that if she made it through this process she could do anything. Then I started doing research on my own and learned about all the things AKA were involved in. I learned that it was not just a social organization, and that they were involved in a lot of community service work—that's what really got me interested. My view of sororities really changed; everyone told me that I should choose Delta, but I thought otherwise.

Activism for BGLOs does vary from chapter to chapter, but there is a sentiment of competition in the responses of Katrina,

Roslyn, and Candice, which hints at feelings of animosity toward DST. There is a deft accounting of the ongoing contribution of Delta Sigma Theta to political mobilization and community interventions; DST's work is a part of the historical record. Although she denounced her local DST chapter, Katrina admitted as much by revealing that she had read DST's history book, which ignited her interest in the political function of Black sororities. Still, the respondents made outright accusations that DST women on their campuses exhibited a lack of leadership. Their comments went beyond the verbal play of step competitions and took a more odious tone. Paradoxically, just as AKA women pointed to a bias toward DST, their responses also revealed external pressures for them to choose DST instead of AKA. This is likely because whatever impression DST's political record constituted among these women, unlike AKA, they did not hold the reputation for being concerned with class status and physical attributes of perceived beauty.

Graduate member of AKA, Janet, explained why AKA was a more viable choice for her rather than a predominately White sorority. Surprisingly, she explained that growing up in a White suburb and attending a nearly all White high school pushed her toward, rather than away from, a Black organization. Her response did point to feelings and issues of isolation among her White peers, but her reasons for pledging, along with her AKA sisters Ellen and Benita, described how sorority membership is an acculturation into "respectable" modes of behavior for Black women:

> JANET: I pledged because I wanted a Black female organization to identify with being that [college] was my first "away from mother experience" of independence. I attended an all-girls private school with ten African American students on the entire campus. I knew that I would pledge an African American organization from the get go. In fact, I never thought about joining any of the predominantly Caucasian sororities. My undergraduate chapter boasted high academic standing as one of the foremost criteria for acceptance into the organization [which] practically sealed my fate. Alpha Kappa Alpha sorority, being the

> first African American sorority, made it all the more attractive. Lastly, the ladies in my chapter were charming, ladylike, educated, welcoming, and kind.
>
> ELLEN: One of the main reasons I joined a sorority was for the strong relationships amongst Black women. I am the only girl in my family, and the relationship I would have with my mother I knew was completely different than a relationship I would have had with a sister. It was important for me to understand the plights of African American women and to appreciate everyone's individuality.
>
> BENITA: At various points in high school, I encountered women that I looked up to, and many of these women were AKAs, so this encouraged me to pursue becoming a member. I saw pledging as a way to put myself in conversation with people that I saw as the best of the best and who knew how to behave in nicer situations and dress for certain occasions. I didn't have that kind of know-how, but I knew that it was part of being successful. I never had the opportunity to take part of things like Inroads and Upward Bound; as I think of it now, I saw the sorority as one way to get the information about how to conduct oneself and surround yourself with positive people and energy.

To attribute all rationales for sorority involvement to isolation, community, and political motivations only would ignore aspects of social and class status that come with being an AKA. Janet's and Benita's responses point to the sorority as an acculturation of pristine womanhood or acceptable behavior for Black women within middle-class circles and the public sphere. Janet's response about AKA being the first sorority and Benita's response about AKA helping her fit in within the ranks of middle-class life indirectly address the cultural capital that arises from being an AKA. That is to say, there is a certain amount of cultural prestige that arises from being a member of an organization that is the "first," "oldest," and, therefore, in some minds, the "best." A sorority is not the only site where one makes such distinctions in taste and participation. Cultural capital is the invisible social hand of decision making in determining which university to attend, which corporation to work for, and which goods and services to consume and expend. Yet when similar practices are applied to the sphere of Greek-letter organizations, such choices appear more sharply related to elitism and, by extension, classism.

The issue of class has concerned much of the scholarship on the public sphere and counterpublics. Scholarship often locates the Black middle class or class elite as initiators of change in the public sphere. How is it, then, that groups that may have the most to gain from the subjugation of poor classes often become their proponents or workers for social change in Black communities? For Black women, class has always been a slippery signifier. In the twenty-first century, the Black sorority remains entrenched in middle-class values, whether or not the actual members identify as being a member of the working or elite classes. The ways in which AKA women experience and negotiate class status today provide a window into how Black counterpublics see and understand the relationship between class, activism, race, and gender.

A few interviewees showed an ambiguous understanding about class and sorority membership by insisting that AKA women come from all classes. Melissa, a lawyer in her early thirties, made special mention to me during our conversations about race and class that "It's a myth to believe that Black sorority girls come from upper-middle-class families." Darlene, an archivist at a public university and graduate member of AKA, echoed Melissa by arguing that AKAs "come from all classes." However, she added the caveat that a member's class status "depends on the local tradition of membership among the chapter involved." Darlene's reference to tradition leaves room for speculation and interpretation. If the formation of a chapter is dependent on tradition, then is that to say that part of some chapter's tradition is to pick women based on middle-to-upper-middle- class status? Two interviewees made a distinction between socioeconomic class in terms of monetary status and class in terms of the cultural and social status that comes from being a college graduate. Linda, a corporate manager and software trainer, placed the distinction between the university, class, and sorority membership in a historical context by noting, "In today's society, I think there is an equal mixture of all classes [in AKA]. This is because all classes have the opportunity to go to college when one time just the upper classes were afforded this opportunity."

Dawson's work on Black counterpublics is again instructive here, as he argues that Black counterpublics hold more class diversity than what appears on the surface because of the historical significance of race. "The Black counterpublic," he writes, "is not a bourgeois sphere . . . Black institutions and publics have been largely multi-class, at least up to 1970, due to the long regime of enforced segregation."[9] Black sororities, then, may exist as organizations with the middle-class values perpetuated by universities and higher education centers, with a diverse membership that upholds, disseminates, or struggles to acculturate to those values. Nevertheless, Linda's idea that all classes have an opportunity to attend college in the twenty-first century ironically highlights one of the accusations hurled at the Black middle class and middle-class organizations: that they have a cultural/class blind spot. Sentiments in her response elide the possibility that class, in terms of monetary comfort, can hinder the ability to acquire and complete a college education, therefore hindering the opportunity to join a sorority at the undergraduate level. One respondent, Ellen, also believes the university is a space of class diversity. Yet she reveals uneasiness with what her own class position may indicate about the class barriers of BGLOs: "To place [AKA] women in a class position," she says, "is almost impossible. For example, you must attend an accredited college or university to even be considered for membership. Therefore, most people at a collegiate level come from all class backgrounds thanks to scholarships, loans, etc. So to place individuals in particular class brackets would be unrealistic because of other extenuating circumstances. However, I myself come from a middle-class family."

Ellen's reluctant admission about her class status and her overall response require brief pause, because she insinuates that it is impossible to bracket sorority women into any particular class. She too makes no distinction between monetary class and class as a historically situated cultural and social system of values and ideals based on a capitalist ethos. Regardless of the amount of money in the pocketbooks of individuals, there is a cultural component to class that seems to go unnoticed by Ellen and many of the AKA women interviewed for this book. Such responses, however, are likely more than class hegemony or class denial at work. As Black women, there is an obscuring of their class status in the public sphere, because being Black and female often signifies "poor" in the popular imagination. Asserting claims of and to middle-class membership may be as much a statement of fact for these women as it is a statement of the right to have equal access to the social benefits of middle-class status.

Pamela, a graduate member of AKA, and Benita, a graduate member of AKA and college professor, reveal their previous working-class status, and the women provide similar and dissimilar insights into these class and culture distinctions. However, both women are more willing to admit to AKA as a middle-class organization with middle-class values. Pamela argues that being a AKA member has a direct connection to monetary means, and Benita makes important ties between class as a process of monetary means, class as an aspect of culture, and how being working class can possibly act as an impediment to success in college and in the sorority:

> PAMELA: I am from a working-class background, but I think mostly AKAs are middle-to-upper-middle class because of the fees for membership. Right now, it is $265 a year. Sometimes the fee is waived or diminished based on income. You are always an AKA, but some women will cease to be financial or their bad experiences will keep them from being in a graduate chapter.
>
> BENITA: I think that most AKAs come from upper-middle-class or solidly middle-class backgrounds. I came from a working-class family, and that certainly made things hard in certain ways. But as I look back and get honest, I have to say that I think I saw pledging as one of the ways that I was making sure that I would not be working class in adulthood. I was the first in my family to go to college, so the pressure was high. Everyone wanted me to succeed, but they didn't really know how to equip me for success. I was always looking for that kind of guidance. There are certain things that people who grow up around college-educated people can take for granted that I could not take for granted. So I was always looking for ways to

> learn the culture of college (and beyond). These are subtle lessons that I tried to pick up through sorority membership. I saw pledging as a way of making reality what I already believed about my ability to make a different kind of life for myself after college.

Benita indicates that class clearly matters, and that sorority membership may help one benefit from postgraduation networking to obtain more opportunities and financial security. Yet some interviewees were less forthright, and many women I spoke to and sent questionnaires to chose not to answer questions concerning class status. I suspect this is because class elitism is a stereotype of sororities in general, and a number of interviewees might perceive this question as crossing an unsaid taboo, similar to the issue of pledging and hazing. An AKA graduate advisor at a Midwestern university said as much by indicating that my questions were intrusive, especially my questions about class, therefore, she refused to let me interview the women within her chapter. If the majority of women came from a middle-class background, from an outside perspective, then this might make the sorority appear classist, or as an organizational structure that perpetuates class bias. Uplift work and respectability is the core of the women's public persona; to show class divisions with those they help would possibly implicate AKA in strengthening the socioeconomic ladder instead of helping the disadvantaged climb up or dismantle the power relations inherent to this ladder. Class, as it relates to Black counterpublics, historically and currently positions participants in these formations as existing between the proverbial hard spot of class ascension, class consciousness, and class change.

Maintaining Hope through Action, Acting on the Prospects of Hope: Voicing and Living the Challenges of Black Counterpublic-Sphere Work

Theories of counterpublics are effective in identifying historical examples of intervention, yet contemporary examples of activism are not as acknowledged in scholarship. This is, in part, because most scholars of the public sphere describe publics as male bourgeois centers, and counterpublics as bodies that respond to bourgeois centers and the confines of the state's ideological apparatuses. The dominant explanation of the relationship between publics and counterpublics relies heavily on historical hindsight, which in turn allows for an assessment of the effectiveness of counterpublic efforts. Placing an overly determinant definition on the work of counterpublics and ignoring their works in progress, however, misses the opportunity to realize the inventive ways youth and adults create spaces to carry out activist work on a day-to-day basis. One might also understand counterpublic-sphere work as a contemporary and daily struggle that encompasses a variety of responses and tactics.

The way in which AKA women articulate and understand their own counterpublic efforts says much about what they think matters in African America. AKAs argue that the sorority's agenda, generically described as "service to all mankind," encompasses strategies to target the daily needs of Black communities and Black women on and off college campuses. Benita, Pamela, and Roslyn provide a list of AKA's work in this regard, which aims to address youth success in education, women's economic disparity, the AIDS crisis, sexual violence, and women's autonomy over their reproductive rights. The women also address the differing resources and impact of undergraduate and graduate chapters in this work:

> BENITA: Right now we are active with raising awareness of rape and rape prevention on campus; we partnered with Planned Parenthood and NOW to support a woman's right to choose via petitions, and we tutor students in the Upward Bound program and other students who were the first in their families to go to college.
>
> PAMELA: We do a lot of events for women's history month and we donate books on women's history to local libraries. We have a tutoring program at a local church where we teach young African American youth how to read. I think that the grad chapters sometimes have a deeper impact because they have more time and money. For example, we had a local YWCA that was going to be closed, but we were able to help financially to keep it open. The graduate chapter I am now in held a candlelight vigil

for battered women, and we just recently received a grant for our Girls-to-Girls Project, where we organized events for young African American women.

ROSLYN: We did turkey dinner donations for female-headed households that could not afford to buy turkey dinners for Thanksgiving. We also had an AIDS awareness dance. We tried to target the African American community because thus far we are underrepresented in terms of information about AIDS and HIV and we're over-represented in terms of having the [HIV] virus.

The work that Roslyn, Pamela, and Benita describe constitutes social program activism. Urgent social issues for women, including their sexual safety, their sexual rights, and the ability to feed their families at times when many celebrate the idea of family, are problems within the reach of the sorority to act upon. Perhaps not as apparent in these efforts is how the sorority aids in furthering the impact individual women may have on other individual women's lives, which case by case has the potential to affect entire communities. An AIDS awareness dance, a few turkey dinners, and teaching youth to read may not solve the national spread of HIV, hunger across America, or illiteracy across the world, yet one movement ahead for Black women and girls impacts the movement of many more in obtaining better circumstances for living well.

Darlene shared that voter registration for her chapter works in a similar vein, insofar as it may initiate participation and affect the democratic process of governship. Darlene's soror in the Southwest, Mary, who is a retiree and former advisor for an undergraduate AKA chapter, similarly describes how AKA women design activities that merge a variety of social concerns with public politics in a nonpartisan fashion:

Our chapter is doing a lot of lectures and workshops. Recently, we had a forum where lawyers came in and gave free legal advice. We also have health seminars where doctors come and give free medical advice. We give many scholarships for students, and we give fashion shows to help fund the workshops. Recently we started giving scholarships to junior college students. Also, we host and sponsor

> political debates between political candidates running for office. Because we are a nonprofit organization, we cannot publicly endorse a candidate, but the debates have really helped the community gain knowledge about the candidates. At the Boulé, the national directors discuss with us the goals for that year.

Mary's list of AKA programs asserts that the work of the sorority continues; the national agenda of the organization in contemporary times aims to address the challenges of the new millennium. An additional example of this work came in 2004, when the Alpha Chapter of AKA participated in a hunger fast and raised $21,000 for AIDS and hunger relief for the Africare organization. In the words of former Alpha Chapter President Rashida Rogers, the women wanted, through their fasting, "to empathize with those who suffer from HIV/AIDS, homelessness, and hunger."[10]

Today, activism for AKA women takes many shapes and forms. Their work runs the gamut from direct, hands-on work to macro-level developmental work. AKA's more modest undergraduate chapter programs, the assertive measures of graduate programs, and their national 2008 centennial march and plan of action for transformation in Black communities are examples of this spectrum. Each respondent during my interviews concentrated on collective action and common plight as the intent of AKA rather than personal transformation of individual members alone. The voicing of their social and political action in the past and in the present brings to focus the type of work the sorority finds prideful. Until the recent media coverage of their centennial and Michelle Obama's induction into AKA, however, their work in the public sphere rarely brought as much attention to the sorority as the private behavior and mistakes that many of the women said they regret.

From the Promise of Public Service to the Discourse of Private Regrets: Voicing the Mistakes of Hazing

Court cases about pledging, the behavior of Old School Pledgers (OSPs), and rationales for pledging provide insight into the process of making a soror. How the women feel after pledging adds to the story of pledging and hazing previously discussed, because it challenges the idea that all women support OSPs and engage in blind compliance and acceptance. My discussions with the women showed there is as much rhetoric about the merits of pledging and aggressive tactics among OSPs as there is ambivalence, anger, and pain among members about their pledgeship. In order to penetrate the core feelings of the women and their experiences, I avoided combative questions such as: "Are you a hazer?" or "Were you hazed?" Such questions, though important and direct, would no doubt emotionally arm the women, which would have likely put an end to our conversation. Self-reflexive ethnography and oral history require the ethnographer and oral historian to exhibit genuine sensitivity to their informants'/interviewees' boundaries in order to create a safe space for observation and dialogue. In a majority of cases, this approach led to rich, thoughtful answers, without having to engage in unnecessary prying and damning cultural and moral judgment. In other cases, no amount of prying or lack thereof would encourage women to say anything about their post-pledge feelings outside of positive or neutral statements.

AKA's reflection on the pledge process led to discussions about the personal community commitments of individuals within AKA, and the regrets of those individuals injured from the process of bringing them into the sisterhood. Graduate and undergraduate members provide nuance and voice to the more amorphous, public proclamations against hazing by AKA headquarters, and the lack of compliance of OSPs to their no-pledge rule. For some, post-initiation led to an immediate immersion in service work. For others, they would have to negotiate disappointments and pain to gather the strength to carry out the work of the sorority. AKA's varying response to how they felt after becoming an AKA is testament to these differences.

In discussing her post-pledge moment, Roslyn said that after her initiation she was very excited and confident because she held a position of leadership in the sorority and made friends. Her happiness, however, soon gave way to the reality concerning the work it takes to sustain an organization:

ROSLYN: I started to realize [that being in a sorority] was a lot of work and there was a lot of business to do. It is not just something fun; if you take it seriously you realize this. I was happy, but I didn't realize it was going to be so much work. [The sorority] has really helped me to grow as a person. Before, I didn't have a lot of female friends, and I really did not feel like I had a connection to my campus. Yet, afterwards, I found I had all these friends that I had spent the last year and a half with that I became close with. Soon, I became outgoing. Before crossing, I was really unsure of myself, and I gained a lot of confidence just interacting with other women and seeing that they were confident. I learned from these women, and we talked about our different backgrounds. I found out that I was not so different at all. I found that when I visited different schools there were people who would immediately relate to me. I didn't feel so alone because I knew wherever I went there would be a soror who would say: "Oh, you're a soror, how are you doing?" or "Let me help you." I no longer feel alienated. I feel like I belong. I know some people think it is superficial to connect with someone just because you share the Greek letters. But, it is a sisterhood and we are all united for the same cause.

Roslyn's positive experience stands out as an example of how making meaningful connections to others may lead to personal transformation and provide the confidence to engage in counter-public-sphere work. Other AKAs, while a part of the efforts to mobilize and complete work in their communities, maintained a veneer, "poker-face confidence" when describing—or, more pointedly, not describing—their feelings after their pledgeship. Indeed, some women were insistent not to let emotion reveal the hand that their pledgeship had dealt them. Polite and carefully worded, many women said that after their initiation into membership they felt curiously euphoric and placidly content:

JANET: [After pledging I felt] the same way I felt before I joined—I couldn't have made a wiser decision. I learned a lot about myself through the pledge process, and I wouldn't have changed a thing.

> ELLEN: After my initiation process I felt elated. I felt like I had found a new family outside of my biological one, whom I trusted, fought with, and believed in.
>
> BENITA: After my initiation I felt excited. I felt a part of something bigger than myself that was also more specific than what came with knowing that I was a Black woman.
>
> DARLENE: [After pledging] I was thrilled to have advanced to an important stage of young adulthood and extremely proud to be a part of a major organization of African American leaders.
>
> MELISSA: I was very pleased with the entire pledge process.

I do not doubt the women's feelings of joy and excitement after becoming an AKA, nor do I believe that the intent of their responses was meant to act solely as propaganda for the sorority. Given that not all chapters engage in difficult pledge rites, and indeed no chapter is supposed to have a pledge period in contemporary times, it is possible that their experiences were wholly positive. Notwithstanding that, their quickly generated and brief responses may also reflect a mixture of fear about disclosing the realities of their pledgeship, which might embarrass or dishonor the sorority. If the former pledge process and underground pledging intend to cultivate the politics of respectability in members, then the self-presentation and silence among many members, as seen earlier, are evidence of the power behind and presence of their enormous dedication to emotional discipline and discretion.

In stark contradiction to the "ready to work" outlook of Roslyn and the said elation of many AKAs, several women admitted to AKA's mistakes and their own feelings of regret after their initiation. Candice, Mary, Troy, Linda, and Pamela articulated vivid feelings of doubt:

> CANDICE: [After my pledgeship] I felt very bitter. I was very mad and had regrets. I felt my pledge process was unorganized. The AKAs that were on my campus when I pledged were founders. I was on their first official line of new initiates. They had never pledged because they founded the chapter, so I think they were not sure how to

> handle a line [of new initiates]. But, I love them now. Some bonding is starting to happen. I think that it takes time to bond, and it is not going to happen right after you cross; it's something you have to work at. I've learned to work with women and no matter what our differences are we have a common goal and we get it done. That's what I'm really getting out of the sorority that I do not get out of my classes. In my classes, if I don't like a student, I can just shut them out. In a sorority, you can't do that. In a sorority, you learn communication techniques and how to deal with differences in personality. We have great diversity in our culture, and you have to tell yourself sometimes that the sorority is business and not just personal. Any personal conflicts between sorority members you handle outside of the sorority.

An interesting contradiction here is that Candice and Roslyn are members of the same AKA chapter; Roslyn was Candice's big sister. There is no evidence that Roslyn was among those who gave Candice a difficult time during her pledgeship, but it is important to note that differing ideas on the outcome of pledging can take place within the same chapter. I asked Candice how she was able to deal with and adjust to her ambivalence and anger after her pledgeship, and she shared that persistence and hard work led to reconciliation with those who hurt her. "I knew I had to hang in there and really get to know these women," she said. "We went to this retreat where we learned listening techniques, and how to use 'I' statements. Afterwards we went shopping. I had to say, 'Let bygones be bygones.' I made a lifetime commitment that I have to stick with. But, I would never do to initiates what was done to me when I pledged."

More than forty years older than Candice, Mary admits to a very strenuous pledgeship in the early 1960s, which caused her to abort her process at a predominately Black college and go through initiation as a graduate member of AKA. She admits:

> To be perfectly frank, I didn't really pledge. I was going through initiation and [AKAs] were being extremely difficult on me. I learned later that they were so hard on me

because when they pledged my sister [who is an AKA] had been really hard on them. They were trying to get back at her through me. So, I decided that it was best that I dropped out of the pledge process. I ended up becoming an AKA at the graduate level. I did not cross at my university. It was also difficult because my father died when I [started the pledge] process. When I dropped out it was not held against me because I had a death in the family.

As Mary's answer illustrates, although legacy influences women to pledge a particular sorority, being a legacy makes it harder, rather than easier, on pledges. One of the OSPs interviewed earlier echoed this predicament and described her pledge process at a historically Black university as very difficult. She attributed this difficulty to her mother being an AKA. Apparently the women in AKA did not want the pledge hopeful to take for granted the possibility of her future membership. Although she did admit to excesses during pledging, she felt these excesses were necessary, and she believed in strenuous pledge periods. In counterdistinction, Troy and Linda more readily admitted to anger and confusion after their pledgeship, while their soror Pamela expressed indirect misgivings:

TROY: After my pledge I felt angry that AKAs felt it was okay to be cruel to others just because it was the pledge process.

LINDA: After my pledge process was completed and I reflected I was fine . . . I did not understand at the time why I had to do things I had to do [when I pledged]. But, after I crossed and time went on, [everything I had to do] all fit together.

PAMELA: In the former pledge process, some people would pledge for fifty-two weeks, others would pledge for four weeks. Now we have the three-day process, and some people consider these women to be "paper AKAs." The pledge process is not always a positive one. I heard horror stories about what pledges were made to do when I came to Vanderbilt—that they had to wear the same clothes and walk in a line. Things are done during the pledge process

> to bring pledges together—there are things done to help the pledges connect to each other. All of the women go through it together.

Pamela, who apparently did pledge after 1990, did not comment about her own pledge, but her response underscores the tension between perceived sorors and members as a silent, implicit division between the women. As Pamela implied, some AKAs still consider women who go through the three-day process of initiation as AKAs in name only. Troy and Candice seemed the most hurt by their pledge process, using words such as "bitter," "regrets," "cruelty," and "anger" to describe their feelings after initiation. Yet Troy, Candice, and Linda did reconcile their misgivings about their pledge period and became active sorors.

AKA's testimonies are a reminder that however contradictory, there remains a great richness and political forethought in their struggles, regrets, and mistakes, as well as their visions for change in communities. Some women were unsure about the means to make them sorors, and others were content. Several AKA women pointed out the problems in their organization and some of their sisters circumvented the problems. Their reasons for becoming a soror included family tradition, yearning for Black sisterhood in isolating environments, and commitment to their disenfranchised communities. All of these reasons showed their different desires, life experiences, and views. AKA voices trouble the idea of one consensus of thought, although they do ascribe to a common ideology of respectability, uplift, reform, and, in some cases, radical social change. In a moment where lessons from counterhegemonic movements are ever-more urgent, it is crucial to think through the Black sorority alongside the types of collective action that may provide the type of transformation necessary in the twenty-first century for Black counterpublics and the communities they serve.

Conclusion

Cultural critic Thomas C. Holt argues that the litmus test for a counterpublic in a Black American context exceeds speech communities and embodies oppositional action. Our ambitious goal as cultural critics and cultural workers, then, is to explain or initiate transformation beyond intellectual discourse and beyond rhetorical proclamations for change in the name of wide-scale social justice. Holt asks that the writer and practitioner consider three primary objectives in assessing the work of contemporary Black counterpublics: (1) that they "facilitate democratic values and justice for all"; (2) that they initiate "resistance and positive change"; and (3) that they provide a "better understanding of how change might be effected."[11] His definition of a working and an effective counterpublic shows how a social, cultural, and political movement may hold potential for broad dissemination, but his parameters leave little room for real-life contradictions and problems that are the result of the human faults of real people who compose real counterpublic formations. AKA's struggles, visions, actions, and regrets provide documentation of the struggles of existing counterpublics, what constitutes counterpublic sphere work, and the attributes that aid in ensuring such work is carried out under real, and at times dubious, conditions.

AKA women are not the White-identified "little sister organization" in *School Daze*, nor are they the marginal socialites in *Stomp the Yard* introduced at the beginning of this book. Rather, the majority of AKA women present themselves as agents of social change and community organizing. Still, AKA voices in this chapter reflect the experiences of a segment of Black women who hold privilege because they are college educated or overwhelmingly middle class, or both. Our conversations about their experience illustrate the becoming, being, and reflecting upon sorority identity formation for a demographic group that may not represent the masses of Black women in America, and certainly do not represent the Black women who reside outside of the United States. AKA's work is paramount, but so too is a social consciousness that feels uncomfortable with and seeks to change sexism, classism, heterosexism, and homophobia with Black communities, as well as the trappings of economic excess and the insularity of the Black professional managerial class. Their subject position and voices document struggle. Indeed, these women continue to experience their foremothers' struggles with racism and sexism. This continued struggle notwithstanding, AKA women who reflect different axes of identification, such as economically disadvantaged, additional ethnic groups, and AKA women from chapters in England, Germany, Africa, Asia, and the Virgin Islands, would surely present similar and dissimilar perceptions of global sorority life. A discussion with and representation of women who are not only marginalized because of gender and race but who are also on the margins of the margins would add further complexity to the discourse here.

I can only imagine the benefits of extending the components of a Black women's movement to a collective commitment to dismantling a broader range of hierarchies of exclusion, including the regression of human rights within our borders in our post-9/11 world, and the very real social inequities within America that remain. Such a collective effort might move beyond traditional modes of relief abroad to bring attention to U.S. and international colonialism and human rights violations beyond our borders, as well as the struggles of aggrieved populations—particularly, but not exclusively, women and girls—throughout Africa and its diaspora. An intervention into these different but equally troubling atrocities requires planning and organized action that benevolence, hunger strikes, protests, marches, village restructuring, and school building—as seen with AKA's work with Africare in the 1980s through today—will not alone end but can certainly act as a launching pad for stronger anticolonialist activism and teachings in the future.

AKA's donations to Africare, educational programs on AIDS and HIV awareness in partnership with the Red Cross, and health seminars are commendable. However, in view of the rising numbers of Black women contracting the HIV virus—64 percent of all new AIDS cases—a localized health initiative on par with the Mississippi Healthcare Project would generate great benefits for today's Black female citizens.[12] In the 1940s, AKA's National Non-Partisan Council on Public Affairs commented on the status quo of exclusion for a variety of groups, such as farmers, the working poor, veterans, Black men and women, women of color, and White women. Similar efforts today might change the face of American politics in the twenty-first century. AKA women continue to work for mass voter registration, but transformation could further result from their stronger efforts of yesteryear, as seen in the immediate post-World War II years and the 1960s.

For the larger part of the twentieth century, the AKA sorority merged theory with praxis in their counterpublic-sphere work to the ends of quantifiable change. Yet in the twenty-first century, their efforts might use less conservative tactics in view of our current historical moment. Given the incarceration of large numbers of Black women and men in the nation's prison-industrial complex, the sorority's work with our prison population and other types of support for radical political countermovements seems urgent. No one social space can serve every social ill, but any group that professes to respond to the urgency of African America, such as AKA, might entertain newer as well as older programs. Such an approach would constitute what cultural critic Manning Marable defines as immediate "non-reformist reform."[13] This type of reform relies on working within the present state and from localized sites to envision significant change across the full spectrum of African America, including the working poor and sexual minorities, and against the hegemonic order, which keeps the nation's masses subordinate. In the tradition of Black counterpublics, this (re)formation would not only join Black intellectuals with the energies of the street, it would also enact change from below and up (a grassroots working-class struggle), rather than from up to below (a middle-class uplift struggle). All of these prescriptions lead to the following questions: What and/or who does the politics of respectability, which Black sorority women continue to engage in through carefully tailored service programs, elide and hide? What are the long-term social and political effects of this invisibility?

One of the strengths in realizing activist and community action through a collective is that it may become harder to engage in and dabble in activist work only to retreat to and find solace within an economically comfortable life. The black professional managerial class and the masses alike will have to venture into a grassroots, organized partnership to educate, penetrate, and intervene in inequitable structural formations in our own local sites within our own particular means and expertise. Although individual members of counterfraternal formations may exhibit and inhabit a wide range of cultural, political, and social consciousnesses, collective action and counterpublic-sphere work encourage ongoing and embodied struggles. Counterfraternal movements such as the Black sorority hold the potential to function as consistent catalysts for change. It is therefore vital to remember what counterfraternal movements are and have been opposing since their inception: oppressive factions within and outside the university that dislocate and isolate, mentally and physically assault, marginalize, and demonize people of African descent, thereby affecting their life chances and access to the most basic of human and civil rights. The AKA sorority has begun, even if not finished, the initiation of work and cultivation of women who may help work toward the difficult and challenging ends of transformation that the twenty-first century demands from us all.

CONCLUSION

Sorority Sisters

Author Tajuana "TJ" Butler is a fiction writer, poet, and activist and leads seminars on sisterhood and the cultivation of Black women's self-esteem. She is also a member of the AKA sorority and has written several fiction books on the social lives of Black women, including *Sorority Sisters*, *Just My Luck*, *The Night before Thirty*, *Hand Me Down a Heartache*, and a collection of poetry, *Desires of a Woman*. Butler's 1999 novel *Sorority Sisters*, which is not autobiographical but seems loosely based on the AKA sorority, centers on how Black sorority membership affects the everyday lives of five different Black American women.[1] This novel was the forerunner of what is now a burgeoning genre of fiction that uses Black sororities and Black college life as its central focus.[2] Butler's sorority women embody and fall between a diverse set of characteristics in *Sorority Sisters*: they are mentors and proto-feminists; sexually naïve and sexually confident; hedonistic materialists and former welfare recipients; women whose lives revolve around their boyfriends, and women who do not define themselves through men; women who are legacies, and women who are the first in the family to attend college and pledge a sorority. I conclude with a brief exploration of *Sorority Sisters* and my interview with Butler because the novel and our discussion address similar arguments put forth in each chapter in this book.[3]

One of the strengths of Butler's *Sorority Sisters* is its ability to present characters from diverse socioeconomic backgrounds. Socioeconomic standing is a point of contention between several of the women who pledge in the book, particularly Tiara, who is from a modest class background, and Stephanie, who is more affluent. For Tiara, class often appears as a point of personal revelation, and for Stephanie, class reflects the desire for social transformation. According to the narrative in Butler's novel, class exists as a determinant in life chances, which some of the women are either unconscious of if they hold material wealth, or seek to overcome if they do not have monetary advantages. In regard to the necessity of economic diversity in the modern-day Black sorority and how class position shapes the sorority experience for Black sorority members, Butler told me that after attending AKA's national conference (The Boulé) in 2000, she

> met so many young ladies who wanted to help others with upward mobility. I think that is the good thing about a sorority. You meet people different from you that you might not ordinarily be friends with. Through the sorority the women can have an active hand in helping others in the community. Because you have so many people from different backgrounds, you begin to see the world through different eyes, either firsthand or secondhand, you learn from those disadvantaged in your sorority what that feels like, which helps you help others outside of the sorority. Different class backgrounds bring diversity to the group; it continues to make our purpose broader.

In addition to class, Butler writes about the politics of sexuality for young Black women in *Sorority Sisters*. She provides several examples of coming into sexual adulthood, as seen with the character Cajen, who contracts herpes from her partner Jason; the character Sidney, who becomes pregnant after being date raped by Scott; and Stephanie, who rethinks her need to find confidence through her sexual relationships with men. Popular fiction in this case breaks through the boundaries of self-representation and respectable images. When asked why she felt it was important to discuss sexuality and sexual themes in *Sorority Sisters*, Butler said this:

> It was very important to talk about sexuality. In Sidney's case, it shows the fine line between date rape and consent. She was intoxicated, and had she not been, the situation would have turned out differently. Her situation can be seen as an educational device. I know parents who are giving my book to their children for this reason, kids who are in high school. Sexuality is not addressed enough. Many young women are sheltered before they enter college. There is so much freedom on a college campus. Young men and women are testing their boundaries. Then they are opened up to sexual situations and faced to make decisions, and they're not prepared to make them. I wanted to show what happens when people do not think through their choices.

Sorority Sisters also represents the social aspects of these organizations and stays true to the genre of a popular, young adult novel. Yet the book manages to illustrate cultural aspects of BGLOs, including stepping, and it alludes to forms of community action in which Black sororities involve themselves, for example, the mentoring of young Black women, community development work, and philanthropy. As Butler said, "For Black sororities, it is important for the women on campus to do community service. I hear a lot of white women say 'I was in a sorority when I was in college.' Black women don't say this, because we remain active after college. We do a lot for education, the arts, and economics. We do work abroad too. My chapter contributed to Rwanda relief efforts [in the 1990s]. Mostly Black sororities do not seek media attention so people do not know what we do in terms of politics and service."

Sorority Sisters also includes a depiction of the pledge process. The book, through a fictional account, lays bare the experience of women during their pledge process and presents contradictions between sorors' expectations, pledges' interpretation of expectations, and the ongoing struggle for pledges to navigate through the testing waters of the process to arrive at the other side: *sororhood*. This inclusion of the pledge process appears less nostalgic than strategic, and more cultural than immaterial. Given popular journalism's tendency to focus on hazing incidents absent of the social and cultural elements inherent in many BGLO pledge processes, Butler's *Sorority Sis*ters provides an imaginary look at aspects of pledging that are reflections of real life. Rather than presenting tantalizing details of hazing in isolation, Butler's fictional text presents pledge scenarios as opportunities to understand loyalty, friendship, perseverance, and performance under pressure and provides insights into the process from the perspective of pledges and sorors alike. In an era of underground pledging that often tips the scale to hazing and threatens the existence of BGLOs, *Sorority Sisters* is a useful reminder of how different a pledge process is from its dangerous, consanguine partner, hazing. When I inquired as to whom Butler intended as her audience and her desire concerning what her intended reader would take away from *Sorority Sisters*, she offered the following:

> My audience was people who had the experience or who were considering pledging, and not necessarily [considering pledging] Alpha Kappa Alpha. However, what I have found is that the audience is much broader. I hope people would come away from the book knowing that no person is without faults, and that you can't judge a book by its cover. You have to really get to know people to form an impression of them. I wanted people to come away with the idea that things you experience in life can be learning tools, and that what an individual does can affect the people around them in a positive way.

Butler makes points worth reiteration: no person is without faults, you cannot judge a book by its cover, you have to get to know people before you form an impression, and experiences in life—good and bad—can act as instructional tools. I restate Butler's main points and include a discussion of *Sorority Sisters* in this book's conclusion because there are significant parallels between the cultural work of *Sorority Sisters*, which is a popular novel aimed at a mass audience, and the intended cultural work of this book, which aims to join academic and mass audiences.

Although our projects represent different genres, both address issues within African America and BGLOs that require reflection and in some cases change: culture, class, and sexual politics. *Disciplining Women* provides a challenge to those who may judge Black sororities by surface interpretations without seeking to understand their history and cultural practices and how these practices can act as learning tools for realizing the promises and disappointments of social life and movements. My examination of AKA accomplishes the additional work of explaining how cultural formations change over historical time and how culture shapes the social components and political work of a Black sorority—pointing out at the same time how the social is profoundly political within the context of a Black women's organization and women's everyday lives.

Disciplining Women intervenes in the laudatory praise of fraternal members and the polemics of anti-fraternalists. It does so by constructing a cultural history of a Black sorority that serves the simultaneous mission of elucidating and arguing for the specificity of Black cultural practices, seeking to change the conversation about the political possibilities of counterfraternal movements, and placing AKA's work within broader concerns of culture and history. The book began with a historical and cultural context to understand the cultural politics of BGLOs and how popular culture envisages BGLO life. This framework set the stage for a detailed discussion of how AKA fits within the discourses of culture and politics. The examination of counterpublic sphere politics that follows this framework situates AKA's work in the dominant and Black Public Sphere as constituting uplift, race, and counterpublic-sphere work that the women perform in a multiplicity of sites at different historical moments. In this regard, their uplift efforts do not cancel out their counterpublic-sphere work, and their reform programs need not diminish their commitments to "the race."

A shift from the representational and historical to the practices of everyday life revealed stepping as an extension of women's work in the public sphere; I describe and analyze this cultural practice as a contradictory site where Black women use public space to perform race, femininity, and sexual politics. An examination of the underground pledge process, and the hazing that follows, extends an understanding of racial and gender performativity in everyday life. In particular, pledging and hazing demonstrate how the women seek to instill a strengthening mechanism in members that is a consequence of and is in a rhetorical conversation with the historical legacy of racism. During underground pledge rites, sorors make arguments for the importance of emotional maturity and strong Black womanhood as an ideal characteristic of AKA, and their arguments become rationalizations for operating outside of the sorority's legitimate power base. What is perhaps most striking about underground pledging is how the *discipline* carried out by Old School Pledgers reifies debilitating notions of Black feminine practice in the popular imagination, thus paradoxically revealing their claims to a *disciplined* respectability that is dubious at best, and, as their critics may assert, nebulous at worst.

Contemporary perceptions of visible AKAs, including First Lady Michelle Obama, as well as undergraduate and graduate women not as well known, articulate AKA women's lived experiences as Black women and as activists. As evidenced in their oral testimonies, they feel concern regarding the negative representations of BGLOs and their sorority, and their work toward and disclosure of hopes for the future of AKA and Black communities aims to challenge that perception and mitigate anti-Black and anti-Greek sentiment. In all, *Disciplining Women* addresses components of their social, political, and counterpublic-sphere work in its insurgent, conservative, and precarious forms. The assertion of AKA's work as carrying elements of a Black counterpublic with both cultural and political effects is vital to understanding the promise and problems that social-political spaces produce and engender. If culture is the adjective that situates the Black sorority as a unique entity in comparison to the dominant culture, then it is also the verb that propels their behavior, and it is the noun that requires careful critique.

Cultural critic bell hooks argues that the constructive critique of cultural productions and formations is most productive by enacting "vital engagement . . . that dares to lovingly unmask, expose, and challenge. [This] . . . is a gesture of respect; it indicates that the work [or formation] has been taken seriously." Hooks adds that cultural criticism should provide "insights that both reveal aspects of a work [or formation]—how it is what it is, what it does or does not do—as well as suggests new directions, new possibilities."[4] In the tradition of the types of cultural criticism hooks notes as ethical and essential, this study is persistent in its illustration of the exciting possibilities of the cultural and counterpublic-sphere work of AKA. Yet it is equally persistent to argue for an increase in consciousness that would overturn oppressive gender, race, ethnic, sexual, and class regimes that remain unattended in many established Black social and political movements. As I argue throughout this study, a Black middle-class collective might more effectively see its work not in terms of uplift of others and inclusion into a capitalistic regime but, rather, in terms of how it might relinquish privilege and redistribute power and resources outside and within its own racial and ethnic formation. AKA is not alone in this struggle; it embodies elements associative with a common dilemma of other Black social and political movements that rally for social change and struggle to remain cognizant of the diverse needs of the aggrieved masses that compose Africa and its diaspora.

Intellectual work that merges history, theory, ethnography, and interdisciplinary paradigms is invigorating, but tricky, intellectual work, for several reasons. To talk about real people and how they live their everyday lives in a cultural, historical, and theoretical context may mean that the subjects of the work will not always relate to or approve of the representative results. Cultural criticism necessitates, though, that life processes are not entirely represented through the lens and cultural truisms of the subjects of analysis. My goal, then, with *Disciplining Women* has been to take AKA cultural truisms and cast them within various contexts in order to extract cultural and historical meanings from the women's lived experiences. Cultural theory has provided the tools to conceptualize AKA as a viable political collective and cultural phenomenon, and narrative has served as the experiential glue that mends testimony, history, and culture together to the ends of a cohesive look at an underexamined social-political group. The potentialities, contradictions, and prescriptions of political and cultural life, I argue, may be seen through my analysis of AKA's history, AKA's popular representation, cultural and counterpublic-sphere work, performative practices, ritualistic expressions, and oral testimonies. As hooks instructs, my analysis of AKA has meant to show how its social, cultural, and political formation "is what it is, what it does or does not do," and at the same time I encourage new directions, new possibilities. Past, current, and ongoing forms of racial, class, gender, and sexual injustice assert that America is in a state of social, economic, and political emergency. Black women's social and political groups can act as immediate models and warnings for our tenuous futures.

APPENDIX

Alpha Kappa Alpha Fact Sheet

ALPHA KAPPA ALPHA (AKA) CREST: A badge with green parameters and a salmon-pink middle stripe that bears the initials AKA horizontally. The green parameters of the badge include two golden hands in the midst of a handshake, a gold bird, a golden human figure holding a globe representation of Earth on its back, a golden book with a teapot atop, and a gold weighing scale.

GREEK LETTERS: AKA

GREEK MOTTO: : ΩΦΕΛΥΟΜΕΝ ΥΠΗΡΕΤΙΔΕΣ

NATIONAL PAN-HELLENIC COUNCIL (NPHC) FRATERNAL NAME: Alpha Kappa Alpha

FOUNDING DATE AND FOUNDERS: January 15, 1908, Howard University. Founders are Ethel Hedgeman Lyle, Lillian Burke, Beulah Burke, Margaret Flagg Holmes, Marie Woolfolk Taylor, Lavinia Taylor, Anna Brown, Lucy Slowe, and Majorie Hill.

TRADITIONS AND INSIGNIA: The colors of the sorority are salmon pink and apple green. Pink is said to represent femininity for AKA, while green represents strength. Their pin is in the shape of an ivy leaf with twenty pearls on the periphery. Ivy leaf for AKA is said to signify the growth, endurance, and strength of members, and the twenty pearls are placed in accordance with the number of founders joined by the incorporators of the sorority. Their flower is the tea rose.

STEPPING CALL: Skkkkeeeeeeeee Weeeeeeee!!

PUBLICATIONS: The sorority publishes the quarterly magazine *The Ivy Leaf* and a manual of procedures. Two fraternal history books exist by Marjorie Parker: *In the Eye of the Beholder* and *Alpha Kappa Alpha through the Years*. Newsletters are also disseminated through the sorority headquarters.

MEMBERSHIP: 975 chapters, with more than 200,000 members

HEADQUARTERS ADDRESS: 5656 South Stony Island Avenue, Chicago, Illinois, 69637

WEB SITE: http://www.aka.1908.com

SPECIFIC NATIONAL PROGRAMS (see chapters 1 and 5 for more examples of chapter programs):

- IVY AKAdemy: Elementary school in the rural part of Swazi Zulu, near Durbin in South Africa
- Africare: Annual support to Africare, wherein each graduate chapter is encouraged to support a South African Village
- Cleveland Job Corps: Provides vocational training to women and educational advancement
- Educational Endowment Fund: Provides scholarships to undergraduate and graduate students
- National Body Healthcare: Extension of its 1930s Mississippi Healthcare Project, wherein a joint venture with state health agencies helps ensure better health care and access to health care for every segment of the population
- National Council on Human Rights: In conjunction with other Greek letter organizations, members study, support, and act on human rights initiatives.
- ONTRACK: Youth program designed to promote citizenship among African Americans

SOCIAL EVENTS: AKA annual cotillion

NOTES

Introduction

1. I use the word "fraternal" to describe the female and male orders that identify as fraternal organizations, although my terminology shifts with historical moment when the word "sorority," "sororal organization," or "women's auxiliary" is appropriate.
2. I discuss the controversy about the AKA cotillion and sorority representation in my analysis of the film *School Daze*. See "The Empty Space of Sorority Representation: Spike Lee's *School Daze*," in *African American Fraternities and Sororities: The Legacy and the Vision*, ed. Tamara Brown et al., 417–36 (Louisville: University Press of Kentucky, 2005).
3. All names of AKA members I interviewed have been changed when appropriate.
4. By ethnic plurality, I mean to describe those women who may have different nationalities (African, Caribbean, Afro-German, etc.) and multiple ethnic heritages but identify as Black, a racial construct that has real implications and salient meaning in people's everyday lives.
5. Otis Graham, *Our Kind of People: Inside America's Black Upper Class* (New York: HarperCollins, 1998); Lawrence Ross, *The Divine Nine: The History of African American Fraternities and Sororities* (New York: Kensington, 2000).

6. Ricky L. Jones, *Black Haze: Violence, Sacrifice, and Manhood in Black Greek-Letter Fraternities* (Albany: State University of New York Press, 2004); Walter M. Kimbrough, *Black Greek 101: The Culture, Customs, and Challenges of Black Fraternities and Sororities* (Madison, WI: Farleigh Dickinson University Press, 2000).
7. Paula Giddings, *In Search of Sisterhood: Delta Sigma Theta and the Challenge of the Black Sorority Movement* (New York: William Morrow, 1988); Marjorie Parker, *Alpha Kappa Alpha through the Years, 1908–1988* (Chicago, IL: Mobium Press, 1990).
8. Teresa Puente, "Getting Organized," *Hispanic* (March 1992): 32; Alex Mejia, "Hispanics Go Greek," *Hispanic* (October 1994): 34.
9. For interracial membership in Black fraternities, see Laurence A. Stains, "Black Like Me: What's Up with White Guys Who Join Black Frats? Are They Trying Too Hard, or Is It Just a Class Thing?" *Rolling Stone*, March 24, 1994, 69.
10. Several cultural historians have explored this important terrain. One provocative examination includes Philip Deloria, *Playing Indian*, Yale Historical Publication Series (New Haven, CT: Yale University Press, 1998).
11. See Shane L. Windmeyer and Pamela W. Freeman, eds., *Out on Fraternity Row: Personal Accounts of Being Gay in a College Fraternity* (Los Angeles, CA: Alyson Publications, 1997); Shane L. Windmeyer and Pamela W. Freeman, eds., *Secret Sisters: Stories of Being Lesbian and Bisexual in a College Sorority* (Los Angeles, CA: Alyson Publications, 2001).
12. Gregory Parks and Craig Torbenson, eds., *Brothers and Sisters: Diversity in College Fraternities and Sororities* (Madison, WI: Farleigh Dickinson University Press, 2008).
13. On hegemony, counterhegemony, and its useful theorization for ethnic studies, see Antonio Gramsci, *Selections from Cultural Writings* (Cambridge, MA: Harvard University Press, 1985); Lisa Lowe, *Immigrant Acts: On Asian American Cultural Politics* (Durham, NC, and London: Duke University Press, 1996), 69; Stuart Hall, "Gramsci's Relevance for the Study of Race and Ethnicity," in *Stuart Hall: Critical*

Dialogues in Cultural Studies, ed. David Morley and Kuan-Hsing Chen, 424–26 (London: Routledge, 1996).

14. George Lipsitz, "Sent for You Yesterday, Here You Come Today: American Studies Scholarship and the New Social Movements," in *The Futures of American Studies*, ed. Donald Pease and Robyn Wiegman, 441–60 (Durham, NC: Duke University Press, 2002), 444; Robin D. G. Kelley, *Freedom Dreams: The Black Radical Imagination* (Boston, MA: Beacon Press, 2002), ix.

Chapter 1

1. For a thorough analysis of *School Daze* and its representation of BGLOs, see Deborah Elizabeth Whaley, "The Empty Space of Sorority Representation: Spike Lee's *School Daze*," in *African American Fraternities and Sororities: The Legacy and the Vision*, ed. Tamara Brown et al., 417–36 (Louisville: University Press of Kentucky, 2005).
2. Spike Lee, with Lisa Jones, *Uplift the Race: The Construction of School Daze* (New York: Simon and Schuster, 1988), 9.
3. The National Pan-Hellenic Council formed in 1929 to act as a unifying governing body for the eight major BGLOs. It serves as the conduit through which the organizations plan, identify, and act upon areas of mutual concern. The National Pan-Hellenic Council is therefore a channel through which they disseminate, discuss, and strategize pertinent ideas to Black American Greek life. See *Baird's Manual*, 41–42, for a description of the National Pan-Hellenic Council.
4. On the formation of historically Black colleges, see Julian B. Roebuck and Komanduri S. Murty, *Historically Black Colleges and Universities: Their Place in American Higher Education* (Westport, CT: Greenwood Press, 1993).
5. James V. Hatch, "Theatre in Historically Black Colleges: A Survey of 100 Years," in *A Source Book of African-American Performance: Plays, People, Movements*, ed. Annemarie Bean, 150–64 (New York: Routledge, 1999).

6. Kathy Russell, Midge Wilson, and Ronald Hall, *The Color Complex: The Politics of Skin Color among African Americans* (New York: Harcourt, Brace, Jovanovich, 1992), 24–40.
7. A. Denita Gadson, "Greek Power! African-American Greek-Letter Organizations Wield Massive Influence after *School Daze*," *Black Collegian* 20:1 (September 1989): 34.
8. Interview with Ellen, 2000.
9. For a thorough history and an analysis of the Links, Girl Friends, and the Boulé, see Deborah Elizabeth Whaley, "Links, Legacies, and Letters," in *Brothers and Sisters*, 46–82; Graham, *Our Kind of People* (n. 5, introduction).
10. On social fraternal groups and working-class consciousness, see Robin Kelley, "'We Are Not What We Seem,'" in *Race Rebels: Culture, Politics, and the Black Working Class*, 38–39 (New York: Free Press, 1996), and for a description of class distinction among social fraternals, see Lawrence Otis Graham, "The Links and Girl Friends: Women Who Govern Society," and "The Boulé, the Guardsmen, and Other Groups for Elite Black Men," in *Our Kind of People* (n. 5, introduction).
11. For a discussion of blue-vein societies and colorism among Black fraternals from the Revolutionary War to the late-twentieth century, see Kathy Russell, Midge Wilson, and Ronald Hall, *The Color Complex: The Politics of Skin Color among African Americans* (New York: Harcourt, Brace, Jovanovich, 1992), 24–25.
12. Edward Franklin Frazier, *Black Bourgeoisie: The Rise of a New Middle Class in the United States* (New York: Free Press, 1965). Franklin published his book during a time when fraternal organizations were under attack for creating disunity through their exclusive networks, despite the ways in which they participated in and funded civil rights struggles.
13. Ibid.
14. The two extremes of assimilation and accommodation were positions attributed to a group of Black intellectuals, including and most notably Booker T. Washington as accommodationist and W. E. B. Du Bois as assimilationist. See Booker T. Washington, *Up From Slavery* (Garden City, NY: Doubleday, 1901; reprint, New York: Dover, 1995), and W.

E. B. Du Bois, *Souls of Black Folk: Essays and Sketches* (Chicago, IL: A. C. McClurg, 1903; reprint, New York: Mass Market Publishers, 1995).

15. Norma Boyd, interview in *Black Women's Oral History Project*, Arthur and Elizabeth Schlesinger Library at Radcliff College, 26.
16. Deborah Gray White, *Too Heavy a Load: Black Women in Defense of Themselves, 1894–1994* (New York: W.W. Norton, 1999), 96.
17. Interview with Pamela, 1999.
18. Interview with Candice, 1993.
19. Quoted in Vernon Thompson, "Fraternities, Sororities from Howard Students Draw Renewed Interest: Clubs Offer On-Campus Social Life to Off-Campus Communities," *Washington Post*, November 16, 1978, DC1.
20. Kenji Jasper, "A Proud Heritage for 'Black Greek' Groups," *San Diego Union Tribune*, February 24, 1998, E4.
21. Quoted in Marilyn Freeman and Tina Witcher, "Stepping into Black Power: Black Fraternities and Sororities Give Their Members Access to a Network of Influence and Power—and Good Times Too. So What's Wrong with That?" *Rolling Stone*, March 24, 1988.
22. White, *Too Heavy a Load*, 157, emphasis added.
23. Edward Franklin Frazier generally argues in his book that middle-class Blacks and their fraternals engage in conspicuous consumption to the detriment of the masses of Blacks. See Frazier, *Black Bourgeoisie*.
24. Thompson, "Fraternities, Sororities from Howard Students," 25. Lawrence C. Ross Jr., "The Achievers Talk," in *The Divine Nine: The History of African American Fraternities and Sororities*, 311–422 (New York: Kensington, 2000).
26. bell hooks, *Where We Stand: Class Matters* (New York: Routledge, 2000), 108. See also AKA member Beulah Whitby's "Today's Challenge to the Privileged Negro," *Ivy Leaf* 14:1 (March 1936).
27. On the political activism of BGLOs, African secret societies, and social fraternals, see Whaley, "Links, Legacies, and Letters."
28. Cornel West, "The New Cultural Politics of Difference," in

Social Theory: The Multicultural and Classic Readings, ed. Charles Lemert, 577–89 (Boulder, CO: Westview Press, 1999), 528.

29. Jacqueline Woodson, "Common Ground," *Essence*, May 1999, 144.
30. Kobena Mercer, "Welcome to the Jungle: Identity and Diversity in Postmodern Politics," in *Welcome to the Jungle: New Positions in Black Cultural Studies*, 259–86 (New York: Routledge, 1994).
31. Patricia Hill Collins, "The Sexual Politics of Black Womanhood," in *Black Feminist Thought: Knowledge, Consciousness, and the Politics of Empowerment*, 123–48 (New York: Routledge, 1991).
32. Stuart Hall, "New Ethnicities," in *Stuart Hall: Critical Dialogues in Cultural Studies*, ed. David Morley and Kuan-Hsing Chen, 441–49 (London: Routledge, 1996).
33. Stuart Hall, "Cultural Identity and Cinematic Representation," in *Black British Cultural Studies: A Reader*, ed. Houston Baker et al., 210–22 (Chicago, IL: University of Chicago Press, 1996).

Chapter 2

1. Michael C. Dawson, "A Black Counterpublic? Economic Earthquakes, Racial Agenda(s), and Black Politics," in *The Black Public Sphere*, ed. Black Public Sphere Collective (Chicago, IL: University of Chicago Press, 1995), 204.
2. The National Women's Party presented Adelaide Johnson's Portrait Monument, which featured the busts of Elizabeth Cady Stanton, Susan B. Anthony, and Lucretia Mott, as a gift to Congress on February 10, 1921. Congress authorized the monument's installation in the Capitol basement. In accordance with House Concurrent Resolution 216, which Congress passed in September 1996, the monument moved to the Capitol Rotunda in May 1997. See *New York Times*, "A Black Group Assails Statue of Suffragists," March 9, 1997, 28.

3. "The Black Public Sphere Collective," preface to *The Black Public Sphere*, Black Public Sphere Collective, 3.
4. On Black American sororal participation, see Parker, *Alpha Kappa Alpha through the Years* (n. 7, introduction), and Giddings, *In Search of Sisterhood* (n. 7, introduction). For more on AKA health care reform, see Susan L. Smith, "Sharecroppers and Sorority Women: The Alpha Kappa Alpha Mississippi Health Project," in *Sick and Tired of Being Sick and Tired: Black Women's Health Activism in America, 1890–1950*, 149–67 (Philadelphia: University of Pennsylvania Press, 1994). Smith mentions, in brief, class divisions between AKA women and those that they helped in health care reform.
5. For a cross-cultural comparison of Black, Jewish, Mormon, and Protestant women's clubs, and literary societies, see Anne Ruggles Gere, *Intimate Practices: Literacy and Cultural Work in U.S. Women's Clubs, 1880–1920* (Urbana and Chicago: University of Illinois Press, 1997), 1–17, 134–70.
6. On Chicana women's clubs, feminist organizations, and their roots within Mexican and Mexican American benevolent groups, see Cynthia E. Orozco, "Beyond Machismo, La Familia, and Ladies Auxiliaries: A Historiography of Mexican-Origin Women's Participation in Voluntary Associations and Politics in the United States, 1870–1990," *Perspectives in Mexican American Studies: Mexican American Women Changing Images* 5 (1995): 1–34; Elvira Valenzuela Crocker, *One Dream, Many Voices: A History of the Mexican American Women's National Association* (San Antonio, TX: Dagen Bela Graphics, 1991); Vicki L. Ruiz, *From Out of the Shadows: Mexican Women in Twentieth-Century America* (London: Oxford University Press, 1998). On Asian American women's organizations, see Lisa Lowe, "Work, Immigration, Gender: Asian 'American' Women," in *Making More Waves: New Writing by Asian American Women*, ed. Elaine H. Kim, Lilia V. Villanueva, and Asian Women United of California, 269–77 (Boston, MA: Beacon Press, 1997); Evelyn Nakano Glenn, *Issei, Nisei, War Bride: Three Generations of Japanese American Women in Domestic Service*

(Philadelphia, PA: Temple University Press, 1988); Lucie Hirati, "Chinese Immigrant Women in Nineteenth-Century California," in *Women of America*, ed. Carol R. Berkin and Mary B. Norton, 223–44 (Boston, MA: Houghton Mifflin, 1979); Mayumi Tsutakawa, "The Asian Women's Movement: Superficial Rebellion?" *Asian Resources*, available from Karl Lo, East Asia Library, Gowen Hall, University of Washington, Seattle; Nancy D. Donnelly, *Changing Lives of Refugee Hmong Women* (Seattle: University of Washington Press, 1994); Karen Hossfeld, "Hiring Immigrant Women: Silicon Valley's 'Simple Formula,'" in *Women of Color in U.S. Society*, Women in the Political Economy, ed. Maxine Baca Zinn and Bonnie Thornton Dill, 65–94 (Philadelphia, PA: Temple University Press, 1994); Marcia Williams, "Ladies on the Line: Punjabi Cannery Workers in Central California," in *Making Waves: An Anthology of Writings by and about Asian American Women*, ed. Asian American Women United of California, 148–58 (Boston, MA: Beacon Press, 1989). For more about WARN, see Rayna Green, "Review Essay: Native American Women," *Signs: Journal of Women in Culture and Society* (Winter 1980): 248–67; Winona La Duke, "In Honor of Women Warriors," *Off Our Backs* 11 (February 1981): 3–4.

7. Priscilla Murolo, "Quests for Respectability, Demands for Respect," in *The Common Ground of Womanhood: Class, Gender, and Working Girls' Clubs, 1884–1928* (Urbana: University of Illinois Press, 1997), 23–36.
8. Chandra Talpade Mohanty, "Cartographies of Struggle: Third World Women and the Politics of Feminism," in *Third World Women and the Politics of Feminism*, ed. Chandra Talpade Mohanty, Lourdes Torres, and Ann Russo, 28–47 (Bloomington: Indiana University Press, 1991), 4.
9. The Republican Mother ideology flourished between 1776 and 1820 and held that the "model republican woman be competent, confident, rational, benevolent, independent, and self-reliant [in order to be] better wives and better mothers for the next generation of virtuous republican citizens." See Linda Kerber, "The Republican Mother," in *Women's America: Refocusing the Past*, 3d ed., ed. Linda

Kerber and Jane Sherron De Hart, 89–92 (New York: Oxford University Press, 1991).

10. Evelyn Brooks Higginbotham, *Righteous Discontent: The Women's Movement in the Black Baptist Church, 1880–1920* (Boston, MA: Harvard University Press, 1993), outlines how African American women adopted the politics of respectability as a way to redefine notions of Black womanhood. White working-class women used this same moral strategy and resisted the notion that their class status made them less womanly. As Priscilla Murolo writes, "This conscious working-class pride suffused club members' embrace of upper-class standards for womanly behavior and sensibilities." See Murolo, "Quest for Respectability," 25.
11. Stephanie Shaw, *What A Woman Ought to Be and to Do: Black Professional Women Workers during the Jim Crow Era* (Chicago, IL: University of Chicago Press, 1996), 15.
12. David Roediger, *The Wages of Whiteness: Race and the Making of the American Working Class* (New York: Verso, 1994), 115–32.
13. Kevin Gaines, *Uplifting the Race: Black Leadership, Politics, and Culture in the Twentieth Century* (Chapel Hill: University of North Carolina Press, 1997), 180–81.
14. See E. P. Thompson, *The Making of the English Working Class* (London: Victor Collancz, 1963), 8–13.
15. Roediger, *Wages of Whiteness*, 12–13.
16. On the Stanton and Anthony adoption of this slogan, see Angela Davis, *Women, Race, and Class* (New York: Vintage Books, 1981), 81.
17. White women's clubs dwindled drastically in numbers after 1920 not only because they won the vote but also because of the changing historical trends of increased industrialization and capitalism. These factors changed the ethos and political focus of white women's activism. See Gere, *Intimate Practices*, 248–69.
18. Davis, *Women, Race, and Class*, 131.
19. Freeman and Witcher, "Stepping into Black Power" (n. 21, chapter 1).
20. This history of AKA is culled from Parker's *Alpha Kappa Alpha through the Years* and Norma Boyd's *A Love That*

Equals My Labors (Chicago, IL: Mobium Press, 1988); also see James Willis Jackson and Anita K. Ritch, *The Search for Something Better: Ida Louise Jackson's Life Story* (Chicago, IL: Mobium, 1989).

21. Giddings, *In Search of Sisterhood*, 19.
22. Parker, *Alpha Kappa Alpha through the Years*, 36.
23. Giddings, *In Search of Sisterhood*, 49.
24. Jürgen Habermas, *The Structural Transformation of the Public Sphere: An Inquiry into a Category of Bourgeois Society* (Cambridge, MA: MIT Press, 1995).
25. Nancy Fraser, "Rethinking the Public Sphere: A Contribution to the Critique of Actually Existing Democracy," in *Habermas and the Public Sphere*, Studies in Contemporary German Social Thought, ed. Craig Calhoun, 109–42 (Cambridge, MA: MIT Press, 1992).
26. See Higginbotham, *Righteous Discontent*; Houston Baker, "Critical Memory and the Black Public Sphere," in *The Black Public Sphere*, ed. Black Public Sphere Collective, 7–37; Mary P. Ryan, "Gender and Public Access: Women's Politics in Nineteenth Century America," in *Habermas and the Public Sphere*, 259–88; Ellen Messer-Davidow, "Manufacturing the Attack on Liberal Higher Education," *Social Text* 36 (Fall 1993): 40–80. For a critical analysis of public sphere theory, see Michael Schudson, "Was There Ever a Public Sphere? If So, When? Reflections on the American Case," in *Habermas and the Public Sphere*, 143–63.
27. The autobiography of member Ida Louise Jackson, who founded the AKA chapter at the University of California, Berkeley, suggests that its chapter formed to create a forum where African American women could act on and voice their concerns about racism and their feelings of alienation on Berkeley's campus. See Jackson and Ritch, *The Search for Something Better*.
28. I do not wish to discount the work of White sororities and White women's clubs. In addition, I want to note the intercultural work between Black and White women's clubs as described in Higginbotham, *Righteous Discontent*. However, I argue that the multiple identities of Black women (race, gender, historically of a poor socioeconomic class, and

descendants of slavery) and the adverse psychological and material effects of racism sharpened their focus toward race work.

29. Parker, *Alpha Kappa Alpha through the Years*, 36.
30. Frantz Fanon, *Wretched of the Earth*, trans., Haakon Chevalier (New York: Grove Press, 1968), 233.
31. These articles include Alice McGhee's "A Soror in Japan," *Ivy Leaf* 13:3 (September 1935); Clayda Jane Williams, "Impressions: A First Trip Abroad," *Ivy Leaf* 10:4 (December 1934): 10; Merze Tate, "Two Sorors at Oxford," *Ivy Leaf* 14:1 (November 1936).
32. Parker, *Alpha Kappa Alpha through the Years*, 163.
33. Anne Meis Knupfer, *Toward a Tenderer Humanity and a Nobler Womanhood: African American Women's Clubs in Turn-of-the-Century Chicago* (New York: New York University Press, 1997), 46–47.
34. "With the Editor: Jane Addams," *Ivy Leaf* 13:1 (March 1935).
35. Parker, *Alpha Kappa Alpha through the Years*, 163.
36. On this program, see Smith, "Sharecroppers and Sorority Women," 149–67; David Beito, "Black Fraternal Hospitals in the Mississippi Delta, 1942–1967," *Journal of Southern History* 56 (February 1999): 109–40; "AKA Ida J. Jackson on the AKA Health Care Project," *Ivy Leaf* 13:3 (September 1935).
37. Jackson and Ritch, *Search for Something Better*, 155.
38. For more on Black Americans and New Deal public policy, see Byron W. Daynes, William D. Pederson, and Michael P. Riccards, eds., *The New Deal and Public Policy* (New York: St. Martin's Press, 1998), 129, 135–49.
39. Jackson and Ritch, *Search for Something Better*, 157–58.
40. Ibid., 146.
41. Dorothy Boulding Ferebee, "Impressions of Negro Life in Mississippi," *Ivy Leaf* 13:4 (December 1935) 4–6.
42. Shaw, *What A Woman Ought to Be and to Do*, 200–201.
43. Project Family was a precursor to their current "Putting Black Families FIRST" project. FIRST stands for Families Involved in Redefined Survival Techniques. The program seeks to "educate" the Black community so it is "informed

about their rights and responsibilities as citizens." An article on the program ran in a later issue of the *Ivy Leaf*. See "Project Family," *Ivy Leaf* 45:1 (February–March 1969).

44. Descriptions of these programs are in the sorority's magazine the *Ivy Leaf*. See "Finer Womanhood Week," *Ivy Leaf* 25:3 (September 1947): 18.
45. For more on Euro-ethnic working clubs, especially Irish American women's working-class conditions and the formations that fought against their exploitation, see Davis, *Women, Race, and Class*, 54–55; Roediger, *Wages of Whiteness*, 82–84.
46. Murolo, "Quest for Respectability," 37.
47. Norma Boyd's summary of the National Non-Partisan Council of Public Affairs, *Ivy Leaf* 22:3 (March 1944).
48. See Dorothy Boulding Ferebee, "Negro Women in the National Defense Program," *Ivy Leaf* 19:2 (June 1941). See also Lawrence Ross, *The Divine Nine: The History of African American Fraternities and Sororities* (New York: Kensington, 2000), 176; Parker, *Alpha Kappa Alpha through the Years*, 241–44.
49. The Job Corps Center disbanded in 2000.
50. *Ivy Leaf* 45:1 (February/March 1969), 17.
51. Parker, *Alpha Kappa Alpha through the Years*, 244.
52. Author unknown, "SCLC Names Rev. TY Rogers Jr. Coordinator of National Commemorative Effort and Confrontation Program," *Ivy Leaf* 45:1 (February/March 1969), 11.
53. *Ivy Leaf* 52:3 (Fall 1976), 2–3.
54. Parker, *Alpha Kappa Alpha through the Years*, 221.
55. Gadson, "Greek Power!" (n. 7, chapter 1).
56. On the Martin Luther King event and work with Africare, see Parker, *Alpha Kappa Alpha through the Years*, 55, 247–49.
57. Alpha Kappa Alpha Sorority, Inc., "National Report on Chapter Activism," http://www.aka1908.com/openletter.com (accessed March 15, 2001).

Chapter 3

1. "Preface," in *The Black Public Sphere*, ed. Black Public Sphere Collective (n. 1, chapter 2), 2–3.

2. I base this characterization of stepping on my years of attending and viewing step shows and from doing ethnographic work at Greek events. The step shows discussed here are drawn from my own field notes, from step show events, and from videos of step performance disseminated by Rawls Entertainment, 1800 South Robertson Blvd., Ste. #274, Los Angeles, CA, 90035. I changed the names of my interviewees for anonymity. Interviews in this chapter are from Deborah Elizabeth Whaley, "By Merit, By Culture: The Cultural and Counter Public Sphere Work of Alpha Kappa Alpha Sorority" (Ph.D. diss., University of Kansas, 2002). Finally, in my thinking through of this expressive practice, representation of all Black sororal organizations is included for general analysis, yet I recognize the benefits of focusing closely on one particular sorority, AKA, as a representative point of departure. Honing in on AKA step performances, while comparing them to the performances of Delta Sigma Theta, Zeta Phi Beta, and Sigma Gamma Rho, unveils the processes by which a particular Black sorority creates diverse identities and situates itself in juxtaposition to other sororal groups.
3. See Gadson, "Greek Power!" (n. 7, chapter 1); Stains, "Black Like Me" (n. 9, introduction), 69; Freeman and Witcher, "Stepping into Black Power" (n. 21, chapter 1), 143.
4. I define *diasporic experience* as cultural practices not bound by a single geographical location or national experience. Diasporic identities are partial, fragmentary, and dispersed, and, as Stuart Hall reminds us, always a process of change and transformation. See Stuart Hall, "What Is This 'Black' in Black Popular Culture?" in *Black Popular Culture*, ed. Gina Dent, 21–33 (a project by Michelle Wallace) (Boston, MA: South End Press, 1994), 28. Yet as Hall is careful to remind us about the term *diaspora*, we must not "clutch on to the word, but to clutch onto certain ideas about it. It is a place where traditions operate but are not closed, where the Black experience is historically and culturally distinctive but is not the same as it was before." Black step performance, I argue, is a tangible example of diasporic cultural traditions.

See Stuart Hall, "Subjects in History: Making Diasporic Identities," in *The House that Race Built: Black Americans, U.S. Terrain*, ed. Wahneema Lubiano (New York: Vintage, 1998), 299.

5. This question is influenced by Hall, "What Is This 'Black' Popular Culture?"
6. Juneteenth is a Black American celebration of the Emancipation Proclamation. These yearly festivals occur in every region in the United States on or near the nineteenth of June. For more information on Juneteenth, see the ethnography by William Wiggins, *O Freedom! Afro-American Emancipation Celebrations* (Knoxville: University of Tennessee Press, 1987).
7. This event generates money through ticket sales and the prize money received by the winner selected by the judges. The groups that perform split the funds generated through ticket sales, while the prize money goes directly to the winner's charitable cause.
8. Yard shows are step shows that are outside, as opposed to being in an auditorium, and are public events that onlookers do not necessarily pay to see.
9. Jacqui Malone, *Steppin' on the Blues: The Visible Rhythms of African American Dance* (Champagne-Urbana: University of Illinois Press, 1996).
10. Annemarie Bean, "Introduction," in *A Source Book of African-American Performance* (n. 5, chapter 1).
11. Interview with Linda, former dean of pledges of an AKA chapter at a university in California, 1993.
12. Freeman and Witcher, "Stepping into Black Power."
13. Elizabeth Fine, "Stepping, Saluting, Cracking, and Freaking: The Cultural Politics of African American Sorority Step Shows," in *A Source Book of African-American Performance* (n. 5, chapter 1), 176.
14. Robert Farris Thompson, "An Aesthetic of the Cool: West African Dance," in *Signifyin(g), Sanctifyin', an Slam Dunking; A Reader in African American Expressive Culture*, ed. Gena Dagel Caponi, 75 (Amherst: University of Massachusetts Press, 1999).
15. See Henry Louis Gates, *The Signifying Monkey: A Theory of*

African American Literary Criticism (New York: Oxford University Press, 1988); Claudia Mitchell-Kernan, "Signifying, Loud-Talking, and Marking," in *Signifyin(g), Sanctifyin', and Slam Dunking*, 309.

16. This step chant is printed in Fine, "Stepping, Saluting, Cracking, and Freaking," 181–83.
17. *Dialogic* refers to the ways in which people communicate with an audience in mind, and the ways in which this verbal translation to the audience is connected to ideas and thoughts communicated in the past. In this instance, there is a provoking of dialogue by the performance. See Mikhail Bakhtin, *The Dialogic Imagination: Four Essays*, ed. C. Emerson, trans. M. Holquist (Austin: University of Texas Press, 1982), 279–80.
18. This step chant is printed in Fine, "Stepping, Saluting, Cracking, and Freaking,"181–83.
19. Stuart Hall, "For Allon White: Metaphors of Transformation," in *Stuart Hall*, ed. Morley and Chen (n. 32, chapter 1), 291–92.
20. See Alabama A&M Step Show Extravaganza, 1995, Rawls Entertainment, 1800 South Robertson Blvd., Ste. #274, Los Angeles, CA, 90035.
21. Interview with Conroy, a member of Kappa Alpha Psi at a Midwestern university, 2000.
22. Interview with Linda, 1993.
23. Interview with members of Zeta Phi Beta Sorority, Lucy and Dana (names changed), who pledged at a California State University campus and were participants at a San Jose State University Step Show. I combined their responses here for coherency.
24. See University of Southern California Millennium Yard Show, spring 2000, Rawls Entertainment, 1800 South Robertson Blvd., Ste. #274, Los Angeles, CA, 90035.
25. Ibid.
26. University of California, Riverside, Step Show, Rawls Entertainment, 1800 South Robertson Blvd., Ste. #274, Los Angeles, CA, 90035.
27. Interview with Linda, 1993.
28. Interview with Lucy and Dana, 2000.

29. On this, see Hazel Carby, "'In the Quiet, Undisputed Dignity of My Womanhood': Black Feminist Thought after Emancipation," in *Reconstructing Womanhood: The Emergence of the Afro-American Woman Novelist*, 95–120 (London: Oxford University Press, 1990). See also Angela Davis, *Women, Race, and Class* (New York: Vintage Books, 1982); Meis Knupfer, *Toward a Tenderer Humanity* (n. 33, chapter 2); Shaw, *What a Woman Ought to Be and to Do* (n. 12, chapter 2); Elsa Barkley Brown, "Negotiating and Transforming the Public Sphere: African American Political Life in the Transition from Slavery to Freedom," in *The Black Public Sphere*, ed. Black Public Sphere Collective (n. 1, chapter 2), 111–50; Anna Julia Cooper's 1925 AKA National Convention Speech, *Ivy Leaf* 5:1 (December 1926).
30. An example of nineteenth-century White violence at Black public celebrations includes Pinkster celebrations and Negro Election Day. Pinkster celebrations were cultural carnivals also attended by working-class Whites, and this element of cultural mixture at a public festival angered White police, city officials, and White vigilantes. Negro Election Day, as the title indicates, was a celebration of enfranchisement for Blacks in the North. See Roediger, *The Wages of Whiteness* (n. 13, chapter 2), 101–103.
31. On neoliberal discourses that espouse conservative ideologies that include claiming that culture is best kept out of the mainstream public sphere, see William Flores, *Latino Cultural Citizenship: Claiming Identity, Space, and Rights* (Berkeley: University of California Press, 1998). On the imposed dress code for NBA players at athletic-related events, see John Eligon, "N.B.A. Dress Code Decrees: Clothes Make the Image," *New York Times*, October 19, 2005; Mike Wise, "Opinions on the NBA Dress Code Are Far from Uniform," *Washington Post*, October 23, 2005.
32. Carby, *Reconstructing Womanhood*, 3.
33. See Jayna Brown, *Babylon Girls: Black Women Performers and the Shaping of the Modern* (Durham, NC, and London: Duke University Press, 2008).
34. On the complexity of everyday practices and popular culture, see Stuart Hall, "Notes on Deconstructing the Popular," in *Cultural Theory and Popular Culture: A Reader*, ed.

John Storey (Athens: University of Georgia Press, 1998), 442–54.

35. On the use of color and clothing in BGLOs, see Lillian O. Holloman, "Black Sororities and Fraternities: A Case Study in Clothing Symbolism," in *Dress and Popular Culture*, ed. Patricia A. Cunningham and Susan Voso Lab, 46–60 (Bowling Green, KY: Bowling Green State University Popular Press, 1991).
36. See Hall's reading of Bakhtin, in "For Allon White," 291–92.
37. Ibid. For further reading, see Mikhail Bakhtin, *Rabelais and His World* (Bloomington: Indiana University Press, 1984).
38. A vernacular community is an extended nuclear community-based group that shares knowledge about the origins and multiple purposes of the practices, norms, and expectations of that formation.
39. Interview with AKA member Janet, 2000.
40. Lawrence W. Levine, *Black Culture and Black Consciousness: Afro-American Folk Thought from Slavery to Freedom* (New York: Oxford University Press, 1977), 5.
41. Stuart Hall, "Who Needs 'Identity'?" in *Questions of Cultural Identity*, ed. Paul du Gay and Stuart Hall (London: Sage, 1996), 4. See also Stuart Hall, "Cultural Identity and Diaspora," in *Identity: Community, Culture and Difference*, ed. Jonathan Rutherford, 222–37 (London: Lawrence and Wishart).
42. On the symbolic importance of ritual, see Peter Stallybrass and Allon White, *The Politics and Poetics of Transgression* (Ithaca, NY: Cornell University Press, 1986), 5.

Chapter 4

1. Steven Gregory, "Race, Identity, and Political Activism: The Shifting Contours of the African American Public Sphere," in *The Black Public Sphere*, ed. Black Public Sphere Collective (n. 1, chapter 2), 151.
2. Based on interviews and participant observation, I hypothesized as to what behavior best fit into the three respective stages of initiation.

3. When pledges are struck with a paddle during the pledge process, sorors refer to it as "taking wood," that is, being able to take or endure wood paddling.
4. I have taken all quotes and the synthesis of the Ohio State Case from the court transcript. See *State of Ohio v. Brown* 90 Ohio 92–P-0055.
5. Hazing is described as "anything done without direct bearing on a pledge's contribution to the organization" and often encompasses psychological and physical punishments for the failure to comply with sorority members' expectations. See Hank Nuwer, *Broken Pledges: The Deadly Rite of Hazing* (Atlanta, GA: Longstreet Press, 1990), 237, and *The Wrongs of Passage: Fraternities, Sororities, Hazing, and Binge Drinking* (Bloomington: Indiana University Press, 1999); John Williams, *Perceptions of the No-Pledge Policy for New Member Intake by Undergraduate Members of Predominantly Black Fraternities and Sororities* (Manhattan, KS: Center for the Study of Pan-Hellenic Issues, Tennessee State University, 1992).
6. For a detailed exploration of the history of the critical race theory movement, see Cornell West, "Introduction," in *Critical Race Theory: The Key Writings that Formed the Movement*, ed. Kimberle Crenshaw et al., xiii-4 (New York: New Press, 1996), and on the multiplicative forms of critical race feminism, see Adrien Katherine Wing, "Brief Reflections toward a Multiplicative Theory and Praxis of Being," *Critical Race Feminism: A Reader*, Critical America Series (New York: New York University Press, 1996), 27–34. On transnational critical race feminism, see Adrien Katherine Wing, "Global Critical Race Feminism for the Twenty-First Century," in *Global Critical Race Feminism: An International Reader*, Critical America Series (New York: New York University Press, 2000), 1–26. For a case study analysis of violence, culture, and power within the critical race feminist movement, see Patricia Williams, "Spirit-Murdering the Messenger: The Discourse of Fingerpointing as the Law's Response to Racism," Regina Austin, "Black Women, Sisterhood, and the Difference/Deviance Divide," and Adrien Katherine Wing and Christine A. Willis, "Sisters in the Hood: Beyond Bloods and Crips," all in *Critical Race Femi-*

nism: A Reader (New York: New York University Press, 1997), 229–36; 237–42; 242–54.

7. Newspapers across the nation covered the ban on pledging. See Barbara Bradley, "A Pledge of Change from Alpha to Omega; Blacks Worry Greek Reforms May Go Too Far," *The Commercial Appeal*, November 15, 1990; Michel Marriott, "Black Fraternities and Sororities End a Tradition," *New York Times*, October 3, 1990, B8; David Mills, "Fraternity Violence: The Pledging Debate: The Greeks: There Is a Move Afoot to Do Away with Hazing and the Traditionalists Are Outraged and Vow to Fight," *Los Angeles Times*, July 24, 1990; David Mills, "The Wrongs of the Rites of Brotherhood; Leaders of Black Fraternities Move to End a Cruel Tradition of Violent Hazing," *Washington Post*, June 18, 1990, B1, B6; Michelle K. Collison, "8 Fraternities and Sororities Announce an End to Hazing," *Washington Post*, February 19, 1990.
8. On definitions and a detailed description of hazing, see Nuwer, *Broken Pledges* and *The Wrongs of Passage*.
9. This incident is reported in a chronology of hazing incidents in Nuwer, *Broken Pledges*, 299.
10. Ibid., 301.
11. "Howard," *USA Today*, April 15, 1988, 10A.
12. National newspapers and magazines covered this incident. See "JSU AKA Sorority Pleads Guilty to Hazing Charges," *Jet*, May 13, 1991, p. 14, and "Jacksonville," *USA Today*, April 18, 1991.
13. "Law and Order," *Atlanta Journal and Constitution*, April 29, 1997; "Georgia State Sorority Pledge Alleges Attack," *Atlanta Journal and Constitution*, April 30, 1997.
14. This incident is described in Nuwer, *The Wrongs of Passage*, 299. Nuwer does not cite the sorority involved, but I confirmed the allegation and was given the name of the sorority, Delta Sigma Theta, by Sgt. Baxter of the Western Illinois University Campus Police Department on January 16, 2001. See also the court case *Wallace v. the State of Illinois*, December 3, 1999, 99 L0 798.
15. Mills, "The Wrongs of the Rites," B6. The Kappa Alpha Psi pledge was pushed to his death, and the Omega Psi Phi

pledge was placed in front of a burning heater, reportedly because Omega members thought his skin complexion should be "darker."

16. Williams, *The Perceptions of Membership Intake among Historically Black Greek Letter Fraternities*, master's thesis, 1994, Kansas State University.
17. Walter Kimbrough, "Notes from Underground: Despite Ban, Pledging Remains," *Black Issues in Higher Education* 17:6 (2000): 36.
18. The hazing incidents and subsequent deaths among White Greek-letter organizations are more frequent than in BGLOs because (1) they have larger numbers and (2) alcohol-related pledging is a core component of White Greek organizational life, which results in alcohol-related deaths in these groups. For more information on this and White Greek-letter organizations' hazing practices, particularly relating to alcohol abuse, see Nuwer, *Broken Pledges* and *The Wrongs of Passage*.
19. I point this out to reveal that this is not the case with fraternities. No matter the racial and ethnic composition, fraternities will refer to themselves as "brothers" or "frats," but the word "soror" is particular to Black Greek-letter sororities.
20. Stuart Hall, "Introduction," in *Representation: Cultural Representations and Signifying Practices*, Culture, Media, and Identities Series, vol. 2 (London: Sage, 1997).
21. Julia B. Purnell, "The Supreme Basileus Speaks," *Ivy Leaf* 40:11 (February–March 1964).
22. "Howard University Bans AKA Sorority (Alpha Kappa Alpha) from Campus until 1966," *New York Amsterdam News*, May 19, 1962, 1.
23. Nuwer, *The Wrongs of Passage*, 178; Giddings, *In Search of Sisterhood* (n. 7, introduction), 284.
24. Marriott, "End a Tradition," B8.
25. See the chronology of hazing incidents from the eighteenth to twentieth centuries in Nuwer, *Broken Pledges*.
26. Malcolm X, "Message to the Grassroots," in *The Eyes on the Prize Civil Rights Reader: Documents, Speeches, and Firsthand Accounts from the Black Freedom Struggle*," ed. Clayborne Carson et al., 248 (New York: Viking, 1991).

27. Trish Eber, "Greek Secrecy Leads to Hazing," *Kent Stater*, January 22, 1992.
28. Ibid.
29. Ibid.
30. Ibid.
31. Dwayne Gentner, "Abuse Tarnishes Greek Image," *Kent Stater*, January 24, 1992.
32. Kenneth Weiss, "Greek System a Simplistic Term," *Kent Stater*, January 24, 1992. I included the exclamation point for emphasis.
33. Kelly McGuire, "Hazing Intolerable," *Kent Stater*, January 22, 1992, emphasis added.
34. Fieldwork for this chapter took place in 1995. Interviewee responses in this chapter are culled from Whaley, "By Merit, By Culture" (n. 2, chapter 3). To proceed ethically and protect my informants' identities, I do not disclose the personal identity of members, pledges, or the chapter.
35. Interview with an OSP during fieldwork, winter 1995.
36. Mills, "Wrongs of the Rites," B6; second quote, interview with an OSP during fieldwork, winter 1995.
37. Ibid.
38. On hazing in Black Greek-letter fraternities, see Jones, *Black Haze* (n. 6, introduction).
39. I agree with Foucault's position on the necessity to evaluate the social function of violence. Nonetheless, I acknowledge Nancy Fraser's reading of Foucault's *Discipline and Punish: The Birth of the Prison* (New York: Vintage, 1977), which paces his theory to illuminate the differing effects of knowledge and power produced through violent means. Fraser writes that "Foucault calls too many different sorts of things power and simply leaves it at that. . . . Granted there can be no social practices without power—but that doesn't follow that all forms of power are normatively equivalent nor that any social practices are as good as any other" (32). See Nancy Fraser, "Foucault On Power," in *Unruly Practices: Power, Discourse and Gender in Contemporary Social Theory* (Minneapolis: University of Minnesota Press, 1989).
40. Foucault, "Hierarchal Observation," *Discipline and Punish*, 170–76.

41. Nada Elia, "Violent Women: Surging into Forbidden Quarters," in *Fanon: A Critical Reader*, ed. Lewis. R. Gordon, 168 (Oxford: Blackwell, 1996).
42. Kimbrough, "Notes from Underground."
43. See "Family of Woman Drowned in Alleged L.A. Hazing Files $100 Mil. Suit against AKA Sorority," *Jet*, October 14, 2002, p. 13; Lenea Austin, "Families Struggle with Deaths of AKA Pledges," *L.A. Sentinel*, October 14, 2002; Kristal Brent Zook, "Swept Away," *Essence*, September 2003, 180.
44. A well-devised solution to revamping the membership intake program in BGLOs is in Tamara Brown and Gregory Parks, "The Fell and Clutch of Circumstance: Pledging and the Black Greek Experience," in *African American Fraternities and Sororities: The Legacy and the Vision*, ed. Tamara Brown et al., 437–64 (Lexington: University Press of Kentucky, 2005).

Chapter 5

1. Higginbotham, *Righteous Discontent* (n. 11, chapter 2), 10.
2. Wendy L. Wilson, "Michelle Obama to Become Honorary Member of Alpha Kappa Alpha Sorority, Inc.; Wife of Presidential Hopeful Says "Yes" to the Pink and Green," *Essence*, July 2008. http://www.essence.com/essence/lifestyle/voices/0,16109,1822967,00.html.
3. Jill Dougherty, "Sisterhood Turns 100: Members of Alpha Kappa Alpha Are Serious about Helping Society," CNN, July 20, 2008.
4. "Alpha Kappa Alpha Unity March on the Capitol," FOX 5 News, July 17, 2008.
5. Lonnae O'Neal Parker and Sindya N. Bhanoo, "A Century of Sisterhood: Almost 25,000 Alpha Kappa Alpha Sorority Members Meet in Washington," *Washington Post*, July 14, 2008, B1.
6. Interviews in this chapter (with the exception of Benita) are culled from Whaley, "By Merit, By Culture" (n. 2, chapter 3); interview with Benita, April 24, 2006. All names are pseudonyms.

7. Dawson makes this point in "A Black Counterpublic?" (n. 1, chapter 2), 219.
8. Austin Bogues, "Sorority Celebrates Michelle Obama's Acceptance," Caucus Blog, *New York Times*, July 14, 2008, http://www.thecaucus.blogs.nytimes.com/author/austin-bogues/.
9. Dawson, "A Black Counterpublic?" 201.
10. *Atlanta Inquirer*, "Alpha Kappa Alpha Donates to Africare," February 7, 2004, 6.
11. Thomas C. Holt, "Afterword: Mapping the Black Public Sphere," *The Black Public Sphere* (n. 1, chapter 2), 325–28.
12. Tricia Rose, "The New AIDS Fight—Race, Sex and Stigmas," *New York Times*, March 1, 2003, 9.
13. Manning Marable, "Conclusion," *How Capitalism Underdeveloped Black America: Problems in Race, Political Economy, and Society*, updated ed. (Cambridge, MA: South End Press, 2000).

Conclusion

1. Tajuana Butler, *Sorority Sisters* (New York: Random House, 1999).
2. See Kayla Perrin's three novels on Black sororities: *The Delta Sisters* (New York: St. Martin's Griffin Press, 2005), *The Sisters of Theta Phi Kappa: A Novel* (New York: St. Martin's Griffin Press, 2002), and *We'll Never Tell* (New York: St. Martin's Griffin Press, 2007). Also see Dorrie Wheeler, *Be My Sorority Sister-Under Pressure* (Virginia Beach, VA: Sparkledoll Productions, 2003).
3. Interview with Tajuana Butler, 2000.
4. bell hooks, "Dialectically Down with the Critical Program," in *Black Popular Culture*, ed. Gina Dent, 54 (n. 3, chapter 4).

GLOSSARY

BENEVOLENT ORGANIZATION Organizations that provide assistance to their and other communities in the name of mutual benefit and interest.

BLACK GREEK-LETTER ORGANIZATIONS (BGLOS) Greek-letter organizations that are historically, not exclusively, African American or Black. The organizations developed out of specific historic and social arrangements, which mark them as cultural-, social-, and service-oriented fraternal apparatuses.

CHAPTER Fraternities and sororities have individual chapters, which are designated in sequence by a letter of the Greek alphabet. A regional director and the national headquarters oversee chapters.

CRACKING Verbal or nonverbal parody during step routines.

CROSSING THE BURNING SANDS A secret and sacred (i.e., highly revered, with religious connotations) ceremony that takes place after initiation.

DROPPING LINE Pledges who drop out of their pledge process.

FOUNDERS Original members who began, chartered, and incorporated their fraternal organizations.

FRATERNAL A social body of men or women, not necessarily Greek in its organizational structure, that convenes in the name of mutual cooperation and fellowship.

FRATERNITY A social body of men that convenes in the name of brotherhood.

FREAKING A moment in step routines where an individual steps outside the synchronized movements to gain attention from a crowd.

GREEK-LETTER ORGANIZATION A social body that uses the Greek alphabet and mythology as organizing principles.

HAMBONING A choreographed movement performed during step routines that involves hand-slapping motions between hands, on thighs, and behind the back of the knees.

HAZING Actions required of pledges by members of Greek-letter organizations that do not have direct bearing upon the pledge's contribution. Hazing often involves emotional and physical abuse.

INCORPORATION OF GREEK-LETTER ORGANIZATIONS All nine African American Greek-letter organizations are nonprofit corporations. Each group thus includes "incorporated" at the end of its fraternal name. For example, AKA is referred to as Alpha Kappa Alpha Sorority, Incorporated.

INITIATION A ceremony that pledges endure to become a member.

IVY CENTER The headquarters of AKA. Its national magazine is named the *Ivy Leaf*.

IVY LEAF One of AKA's primary symbols, which for them represents the growth, strength, and endurance of members.

IVY PLEDGE CLUB During the official pledge process, initiates were referred to as a "club of women" in the process of becoming an "ivy," which is synonymous with an AKA.

IVY PRIMER The pledge handbook given to initiates during official pledge processes.

LINE OF INITIATES Pledges are referred to as a sequential line, wherein each person has a "line number." The idea of having a line of pledges is taken from military lineups, wherein one stands at attention to take orders from those in a position of power.

LINE SISTER/BROTHER Pledges refer to each other as such if they pledged at the same time.

MUTUAL AID BENEFIT SOCIETY A social body organized to provide life insurance and benefits for members of its organizing body and its larger communities.

OLD SCHOOL PLEDGERS Men and women in Black Greek-letter organizations who engage in post-1990 pledge rites.

ON LINE The former pledge process.

PADDLING Striking a pledge or member of a fraternal with a wooden paddle, often during pledging. Paddling is also referred to as "taking wood."

PLEDGES Potential fraternal initiates.

PLEDGE SESSIONS A process wherein members and pledges convene to review the aims and objectives of their organization through tests and rites.

PLEDGESHIP The duration that pledges go through to become a member.

PLEDGING A process that men and women go through to become a member of a fraternal. This process is usually secret, and its intricacies are kept within the respective organizations.

RUSH A series of parties or get-togethers wherein fraternals court potential members.

SALUTING A ritualized greeting or verbal call done in Black Greek-letter organizations to other members. Saluting is often done during step performance.

SANDS Members who cross the burning sands together.

SECRET SOCIETY A social body of men or women that convenes in secret and uses rites, ritual, and symbols to create a collective identity and purpose.

SOROR Members of Black sororities; a Black sister among members.

SORORITY A social body of women that convenes in the name of sisterhood.

STEPPING Choreographed dance and marching movements that involve chanting, signifying, and innuendo.

TAKING WOOD See Paddling.

TURN BACK NIGHT The night before initiation in Black fraternities and sororities; also known as "hell night" in White sororities and fraternities, wherein pledges are put through a series of difficult rites to weed out weaker pledges from being initiated.

BIBLIOGRAPHY

Abel, Elizabeth. *Female Subjects in Black and White: Race, Psychoanalysis, Feminism.* Berkeley: University of California Press, 1997.

Addams, Jane. *Twenty Years at Hull House.* Urbana: University of Illinois Press, 1910. Reprint. With introduction and notes by James Hurt. Prairie State Books. Urbana: University of Illinois Press, 1990.

Applebome, Peter. "Lawsuit Shatters Silence over Hazing in Black Fraternities." *New York Times*, December 21, 1994.

Aptheker, Bettina. *Women's Legacy: Essays On Race, Class and Sex in American History.* Amherst: University of Massachusetts Press, 1982.

Atkinson, Paul, and Martyn Hammersly. *Ethnography: Principles and Practice.* New York: Tavistock, 1983.

Atlanta Journal and Constitution. "Law and Order," April 29, 1997.

Baird, William R. *Baird's Manual of American College Fraternities.* Menasha, WI: Baird's Manual Foundation, 1977.

Baker, Houston, Manthia Diawara, and Ruth Lindenberg, eds. *Black British Cultural Studies: A Reader.* Chicago, IL; University of Chicago Press, 1996.

Baker, Houston A. "Critical Memory and the Black Public Sphere." In *The Black Public Sphere*, ed. Black Public Sphere Collective. 5–38. Chicago, IL: University of Chicago Press, 1995.

Bakhtin, Mikhail. *The Dialogical Imagination.* Edited by C. Emerson and translated by M. Holmquist. Austin: University of Texas Press, 1982.

Bakhtin, Mikhail. *Rabelais and His World.* Bloomington: Indiana University Press, 1984.

Baltimore Afro-American. "The Price of Membership," April 18, 1998.

Banks, Ingrid. *Hair Matters.* New York: New York University Press, 1999.

Barthes, Roland. *Mythologies.* Translated by Annette Laverse. New York: Noonday Press, 1972.

Bay, Betty Winston. "Hazing: An Ugly Throwback?" *The Courier-Journal*, April 23, 1998.

Bean, Anna Marie. *A Source Book of African American Performance: Plays, Peoples, Movements.* New York: Routledge, 1999.

Beito, David. "Black Fraternal Hospitals in the Mississippi Delta, 1942–1967." *Journal of Southern History* 56 (February 1999): 109–40.

Blair, Karen. *The Clubwoman as Feminist: True Womanhood Redefined, 1868–1914.* Amherst: University of Massachusetts Press, 1982.

Bowan, Mary D. *Educational Work of a National Professional Sorority of Negro College Women.* Master's thesis, University of California, Berkeley, 1935.

Boyd, Norma. *A Love That Equals My Labors.* Chicago, IL: Mobium, 1988.

Bradley, Barbara. "A Pledge of Change from Alpha to Omega; Blacks Worry Greek Reforms May Go Too Far." *The Commercial Appeal*, November 15, 1990.

Brockman, Lance. *Theater of the Fraternity: Staging the Ritual of Space 1896–1929.* Jackson: University Press of Mississippi, 1996.

Brown, Jayna. *Babylon Girls: Black Women Performers and the Shaping of the Modern.* Durham, NC, and London: Duke University Press, 2008.

Brown, Tamara, et al. *African American Fraternities and Sororities: The Legacy and the Vision.* Lexington: University Press of Kentucky, 2005.

Bryan, William. *The Eighties: Challenges for Fraternities and Sororities*. Carbondale: Southern Illinois University Press, 1983.

Butler, Tajuana. *Sorority Sisters*. New York: Random House, 1999.

Butt-Thompson, and F. W. Captain. *West African Secret Societies: Their Organization, Officials, and Teachings*. London: H.F. & G Witherby, 1929; reprint, New York: Argosy-Antiquarian, 1969.

Callhoun, Craig, ed. *Habermas and the Public Sphere*. Cambridge, MA: MIT Press, 1992.

Caponi, Gina. *Signifyin,' Sanctifyin,' and Slam Dunking: A Reader in African American Expressive Culture*. Amherst: University of Massachusetts Press, 1999.

Caraway, Nancie. *Segregated Sisterhood: Racism and the Politics of American Feminism*. Knoxville: University of Tennessee Press, 1991.

Carby, Hazel. *Reconstructing Womanhood: The Emergence of the Afro-American Woman Novelist*. London: Oxford University Press, 1990.

Case, Douglas. "A Glimpse of the Invisible Membership: A National Survey of Lesbigay Greek Members." *Perspectives* 23:3 (1996).

Collins, Patricia Hill. *Black Feminist Thought: Knowledge, Consciousness, and the Politics of Empowerment*. New York: Routledge, 1990.

Collison, Michele. "Eight Major Black Fraternities and Sororities Agree to End the Practice of Pledging." *Chronicle of Higher Education*, February 28, 1990.

Cott, Nancy F. *Bonds of Womanhood: Women's Sphere in New England 1780–1835*. New Haven, CT: Yale University Press, 1977.

Crenshaw, Kimberle. *Critical Race Theory: The Key Writings that Formed the Movement*. New York: New Press, 1995.

Crocker, Elvira Valenzuela. *One Dream, Many Voices: A History of the Mexican American Women's National Association*. San Antonio, TX: Dagen Bela Graphics, 1991.

Davis, Angela Y. *Women, Culture and Politics*. New York: Random House, 1989.

———. *Women, Race and Class*. New York: Vintage Books, 1982.

Davis, Sandra. "U.S. Fraternities Working to Clean Up Their Acts." *The Toronto Star*, April 22, 1989.

Dawson, Michael C. "A Black Counterpublic? Economic Earthquakes, Racial Agenda(s), and Black Politics." In *The Black Public Sphere*, ed. Black Public Sphere Collective. Chicago, IL: University of Chicago Press, 1995.

Daynes, Byron W., William D. Pederson, and Michael P. Riccards, eds., *The New Deal and Public Policy*. New York: St. Martin's Press, 1998.

de Lauretis, Teresa. *Alice Doesn't: Feminism, Semiotics and Cinema*. Bloomington: Indiana University Press, 1984.

———. *Technologies of Gender: Essays on Theory, Film and Fiction*. Bloomington: Indiana University Press, 1987.

Deloria, Philip. *Playing Indian*. Yale Historical Publication Series. New Haven, CT: Yale University Press, 1998.

Dent, Gina (a project by Michelle Wallace). *Black Popular Culture*. Seattle, WA: Bay Press, 1992.

Desmond, Jane. *Meaning in Motion: New Cultural Studies of Dance*. Durham, NC, and London: Duke University Press, 1997.

Diawara, Manthia. *Black American Cinema*. New York: Routledge, 1994.

Dill, Bonnie Thorton. "The Dialectics of Black Womanhood." *Signs* 4:2 (1979): 425–88.

Doane, Mary Ann. *Desire to Desire*. Bloomington: University of Indiana Press, 1987.

Donnelly, Nancy D. *Changing Lives of Refugee Hmong Women*. Seattle: University of Washington Press, 1994.

Du Bois, Ellen Carol, and Vicki Ruiz, eds. *Unequal Sisters: A Multicultural Reader in U.S. Women's History*. New York: Routledge, 1990.

Du Bois, W. E. B. *Souls of Black Folk: Essays and Sketches*. Chicago, IL: A. C. McClurg, 1903; reprint, New York: Mass Market Publishers, 1995.

Dunbar, Donnette. "Convention Marketing: African American Entrepreneurs Want to Become Licensed Vendors at Black

Fraternities and Sororities Convention." *Black Enterprise*, July 1991.

Duster, Alfreda M. *Crusade for Justice: The Autobiography of Ida B. Wells*. Chicago, IL: University of Chicago Press, 1970.

Ebony. "Kappa Alpha Psi: Fraternity Founded at Indiana University Stresses Individual and Group Achievement," May 1990.

———. "Omega Psi Phi," September 1993.

———. "Phi Beta Sigma," March 1992.

———. "Sigma Gamma Rho: Motto of the Youngest Black Greek Letter Organizations Is Greater Service, Greater Progress," February 1991.

———. "Zeta Phi Beta: Founded at Howard University, Group Celebrates 71st Anniversary with Innovative Programs," May 1991.

Elia, Nada. "Violent Women: Surging into Forbidden Quarters." In *Fanon: A Critical Reader*, ed. Lewis. R. Gordon. Oxford: Blackwell, 1996.

Ellis, Clyde. "Hazing Incidents Are a Moral Affront." *Chronicle of Higher Education*, November 14, 1990.

Emery, Lynne Fauley. *Black Dance in the United States from 1619 to Today*. New York: Dance Horizons Publishers, 1972; 1988.

Espiritu, Yen Le. *Asian American Panethnicity: Bridging Identities and Institutions*. Philadelphia, PA: Temple University Press, 1992.

Evans, Sara M., and Harry C. Boyte. *Free Space: The Sources of Democratic Change in America*. New York: Harper & Row, 1986.

Evans, Sherrell. "Georgia State Sorority Pledge Alleges Attack." *Atlanta Constitution*, April 30, 1997.

Everton, Leslie. "Blacks Need Not Apply: An Incident at Georgia Shows Little Has Changed among Segregated College Sororities." *Time*, November 6, 2000.

Fanon, Frantz. *Wretched of the Earth*. Translated by Haakon Chevalier. New York: Grove Press, 1968.

Ferguson, Margaret, and Jennifer Wicke, eds. *Feminism and Postmodernism*. Durham, NC: Duke University Press, 1994.

Fine, Elizabeth. "Stepping Saluting, Cracking, and Freaking: The Cultural Politics of African American Step Shows." *Drama Review* 35:2 (1991): 39–57.

Firth, Raymond. *Adaption and Symbolism: Essays on Social Organization*. Honolulu: University of Hawaii Press, 1978.

Fischer, Lucy. *Shot/Countershot: Film Tradition and Women's Pictures*. Bloomington: Indiana University Press, 1989.

Flores, William. *Latino Cultural Citizenship: Claiming Identity, Space, and Rights*. Berkeley: University of California Press, 1998.

Ford, M. G. "The Greek Rites of Exclusion." *The Nation*, July 4, 1987.

Foucault, Michel. *Discipline and Punish: The Birth of the Prison*. New York: Vintage, 1977.

Fox, Stephen R. *The Alpha Au Chapter of Beta Theta Pi: 1873–1973*. Lawrence: University of Kansas Press, 1976.

Fox, Susan. "Heterosexual Bastions: For Gay Collegiates, Going Greek Can Be a Risky Venture." *Washington Blade*, June 21, 1996.

Fraser, Nancy. "Foucault on Modern Power: Empirical Insights and Normative Confusions." In *Unruly Practices: Power, Discourse and Gender in Contemporary Social Theory*, 17–36. Minneapolis: University of Minnesota Press, 1989.

Fraser, Nancy. "Rethinking the Public Sphere: A Contribution to the Critique of Actually Existing Democracy." In *Habermas and the Public Sphere*, Studies in Contemporary German Social Thought, ed. Craig Calhoun, 109–42 (Cambridge, MA: MIT Press, 1992).

Frazier, Edward Franklin. *Black Bourgeoisie: The Rise of a New Middle Class in the United States*. New York: Free Press, 1965.

Freeman, Marilyn, and Tina Witcher. "Stepping into Black Power: Black Fraternities and Sororities Give Their Members Access to a Network of Influence and Power—and Good Times Too. So What's Wrong with That?" *Rolling Stone*, March 24, 1988.

Fregoso, Rosa Linda. *The Bronze Screen: Chicana and Chicano Film Culture*. Minneapolis: University of Minnesota Press, 1995.

Gadson, A. Denita. "Greek Power! African American Greek-Letter Organizations Wield Massive Influence after *School Daze*." *Black Collegian* 20:1 (September 1989): 34–36.

Gaines, Kevin. *Uplifting the Race: Black Leadership, Politics, and Culture in the Twentieth Century*. Chapel Hill: University of North Carolina Press, 1997.

Gans, Herbert. *Essays in Honor of David Riesman*. Philadelphia: University of Pennsylvania Press, 1979.

Gates Jr., Henry Louis. *The Signifying Monkey: A Theory of African American Literary Criticism*. New York: Oxford University Press, 1988.

———, ed. *Reading Black, Reading Feminist: A Critical Anthology*. New York: Meridian, 1990.

———, with Cornell West. "Parable of the Talents." *The Future of the Race*. New York: Vintage, 1996.

Geertz, Clifford. *The Interpretations of Cultures*. New York: Basic Books, 1973.

Gere, Ann Ruggles. *Intimate Practices: Literacy and Cultural Work in U.S. Women's Clubs, 1880–1920*. Urbana and Chicago: University of Illinois Press, 1997.

Gibson, Aliona. *Nappy*. New York: Random House, 1998.

Gibson Sr., W. H. *History of the United Brothers of Friendship and Sisters of the Mysterious Ten, in Two Parts: A Negro Order*. Freeport, NY: Books for Libraries Press, 1971.

Giddings, Paula. *In Search of Sisterhood: Delta Sigma Theta and the Challenge of the Black Sorority Movement*. New York: William Morrow, 1988.

———. "Sorority Sisters." *Essence* (July 1988): 36.

———. *When and Where I Enter: The Impact of Black Women on Race and Sex in America*. New York: William Morrow, 1984.

Gilroy, Paul. *The Black Atlantic: Modernity and Double Consciousness*. Cambridge, MA: Harvard University Press, 1993.

———. *Without Guarantees: In Honour of Stuart Hall*. London: Verso, 2000.

Glenn, Evelyn Nakano. *Issei, Nisei, War Bride: Three Generations of Japanese American Women in Domestic Service*. Philadelphia, PA: Temple University Press, 1988.

Gordon, Ann, Bettye Collier-Thomas, and John Bracey, eds. *African American Women and the Vote: 1837–1965*. Amherst: University of Massachusetts Press. 1997.

Gordon-Hazzard, Katrina. *Jookin': The Rise of Social Dance Formations in African American Culture*. Philadelphia, PA: Temple University Press, 1990.

Gottschild, Brenda Dixon. *Digging the Africanist Presence in American Performance; Dance and Other Contexts*. Westport, CT: Greenwood Press, 1996.

Graham, Otis. *Our Kind of People: Inside America's Black Upper Class*. New York: HarperCollins, 1998.

Gramsci, Antonio. *Selections from Cultural Writings*. Cambridge, MA: Harvard University Press, 1985.

Gray, Herman. *Watching Race: Television and the Struggle for Blackness*. Minneapolis: University of Minnesota Press, 1995.

Green, Rayna. "Review Essay: Native American Women." *Signs:* Journal *of Women in Culture and Society* (Winter 1980): 248–67.

Habermas, Jürgen. *The Structural Transformation of the Public Sphere: An Inquiry into a Category of Bourgeois Society*. Cambridge, MA: MIT Press, 1995.

Hall, Ronald, Kathy Russell, and Midge Wilson. *The Color Complex: The Politics of Skin Color among African Americans*. New York: Harcourt Brace Jovanich, 1992.

Hall, Stuart. "Gramsci's Relevance for the Study of Race and Ethnicity." In Morley and Chen.

———. "Deconstructing the Popular." In *Cultural Theory and Popular Culture: A Reader*, ed. John Storey, 442–53. Athens: University of Georgia Press, 1998.

———. "Encoding/Decoding." *Culture, Media, Language*. London: Hutchinson/Centre for Contemporary Cultural Studies, 1980.

———. "Global, Local, and the Return to Ethnicity." In *Social Theory: The Multicultural and Class Readings*, ed. Charles Lemert, 626–34. Boulder, CO: Westview Press, 1999.

———. *Questions of Cultural Identity*. London: Sage, 1996.

———. "Signification, Representation, Ideology: Althusser and the Post Structuralist Debates." *Critical Studies in Mass Communication* 2:2 (June 1985): 91–114.

———. "Subjects in History: Making Diasporic Identities." In *The House that Race Built*, ed. Wahneema Lubiano, 289–300. New York: Vintage, 1998.

Hamilton, Tullia Kay Brown. *The National Association of Colored Women, 1896–1920*, Ph.D. dissertation, Emory University, 1978.

Hanauer, Cindy. "Behind Closed Doors at Sorority Rush." *Seventeen*, September 1989.

Harris Jr., Robert. "Early Black Benevolent Societies, 1780–1830." *Massachusetts Review 20* (Autumn 1979): 603–25.

Harris, Rosemary Banks. "College Love Affair/Sorority, Fraternity Affiliations Lasting." *St. Petersburg Times*, April 15, 1988.

Haskins, James. *Black Dance in America: A History through Its People*. New York: HarperCollins, 1990.

Hatch, James V. "Theatre in Historically Black Colleges: A Survey of 100 Years." In *A Source Book of African-American Performance: Plays, People, Movements*, ed. Annemarie Bean, 150–64. New York: Routledge, 1999.

Haynes, Karima A. "The Women of Spelman." *Ebony*, March 1993.

Hernandez, Rornell. "Racial Incident Calls OSU Diversity Efforts into Question." *The Oregonian*, May 12, 1999.

Higginbotham, Evelyn Brooks. *Righteous Discontent: The Women's Movement in the Black Baptist Church, 1880–1920.* Boston, MA: Harvard University Press, 1993.

Hine, Darlene Clark. *Black Women in United States History: From Colonial Times to the Present.* 16 vols. Brooklyn, NY: Carlson, 1990.

———. *Hine Sight: Black Women and the Reconstruction of American History*. New York: Carlson, 1994.

———. *A Shining Thread of Hope: The History of Black Women in America*. New York: Broadway Books, 1998.

Hirati, Lucie. "Chinese Immigrant Women in Nineteenth-Century California." In *Women of America*, ed. Carol R. Berkin and Mary B. Norton, 223–44. Boston, MA: Houghton Mifflin, 1979.

Holloman, Lillian O. "Black Sororities and Fraternities: A Case Study in Clothing Symbolism." In *Dress and Popular Culture*, ed. Patricia A. Cunningham and Susan Voso Lab, 46–60. Bowling Green, KY: Bowling Green State University Popular Press, 1991.

hooks, bell. *Ain't I a Woman: Black Women and Feminism*. Boston, MA: South End Press, 1981.

———. *Black Looks: Race and Representation*. Boston, MA: South End Press, 1992.

———. *Feminist Theory from Margin to Center*. Boston, MA: South End Press, 1984.

———. *From Reel to Real: Race, Class, and Sex at the Movies*. New York: Routledge, 1997.

———. *Talking Back: Think Feminist, Thinking Black*. Boston, MA: South End Press, 1989.

———. *Teaching to Transgress: Education as the Practice of Freedom*. New York: Routledge, 1994.

———. *Where We Stand: Class Matters*. New York: Routledge, 2000.

hooks, bell, and Cornell West. *Breaking Bread: Insurgent Black Intellectual Life*. Boston, MA: South End Press, 1991.

Hossfeld, Karen. "Hiring Immigrant Women: Silicon Valley's 'Simple Formula.'" In *Women of Color in U.S. Society*, Women in the Political Economy, ed. Maxine Baca Zinn and Bonnie Thornton Dill, 65–94. Philadelphia, PA: Temple University Press, 1994.

Hurteau, Teresa. "In Step with a Tradition." *San Jose Mercury News*, February 24, 1993.

Jackson, James Willis, and Anita K. Ritch. *The Search for Something Better: Ida Louise Jackson's Life Story*. Chicago, IL: Mobium, 1989.

Jasper, Kenji. "A Proud Heritage for Black Greek Groups." *San Diego Union Tribune*, February 24, 1998.

Jones, Gavin. "Whose Line Is It Anyway? WEB Du Bois and the Language of the Color Line." *Race Consciousness: African American Studies for the New Century*. New York: New York University Press, 1997.

Jones, Lisa. *Bulletproof Diva: Tales of Race, Sex and Hair*. New York: Doubleday, 1994.

Jones, Ricky L. *Black Haze: Violence, Sacrifice and Manhood in Black Greek-Letter Fraternities*. Albany: State University of New York Press, 2004.

Kelly, Robin D. G. *Race Rebels: Culture Politics, and the Black Working Class*. New York: Free Press, 1994.

———. *Freedom Dreams: The Black Radical Imagination*. Boston, MA: Beacon Press, 2002.

Kerber, Linda, and Jane Sherron De Hart, eds. *Women's America: Refocusing the Past*. New York: Oxford University Press, 1991.

Kimbrough, Walter M. *Black Greek 101: The Culture, Customs, and Challenges of Black Fraternities and Sororities*. Madison, WI: Farleigh Dickinson University Press, 2000.

———. "Notes from Underground: Despite Ban, Pledging Remains." *Black Issues in Higher Education*, May 11, 2000.

Kimmel, Michael, and Michael Messner. *Men's Lives*. 5th ed. New York: Allyn and Bacon, 2000.

Kincheloe, Joe, et al. *White Reign: Deploying Whiteness in America*. New York: St. Martin's Griffin, 1998.

Knupfer, Anne Meis. *Toward a Tenderer Humanity and a Nobler Womanhood: African American Women's Clubs in Turn-of-the-Century Chicago*. New York: New York University Press, 1997.

Kobbs, Kamina. "Steppin' Out: African American Fraternities and Sororities Practice Stepping for Show, Unity, and Communication." *Black Collegian*, February 10, 1998.

Konigsber, Eric. "The Fall of Animal House for Dartmouth's Alpha Delta Fraternity: The Choice Is Change or Die." *Rolling Stone*, September 17, 1992.

La Duke, Winona. "In Honor of Women Warriors." *Off Our Backs* 11 (February 1981): 3–4.

Lee, Spike, with Lisa Jones. *Uplift the Race: The Construction of* School Daze. New York: Simon and Schuster, 1988.

Leemon, Thomas A. *The Rites of Passage in a Student Culture: A Study of the Dynamics of Transition*. New York: Teachers College Press, Columbia University Press, 1972.

Lerner, Gerda, ed. *Black Women in White America: A Documented History*. New York: Vintage Press, 1992, c. 1972.

Levine, Lawrence W. *Black Culture and Black Consciousness: Afro-American Folk Thought from Slavery to Freedom*. New York: Oxford University Press, 1977.

Lewis, Benoit Denizet. "Viewing Fraternity Life from the Three-B Perspective." *Contra Costa Times*, February 24, 1998.

Lichtblau, Eric. "Trial Opens on Fullerton Bid to Oust Frat Houses." *Los Angeles Times*, August 8, 1989.

Lipsitz, George. *The Possessive Investment in Whiteness: How White People Profit from Identity Politics*. Philadelphia, PA: Temple University Press, 1998.

———. "Sent for You Yesterday, Here You Come Today: American Studies Scholarship and the New Social Movements." In *The Futures of American Studies*, ed. Donald Pease and Robyn Wiegman, 441–60. Durham, NC: Duke University Press, 2002.

Lorde, Audre. *Sister Outsider*. New York: Crossing Press, 1984.

Lowe, Lisa. *Immigrant Acts: On Asian American Cultural Politics*. Durham, NC, and London: Duke University Press, 1996.

——. "Work, Immigration, Gender: Asian 'American' Women." In *Making More Waves: New Writing by Asian American Women*, ed. Elaine H. Kim, Lilia V. Villanueva, and Asian Women United of California, 269–77. Boston, MA: Beacon Press, 1997.

Lowe, Lisa, and David Lloyd. *The Politics of Culture in the Shadow of Capital*. Durham, NC, and London: Duke University Press, 1997.

Lyman, M. Stanford. *Social Movements: Critiques, Concepts, Case Studies*. New York: New York University Press, 1995.

Lystra, Karen. "Clifford Geertz and the Concept of Culture." *Prospects* 8 (October 1983): 31–47.

Maddox, Lucy. *Locating American Studies: The Evolution of American Studies*. Baltimore, MD, and London: Johns Hopkins University Press, 1999.

Magner, Denise K. "Howard University: A Year after a Tense Campus Sit-in, Awaits the Arrival of a New President Who Faces Tough, Myriad Issues." *Chronicle of Higher Education*, March 7, 1990.

Malcolm X. "Message to the Grassroots." In *The Eyes on the Prize Civil Rights Reader: Documents, Speeches, and Firsthand Accounts from the Black Freedom Struggle*," ed. Clayborne Carson et al. New York: Viking, 1991.

Malone, Jaquie. *Stepping on the Blues: The Visible Rhythms of African American Dance*. Champagne-Urbana: University of Illinois Press, 1996.

Marable, Manning. *How Capitalism Underdeveloped Black America: Problems in Race, Political Economy, and Society*. Cambridge, MA: South End Press, 2000.

Marshall, Marilyn. "Delta Sigma Theta: Sorority Founded at Howard University Stresses Service, Scholarship and the Arts." *Ebony*, February 1990.

Mayne, Judith. *The Woman at the Keyhole: Feminism and Women's Cinema*. Bloomington: Indiana University Press, 1990.

McDowell, Deborah E. *The Changing Same: Black Women's Literature, Criticism, and Theory*. Bloomington: Indiana University Press, 1995.

Mejia, Alex. "Hispanics Go Greek. *Hispanic* (October 1994): 34.

Mercer, Kobena. *Welcome to the Jungle: New Positions in Black Cultural Studies*. New York: Routledge, 1994.

Messer-Davidow, Ellen. "Manufacturing the Attack on Liberal Higher Education." *Social Text* 36 (Fall 1993): 40–80.

Mills, David. "The Wrongs of the Rites of Brotherhood: Leaders of Black Fraternities Move to End a Cruel Tradition of Violent Hazing." *Washington Post*, June 18, 1990.

Mohanty, Chandra Talpade. "Cartographies of Struggle: Third World Women and the Politics of Feminism." In *Third World Women and the Politics of Feminism*, ed. Chandra Talpade Mohanty, Lourdes Torres, and Ann Russo, 28–47. Bloomington: Indiana University Press, 1991.

Moore, Sally, and Barbara Myeroff. *Secular Ritual*. Assen, Austria: Van Gorcum, 1977.

Moraga, Cherrie, and Gloria Anzaldua. *This Bridge Called My Back: Writings By Radical Women of Color*. Watertown, MA: Persphone, 1981.

Morley, David, and Kuan-Hsing Chen. *Stuart Hall: Critical Dialogues in Cultural Studies*. London: Routledge, 1996.

Morrison, Toni, ed. *Racing Justice, Engendering Power: Essays on Anita Hill, Clarence Thomas, and the Construction of Social Reality*. New York: Pantheon, 1992.

Muhammed, Askia. "From Capital Hill: How to Start a Quiet Riot." *Washington Informer*, September 6, 1993.

Muhammed, Lawrence. "U of L Greek Letter Groups Step Out at Dance Show." *Courier-Journal*, October 14, 1990.

Mulvey, Laura. *Visual and Other Pleasures*. Bloomington: Indiana University Press, 1989.

Murolo, Priscilla. *The Common Ground of Womanhood: Class, Gender, and Working Girls' Clubs, 1884–1928*. Urbana: University of Illinois Press, 1997.

Murry, Thomas E. "Social Structure and Phonological Variation on a Midwestern College Campus." *American Speech* 67:2 (Summer 1992): 163–74.

Naisbitt, John. *In the Spirit of Black Women's Clubs: Alpha Kappa Alpha and the Civil Rights Movement*. Master's thesis, Syracuse University, 1994.

Neal, Erika. "Search for Brotherhood Ends in Death." *St. Louis Post Dispatch*, February 23, 1994.

Newitz, Annalee, and Matt Wray. *White Trash: Race and Class in America*. New York: Routledge, 1997.

New York Amsterdam News. "Howard University Bans AKA Sorority (Alpha Kappa Alpha) from Campus Until 1966," May 19, 1962, p. 1.

New York Times. "Omega to Hazing Sought," September 3, 1989.

———. "Two Expulsions in Hazing Death," October 25, 1989.

Nuwer, Hank. *Broken Pledges: The Deadly Rite of Hazing*. Atlanta, GA: Longstreet Press, 1990.

———. *The Wrongs of Passage: Fraternities, Sororities, Hazing, and Binge Drinking*. Bloomington: Indiana University Press, 1999.

Orozco, Cynthia E. "Beyond Machismo, La Familia, and Ladies Auxiliaries: A Historiography of Mexican-Origin Women's Participation in Voluntary Associations and Politics in the United States, 1870–1990," *Perspectives in Mexican American Studies: Mexican American Women Changing Images* 5 (1995).

Palmer, Edward. "Negro Secret Societies." *Social Forces* 23:2 (December 1944): 207–12.

Parker, Marjorie Holloman. *Alpha Kappa Alpha through the Years 1908–1988*. Chicago, IL: Mobium Press, 1990.

Parks, Gregory, and Craig Torbenson. *Brothers and Sisters: Diversity in College Fraternities and Sororities*. Madison, WI: Farleigh Dickinson University Press, 2008.

Pascarella, Ernest. *Cognitive Effects of Greek Affiliation during the First Year of College*. Washington, DC: U.S. Department of Education Press, 1994.

Paul, Deborah. "Join the Club." *Indianapolis Monthly*, January 1998.

Puente, Teresa. "Getting Organized." *Hispanic* (March 1992): 32.

Radway, Janice. "*Reading* Reading the Romance." In *Cultural Theory and Popular Culture: A Reader*, ed. John Storey, 215–31. Athens: University of Georgia Press, 1998.

Reed, Adolph. *W. E .B. Du Bois and American Political Thought: Fabianism and the Color Line*. Oxford: Oxford University Press, 1997.

Riggs, Marcia Y. *Awake, Arise and Act: A Womanist Call for Black Liberation*. Cleveland, OH: Pilgrim Press, 1994.

Right, Evan. "Sister Act: Deep Inside the Secret Life of Sorority Girls at Ohio State University." *Rolling Stone*, October 14, 1999.

Roebuck, Julian B., and Komanduri S. Murty. *Historically Black Colleges and Universities: Their Place in American Higher Education*. Westport, CT: Greenwood Press, 1993.

Roediger, David. *The Wages of Whiteness: Race and the Making of the American Working Class*. New York: Verso, 1994.

Rooks, Knowlie. *Hair-raising: Beauty, Culture, and Power*. New Brunswick, NJ: Rutgers University Press, 1996.

Rosenberg, Rosalind. *Beyond Separate Spheres: Intellectual Roots of Modern Feminism*. New Haven, CT: Yale University Press, 1982.

Ross Jr., Lawrence C. *The Divine Nine: The History of African American Fraternities and Sororities*. New York: Kensington, 2000.

Ruiz, Vicki L. *From Out of the Shadows: Mexican Women in Twentieth-Century*. America. London: Oxford University Press, 1998.

Russell, Kathy, and Midge Wilson. *Divided Sisters: Bridging the Gap between Black Women and White Women*. New York: Anchor Books, 1996.

Russell, Kathy, Midge Wilson, and Ronald Hall. *The Color Complex: The Politics of Skin Color among African Americans*. New York: Harcourt, Brace, Jovanovich, 1992.

Said, Edward. *Orientalism*. New York: Vintage Books, 1979.

Sanaday, Peggy R. *Fraternity Gang Rape: Sex, Brotherhood, and Privilege on Campus*. New York: New York University Press, 1990.

Schwartz, Martin. "Fraternity Membership, Rape Myths, and Sexual Aggression on College Campus." *Violence against Women* 2:2 (June 1996): 148–62.

Shaw, Stephanie. *What a Woman Ought To Be and To Do: Black Professional Women Workers during the Jim Crow Era*. Chicago, IL: University of Chicago Press, 1996.

Silverman, Geneva. *Talkin' and Testifyin': The Language of Black America*. Detroit, MI: Wayne State University Press, 1977.

Smith, Susan L. "Sharecroppers and Sorority Women: The Alpha Kappa Alpha Mississippi Health Project," in *Sick and Tired of Being Sick and Tired: Black Women's Health Activism in Amercia, 1890–1950*, 149–67 (Philadelphia: University of Pennsylvania Press, 1994).

Springer, Kimberly, ed. *Still Lifting, Still Climbing: African American Women's Contemporary Activism*. New York: New York University Press, 1999.

Stains, Laurence A., "Black Like Me: What's Up with White Guys Who Join Black Frats? Are They Trying Too Hard, or Is It Just a Class Thing?" *Rolling Stone*, March 24, 1994.

Stallybrass, Peter, and Allon White. *The Politics and Poetics of Transgression*. Ithaca, NY: Cornell University Press, 1986.

Thomas, Melvin. "Anything But Race: The Social Science Retreat From Racism." *Perspectives* 6:3: 248–55.

Thompson, Brian. "Steppin' with Jerald Harkness." *Indianapolis Recorder*, May 22, 1993, N21.

Thompson, E. P. *The Making of the English Working Class*. London: Victor Collancz, 1963.

Thompson, Robert Farris. "An Aesthetic of the Cool: West African Dance." In *Signifyin(g), Sanctifyin', an Slam Dunking; A Reader in African American Expressive Culture*, ed. Gena Dagel Caponi. Amherst: University of Massachusetts Press, 1999.

Thompson, Vernon. "Fraternities, Sororities from Howard Students Draw Renewed Interest: Clubs Offer On-Campus Social Life to Off-Campus Communities." *Washington Post*, November 16, 1978.

Thorpe, Edward. *Black Dance*. New York: Overlook Press, 1990.

Tifft, Susan. "Waging War on the Greeks: Fraternities and Sororities Are Being Forced to Clean Up Their Acts." *Time*, April 16, 1990.

Townes, Emilie M. *Womanist Justice, Womanist Hope*. Atlanta, GA: Scholars Press, 1993.

Turner, Victor W. *Blazing the Trail Way: Marks in the Exploration of Symbols*. Tucson: University of Arizona Press, 1992.

———. *Celebration: Studies in Festivity and Ritual*. Washington, DC: Smithsonian, 1982.

USA Today. "Howard," April 15, 1988.

Walker, Alice. *In Search of Our Mother's Gardens*. New York: Harcourt Brace Jovanovich, 1983.

Wallace, Michelle. *Black Macho and the Myth of the Superwoman*. London: Verso, 1991, c. 1979.

———. *Black Popular Culture*. Seattle, WA: Bay Press, 1994.

———. *Invisibility Blues: From Pop To Theory*. London: Verso, 1990.

Washington, Booker T. *Up From Slavery*. Garden City, NY: Doubleday, 1901; reprint, New York: Dover, 1995.

Weare, Walter, "Fraternal Orders, Black." In *The Encyclopedia of Southern Culture*, ed. Charles Reagan Wilson and William Ferris, 92–94. Chapel Hill: University of North Carolina Press, 1989.

Weiner, John. "Racial Hatred on Campus." *The Nation*, February 27, 1989.

Welsch, Janice, ed. *Multiple Voices in Feminist Film Criticism*. Minneapolis: University of Minnesota Press, 1994.

Wesley, Charles. *The History of Alpha Phi Alpha: A Development in Negro College Life*. Washington, DC: Foundation Publishers, 1948.

West, Cornell. "The New Cultural Politics of Difference." In *Social Theory: The Multicultural and Classic Readings*, ed. Charles Lemert, 521–31. Boulder, CO: Westview Press, 1999.

Whaley, Deborah E. "By Merit, By Culture: The Cultural and Counter Public Sphere Work of Alpha Kappa Alpha Sorority." Ph.D. diss., University of Kansas, 2002.

———. "The Empty Space of Sorority Representation: Spike Lee's *School Daze*. In *African American Fraternities and Sorori-*

ties: The Legacy and the Vision, ed. Tamara Brown et al., 417–36. Lexington: University Press of Kentucky, 2005.

———. "Links, Legacies, and Letters: A Cultural History of African American Fraternities and Sororities." In *Brothers and Sisters: Diversity in the College Fraternity and Sorority*, ed. Craig Torbenson and Gregory S. Parks, 46–82. Madison, WI: Farleigh Dickson University Press, 2009.

———. "We Strive and We Do: The Counterpublic Sphere Work of Alpha Kappa Alpha Sorority." *Contours* 3:2 (Fall 2005): 139–62.

Whitby, Beulah. "Today's Challenge to the Privileged Negro," *Ivy Leaf* 14:1 (March 1936).

White, Deborah Gray. *Too Heavy a Load: Black Women in Defense of Themselves 1894–1994*. New York: W.W. Norton, 1999.

Wiggins, William. *O Freedom! Afro-American Emancipation Celebrations*. Knoxville: University of Tennessee Press, 1987.

Wilkerson, Isabel. "Black Fraternities Thrive, Often on Adversity." *New York Times*, October 2, 1989.

Williams, John. *Perceptions of the No-Pledge Policy for New Member Intake by Undergraduate Members of Predominantly Black Fraternities and Sororities*. Manhattan, KS: Center for the Study of Pan-Hellenic Issues, 1992.

Williams, John. *A Study of the No Pledge Policy in Historically Black Sororities and Fraternities*. Master's thesis, Tennessee State University, 1996.

Williams, Marcia. "Ladies on the Line: Punjabi Cannery Workers in Central California." In *Making Waves: An Anthology of Writings by and about Asian American Women*, ed. Asian American Women United of California, 148–58. Boston, MA: Beacon Press, 1989.

Wilson, Wendy L. "Michelle Obama To Become Honorary Member of Alpha Kappa Alpha Sorority, Inc.; Wife of Presidential Hopeful Says "Yes" to the Pink and Green." *Essence* Online. http://www.essence.com/essence/lifestyle/voices/0,16109,1822967,00.html# (accessed August 1, 2008).

Windmeyer, Shane, ed. *Out on Fraternity Row: Personal Accounts of Being Gay in a College Fraternity*. New York: Alyson Publications, 1998.

Windmeyer, Shane L., and Freeman, Pamela W., eds. *Secret Sisters: Stories of Being Lesbian and Bisexual in a College Sorority.* Los Angeles, CA: Alyson Publications, 2001.

Woodson, Jacqueline. "Common Ground." *Essence*, May 1999.

Zill, Baca, and Thorton Dill. *Women of Color in U.S. Society.* Philadelphia, PA: Temple University Press, 1994.

Zott, Stacey. "Out. Proud. Greek?" *Indiana Daily*, February 2, 1998.

Special Collections

The following AKA *Ivy Leaf* issues were consulted: 1:1 (December 1921); 4:1 (December 1925); 5:1 (December 1926); 8:4 (December 1930); 13:1 (March 1935); 13:2 (June 1935); 13:3 (September 1935); 13:4 (December 1935); 14:1 (March 1936); 14:2 (June 1936); 15:3 (September 1937); 16:3 (September 1938); 17:2 (June 1939); 18:3 (September 1940); 19:1 (March 1941); 19:2 (June 1941); 19:3 (September 1941); 21:1 (March 1943); 21:2 (June 1943); 21:3 (September 1943); 21:4 (December 1943); 25:1 (March 1947); 25:2 (June 1947); 40:11 (February/March 1964); 45:1 (February/March 1969); 45:3 (September/October 1969); 45:4 (November/December 1969); 46:1 (Spring 1970); 46:2 (Summer 1970); 48:1 (February 1972); 49:1 (February 1973); 49:2 (Spring/Summer 1973); 51:4 (Winter 1975); 52:1 (Spring 1976); 52:2 (Summer 1976); 61:4 (Winter 1984); 62:1 (June 1985); 62:2 (Summer 1985); [*Sorority* magazine archived at Alpha Kappa Alpha headquarters (Ivy Center), Lorraine R. Green Drive/57th Street and South Stony Island Ave, Chicago, Illinois, and Howard University.]

Hill, Ruth Edmonds. *The Black Women Oral History Project: From the Arthur and Elizabeth Schlesinger Library on the History of Women in America*, Radcliffe College. Westport: Meeckler, 1991.

University of Kansas Collection on Black History

Dorothy Hodge Johnson collection, Kansas Collection, University of Kansas Libraries.

Laurvenia E. Kiser collection, Kansas Collection, University of Kansas Libraries.

Olga Heavan collection, Kansas Collection, University of Kansas Libraries.

Electronic Sources

Kappa Alpha Theta home page: http://www.emory.edu/kat/kat/

Order of The Eastern Star home page (African American chapters): http://www.csra.net/tamu/oes.htm

Alpha Kappa Alpha home pages:
http://www.aka1908.com/
http://www.mit.edu:8001/ctivities/akas/home2.html
http://www.umr.edu/edu/xidelta/founders.html

INDEX

Note: Page numbers in italics indicate figures.

Addams, Jane, 43
African dance, 61, 63–64, 84, 165n4
African Village Development Program, 51
Africare organization, 51, 132, 140
AIDS education, 52, 130–132, 140
alcohol abuse, 172n18
Alpha Kappa Alpha (AKA), 2–12, 17, 146–150
  activist programs of, 47–51
  Boulé national conference of, 117, 119, 132, 144
  civil rights movement and, 49–50
  colors of, 70
  community programs of, 42–46
  Delta Sigma Theta and, 38–39, 66–67, 121–123
  fact sheet on, 151–152
  future of, 117–142
  goals of, 38, 41–43, 97, 106–108
  hazing in, 2, 87–115
  historical roots of, 36–39
  incorporation of, 38
  international chapters of, 37, 43, 140
  photographs of, 55–58
  Sojourner Truth Monument Crusade and, 29–30
  step dancing by, 59–61, 64–77, 165n2
  stepping call of, 59, 68, 74
  U.S. chapters of, 39, *55–58*
Alpha Phi Alpha, 4, 17, 25, 98
Alpha Suffrage Club, 33
Anthony, Susan B., 35–36
anti-apartheid movement, 50–51, 53
antilynching campaigns, 29, 33, 34, 45
anti-violence programs, 72
Asian Americans, 5, 31, 32, 159n6
step dancing by, 84
Asian Immigrant Women Advocates (AIWA), 32

Baker, Houston, 40
Bakhtin, Mikhail, 69, 81–82, 167n17
Bean, Annemarie, 62
Bethune-Cookman College, 21
Bethune, Mary McLeod, 33
BGLOs. *See* Black Greek-letter organizations
Black Christian Women's Association, 32
Black counterpublics, 40–53, 147
  assessment of, 139
  challenges of, 129–132

Black counterpublics (*cont.*)
Dawson on, 29
definition of, 30, 40
future of, 117–142
Gregory on, 87
hazing and, 96
making of, 120–129
public sphere and, 39–42, 79, 83
Black Greek-letter organizations (BGLOs), 2–6, 147–150
academic performance of, 37–38
colorism within, 19–24
cultural politics of, 24–27
development of, 16–18
films about, 13–17
future of, 117–142
pledge process and hazing by, 87–115
step dancing and, 61–85
women's clubs and, 31–36
Black Public Sphere Collective (BPSC), 30, 59
Black Women's Sojourner Truth Monument Crusade, 29–30
blue vein test, 20
See also colorism
Boulé (AKA's national conference), 117, 119, 132, 144
Boulé (social fraternity), 4, 20
Boyd, Norma, 23, 33, 45, 47, 52
Brown, Anna Easter, 37
Brown, Jayna, 80
Brown, Tamara, 174n44
Brown, William C., 25
Burke, Beulah, 37
Burke, Lillie, 37
Butler, Tajuana "TJ," 143–147
Butler University, 17, 75

Calhoun, John C., 38
California State University, Los Angeles, 114
call and response, 16, 65, 68, 82
calls, stepping, 59, 68, 74
Carby, Hazel, 77
carnivalesque
in hazing, 112
in step dancing, 69, 81–82
Chicanas, 31, 32, 159n6
See also Latinos
Christian Endeavor, 37
civil rights movement, 24
Black sororities and, 31, 42, 48–50, 98, 108
women's clubs and, 33–34
class, 35, 46–47, 144
color and, 18–21, 23–24, 28
cultural conundrum of, 120–129
cultural politics of, 24–27
hooks on, 26
Cleophan Club, 31–32
Cleveland Job Corps Center, 48–50, 164n49
Clinton, George, 70–71
Clinton, Hilary Rodham, 117
Collins, Patricia Hill, 27
colorism
within BGLOs, 19–24
class and, 18–21, 23–24, 28
definition of, 19
tests of, 20
community development programs, 25–26, 42
Cooper, Anna Julia, 77, 80
Cornell University, 17
cotillions, 2, 25, 153n2
counterhegemony, 6–7
counterpublics. *See* Black counterpublics
critical race theory, 90, 170n6
cultural politics, 3, 24–27
cultural theory, 42, 61, 81, 149–150
See also specific writers, e.g., Hall, Stuart
"cutting," 70, 72–75, 82
See also step dancing

Daughters of Labor, 32–33
Davis, Angela, 36
Dawson, Michael C., 29, 121
Delta Chi, 104–105
Delta Sigma Theta, 4, 17, 118
Alpha Kappa Alpha and, 38–39, 66–67, 121–123

colors of, 70
founding of, 38–39, 67
hazing and, 92–94, 98, 171n14
Sojourner Truth Monument Crusade and, 29–30
step dancing by, 59–60, 69–77, 165n2
stepping call of, 59, 68
Delta Upsilon, 104
diasporic experience, 41
definition of, 165n4
step dancing and, 61, 63–64, 83–84
domestic violence, 52, 130–131
Dougherty, Jill, 118
"dozens," 70, 72–75, 82
See also step dancing
Du Bois, W. E. B., 156n14
Durkee, J. Stanley, 18

education, 18, 48, 51
bilingual, 79
rural, 44, 45
Elia, Nada, 113
elitism, 19–21, 23–24
See also class
ethnicity, 79, 153n4

Fanon, Frantz, 42
Ferebee, Dorothy Boulding, 44, 45
Fine, Elizabeth, 63–67, 69
Fisk University, 18
Floyd, Dea, 100–103
Foucault, Michel, 111, 173n39
Fraser, Nancy, 40, 173n39
Frazier, Edward Franklin, 25–26, 157n23
"freaker," 63, 70, 74–76, 81
See also step dancing
Fry, Genelle, 50–51

Gaines, Kevin, 34–35
Gates, Henry Louis, 65
gender, 21
hazing rituals and, 88–90, 94–97, 108, 114–115
race and, 33–36, 46–47
step dancing and, 60–61, 69–79
See also sexuality(ies)
General Federation of Women's Clubs, 32
Georgia State University, 93
Gere, Anne Ruggles, 36
Giddings, Paula, 4–5, 37–38, 98
Girl Friends (social sorority), 20
Graham, Otis, 4
Gramsci, Antonio, 154n13
Gregory, Steven, 87
Guardsman (social fraternity), 20

Habermas, Jürgen, 39–40
Hall, Katie, 50
Hall, Stuart, 28, 61
on carnivalesque, 81
on diaspora, 165n4
on identity, 84, 96
on symbolic categories, 69
hazing, 2, 87–115
definitions of, 91, 170n5, 171n8
elimination of, 113–115
legal discourse of, 92, 100–106, 115
motivations for, 110–111
pledging versus, 91–92, 146
politics of respectability and, 89, 99, 107, 112, 148
"turn back night" and, 109
unofficial, 94–97, 100–115, 146, 148
voicing mistakes of, 132–138
Hedgeman Lyle, Ethel, 37, 118
hegemony, cultural, 6–7, 22, 154n13
Higginbotham, Evelyn Brooks, 117, 161n10
Hill, Marjorie, 37
Hispanics. *See* Latinos
HIV disease, 52, 130–132, 140
Holmes, Margaret Flagg, 37
Holt, Thomas C., 138–139
hooks, bell, 26, 148–150
Hooks, Benjamin, 37
Howard University, 17–18, 22, 119
Alpha Kappa Alpha at, 37
Delta Sigma Theta at, 38
hazing at, 93, 98
Minor Hall at, 69

Indiana University, 17
Indigenous Nations, 31, 32, 106n6
Iota Phi Theta, 17
Irish Americans, 164n45
Ivy Center, 37
Ivy Leaf (periodical), 43–44, 97–98
Ivy Pledge Club, 91, 102

Jack and Jill social club, 20
Jackson, Ida, 44–45
Jackson, Maxine, *56*
Jackson, Sojourner, 24–25
Jacksonville State University, 93
job training programs, 48–50
Johnson, Dorothy Hodge, *56*
Johnson, James Weldon, 60
Jones, Ricky, 4
Juneteenth festival, 61, 166n6

Kansas State University, 94
Kappa Alpha Psi, 3, 17
  funding of, 25–26
  hazing death in, 94
  step dancing by, 71
Kappa Alpha Theta, 41
Kelley, Robin, 11
Kent State University, 87–89, 95, 100–107, 109
Kimbrough, Walter M., 4, 94, 113–114
King, Coretta Scott, 33
King, Martin Luther, Jr., 50
King, Rodney, 105

Lambda 10, 6
Latinos, 5, 31, 32, 84, 159n6
  bilingual education and, 79
Lee, Spike, 14–17, 23–24, 28, 139, 153n2
Levine, Lawrence, 83
"Lift Every Voice and Sing" (anthem), 60
Links (social sorority), 20
Lipsitz, George, 11
Lyle, Ethel Hedgeman, 37, 118
lynching. *See* antilynching campaigns

Malcolm X, 49, 99
Malone, Jacqui, 62, 64
Marable, Manning, 141
McKenzie, Barbara A., 118–119
McKinney, Cynthia, 29
Mercer, Kobena, 27
Messer-Davidow, Ellen, 40
Mexican Revolution, 32
Mississippi Health Project, 44–45, 140
Mitchell-Kernan, Claudia, 65
Mohanty, Chandra Talpade, 32–33
Moore, Lela, 50–51
Mormons, 31–32
Motherhood, Republican, 33–34, 160n9
multiculturalism, 19, 31, 79, 84
Murolo, Priscilla, 161n10

National Association for the Advancement of Colored People (NAACP), 29, 39, 45
National Association of Colored Women, 32
National Basketball Association (NBA), 79
National Council for Jewish Women, 31–32
National Council of Negro Women, 52
National Non-Partisan Council on Public Affairs, 47–48, 50, 140
National Organization of Women (NOW), 130
National Pan-Hellenic Council (NPHC), 17, 155n3
  pledge process and, 90–92, 96–97
National Urban League, 52
Negro Election Day, 168n30
Negro Teachers Program, 44, 45
Negro Women's Club Movement, 29
neoliberalism, 79, 168n31
Norman, Lavinia, 37
Nuwer, Hank, 98, 171n14

Obama, Barack, 117
Obama, Michelle, 118–119, 122, 148

"Old School Pledgers" (OSPs), 96, 100–115, 132–138, 148
  See also pledge process
Omega Psi Phi, 17, 25, 37
  step dancing by, 70–71
ONTRACK program, 52
Orozco, Cynthia, 32
OSPs. *See* "Old School Pledgers"

paper bag test, 20, 23
  See also colorism
Parker, Lonnae O'Neal, 119
Parker, Marjorie, 4–5, 38
Parks, Gregory, 6, 174n44
Parks, Rosa, 33
Pelosi, Nancy, 119
Phi Beta Kappa, 36–37
Phi Beta Sigma, 17, 71–72
Pinkster festival, 168n30
Planned Parenthood, 130
pledge process, 87–115
  Butler on, 145–146
  dropping out of, 88, 109, 137
  hazing versus, 91–92, 146
  secrecy of, 102–107
  unofficial, 94–97, 100–115, 146, 148
  voicing mistakes of, 132–138
Project Family, 46, 163n43
Purnell, Julia, 97–98
Putting Black Families FIRST, 163n43

Quander, Nellie, 38
queer fraternals, 5–6, 27

race. *See* colorism
rape, 34, 130
Reagan, Ronald, 50
Red Cross, 52, 140
Republican Motherhood, 33–34, 160n9
respectability, politics of, 71, 75
  hazing and, 89, 99, 107, 112, 148
  rites of passage, 91, 101
  women's clubs and, 34
Roediger, David, 34, 79
Roosevelt, Eleanor, 43
Ross, Lawrence, 4
Rural Negro Teachers Program, 44, 45
Ryan, Mary P., 40

Saxton-Ross, Autumn, 119
School Daze (film), 14–17, 23–24, 28, 139, 153n2
secrecy, 20
  of pledging, 103–107
Senegal, 51
settlement houses, 32, 46
sexuality(ies), 21, 144–145
  cultural politics of, 27
  Greek-letter organization and, 5–6
  step dancing and, 60–61, 69–80
  See also gender
Shaw, Stephanie, 34
Sigma Gamma Rho, 17
  colors of, 70
  motto of, 75
  Sojourner Truth Monument Crusade and, 29–30
  step dancing by, 59–60, 69–77, 165n2
  stepping call of, 59, 68, 74
Sigma Pi Phi, 4, 20
signifying practices, in step dancing, 61, 65–69, 73, 78–80, 84–85
Slowe, Lucy, 37
Smith, Roger (actor), 15–16
Smith, Susan L., 159n4
Sociedad Beneficiencia, 32
"soror," 95–96, 102, 106, 133–138, 145–146, 172n19
Sorority Sisters (Butler), 143–147
South Africa, 52, 63, 95
  anti-apartheid movement and, 50–51, 53
Southern Christian Leadership Conference, 51
Spelman College, 18
Stallybrass, Peter, 84
Stanton, Elizabeth Cady, 35–36

step dancing, 59–85, 147–148
  carnivalesque in, 69, 81–82
  diasporic experience in, 61, 63–64, 83–84, 165n4
  films about, 13–17, 23–24, 28, 139, 153n2
  gender issues with, 60–61, 69–79
  historical foundations of, 61–64
  multicultural participation in, 79, 84
  sexuality and, 60–61, 69–80
  signifying practices in, 61, 65–69, 73, 78–80, 84–85
stepping calls, 59, 68, 74
Stomp the Yard (film), 13–15, 28, 139
suffrage, women's, 35–36, 42, 43, 52
  See also voter registration drives
Sutton, Ozell, 25

Taylor, Marie Woolfolk, 37
Tennessee State University, 92
Terrell, March Church, 33, 77
Thompson, E. P., 34
Thompson, Robert Farris, 63–64
Torbenson, Craig, 6
Transafrica organization, 50–51
transgression, in step dancing, 81–82
Traveler's Aid Society, 44
Truth, Sojourner, 29–30
Tucker, C. Delores, 29–30
"turn back night," 109
Tuskegee Institute, 21

United Negro College Fund, 52
University of Kansas, *55–58*
University of Texas at Austin, 92–93

violence
  community programs against, 72
  domestic, 52, 130–131
  Elia on, 113
  Fraser on, 173n39
  hazing, 88, 92–94, 101, 110–115
  power and, 89–90, 111
  sexual, 34, 130
voter registration drives, 48, 53, 140–141

Washington, Booker T., 156n14
Wells, Ida B., 29, 33, 77
West, Cornell, 26
Western Illinois University, 93–94
White, Allon, 84
White, Angela, 118
White, Deborah Gray, 23, 25
White, Linda M., 114
White, Sylvain, 14–15, 28, 139
Wilberforce University, 18
Women of All Red Nations (WARN), 32, 160n6
women's clubs, 31–36, 46–47, 51–52
  decline of, 161n17
Woodson, Jacqueline, 26–27
World War II, 47–48, 141

Yancey, Shawn, 118–119
yard step shows, 62, 73, 166n8
Young, Andrew, 98
Young, Phyllis, 50–51
Young Women's Christian Association (YWCA), 32
  Alpha Kappa Alpha and, 37, 39, 42, 130
  desegregation of, 56

Zeta Phi Beta, 17, 24–25
  colors of, 70
  Phi Beta Sigma and, 71–72
  Sojourner Truth Monument Crusade and, 29–30
  step dancing by, 59–60, 69–77, 165n2
  stepping call of, 59, 68

61628888R00125

Made in the USA
Lexington, KY
15 March 2017